REFERENCE

DISCARDED

The Islamic World

Past and Present

The Islamic World

Past and Present

VOLUME 1

John L. Esposito, *Editor in Chief*

Associate Editors

Abdulaziz Sachedina

Tamara Sonn

John O. Voll

OXFORD UNIVERSITY PRESS
2004

Oxford University Press

Oxford New York

Auckland Bangkok Buenos Aires Cape Town Chennai Dar es Salaam
Delhi Hong Kong Istanbul Karachi Kolkata Kuala Lumpur Madrid Melbourne
Mexico City Mumbai Nairobi São Paulo Shanghai Taipei Tokyo Toronto

Copyright © 2004 by Oxford University Press

Published by Oxford University Press, Inc.
198 Madison Avenue, New York, 10016
http://www.oup.com

Developed for Oxford University Press by Visual Education Corporation, Princeton, NJ

For Oxford
PUBLISHER: Karen Day
EDITORIAL DEVELOPMENT DIRECTOR: Timothy DeWerff
EDITOR: Meera Vaidyanathan
EDITORIAL, DESIGN, AND PRODUCTION DIRECTOR: John Sollami
PROJECT EDITOR: Erica Pirrung
INTERIOR DESIGN: Maxson Crandall
COVER DESIGN: Mary Belibasakis

For Visual Education Corporation
PROJECT DIRECTORS: Jewel Moulthrop, Darryl Kestler
EDITORS: Carol Ciaston, Lauren Hauptman, Doriann Markey
ASSOCIATE EDITOR: Sarah Miller
WRITERS: Jean M. Brainard, John Haley, Kent M. Krause, Elizabeth Shostak
COPYEDITORS: Helen Castro, Maureen Pancza
ELECTRONIC PREPARATION: Fiona Shapiro
PHOTO RESEARCH: Susan Buschhorn
MAPS: Patti Isaacs, Parrot Graphics

Library of Congress Cataloging-in-Publication Data
The Islamic world : past and present / John L. Esposito, editor in chief ;
associate editors, Abdulaziz Sachedina . . . [et al.].
    p. cm.
Includes bibliographical references and index.
   ISBN 978-0-19-516520-3 (hardcover 3 vol. set)
   ISBN 978-0-19-517592-9 (vol. 1)
   ISBN 978-0-19-517593-6 (vol. 2)
   ISBN 978-0-19-517594-3 (vol. 3)
   1. Islamic countries—Encyclopedias. 2. Islam—Encyclopedias.
I. Esposito, John L. II. Sachedina, Abdulaziz Abdulhussein, 1942-
   DS35.53 .I86 2004
909'.097671'003—dc22
                                        2003019665

Contents

 **VOLUME 1**

Contents

═══════════════ **VOLUME 2** ═══════════════

VOLUME 3

Contents

Preface

Islam and the Islamic world have played and continue to play a major role in world history. In the century following the death of the Prophet Muhammad in 632 C.E., Islam spread widely and Muslim rulers created an empire that extended from North Africa to South Asia. The empire was greater than that of Rome at its zenith. While the West passed through its Dark Ages, Islamic civilization flourished, making major contributions to mathematics (Arabic numerals, algebra, geometry), philosophy, medicine and other sciences, art, and architecture.

Today Islam is the second largest of the world's religions, encompassing one-fifth of the world's population. The 1.2 billion Muslims live in some 56 Muslim countries, where they make up a majority of the population. Moreover, if Islam and Muslims seemed invisible in Europe and America only a few decades ago, today Islam is the second largest religion in Europe and the third largest in the United States.

Awareness of Islam and Muslim politics came suddenly to many in America and other parts of the world with the shock of Iran's "Islamic revolution" of 1978-1979, which revealed the West's limited knowledge of Islam and the Islamic world. Ignorance and stereotypes of Islam and Muslims were compounded by the astonishing lack of coverage of Islam in schools and universities, the media, publications, and political analysis. The result over the past two decades has been a flurry of studies, conferences, and media coverage, as well as the introduction of coverage of Islam and the Muslim world in educational curricula.

The terrorist attacks of September 11, 2001, against New York's World Trade Center and the Pentagon in Washington, D.C., and the resultant war against terrorism have increased interest, coverage, and the need to know more about the faith, history, politics, and culture of Islam and Muslims. Now, more than ever, it is important to understand the faith of Islam, its enormous contributions to world history and civilizations, the issues that affect the development of Muslim society, and the

factors that shape and determine international politics and relations.

Over the years, Oxford University Press has become a major source of information and education about Islam and the Islamic world. Its publications have included major reference works, such as *The Oxford Encyclopedia of the Modern Islamic World*, *The Oxford History of Islam*, and *The Oxford Dictionary of Islam*. However, despite the vast amount of materials produced, we still lacked a major reference work for young adults. *The Islamic World: Past and Present* has been designed to meet this important need.

Understanding Islam and Muslim societies, yesterday and today, is a fascinating trip across time and space. The starting point for *The Islamic World: Past and Present* was *The Oxford Encyclopedia of the Modern Islamic World (OEMIW)*, for which I was editor in chief. The 750 articles of this four-volume encyclopedia were authored by more than 450 Muslim and non-Muslim scholars of religion, history, politics, anthropology, sociology, art, and architecture. To make the new student encyclopedia more accessible, many articles from *OEMIW* have been rewritten. To provide coverage of the past as well as the present, *OEMIW* entries have been updated and new entries on historical and current topics have been added, broadening the coverage significantly. We hope that students and teachers will find *The Islamic World: Past and Present* an exciting and engaging gateway to knowledge and understanding of Islam and the Islamic world.

The Islamic World: Past and Present includes a number of useful features. In the margin next to the text column, the reader will find definitions of unfamiliar terms used in the articles, as well as sidebars that focus on interesting people, places, and traditions. Cross references to related entries appear at the end of each article. The front matter of each volume contains a Chronology of the Islamic World. A list of People and Places of the Islamic World and a Glossary of Arabic and Islamic Terms appear at the end of each volume; and a comprehensive index can be found at the back of volume 3. The encyclopedia also includes color inserts in each volume that illustrate Daily Life, Art and Architecture, and the Culture of the Islamic World, respectively.

As with any major project of this magnitude, many people were required to make it happen. Karen Day, the publisher for this work, had the foresight to recognize the need for this project. This has been a collaborative process from start to finish between our board of editors, Oxford University Press, and Visual Education Corporation of McGraw-Hill. Oxford's Timothy J. DeWerff, Director of Editorial Development, and Jewel Moulthrop

and her successor, Darryl Kestler, of Visual Education have worked as an excellent professional team in managing the editorial and production process and keeping it on schedule. Meera Vaidyanathan of OUP has been especially helpful in the late stages of the project. Finally, I want to thank the boards of editors, advisers, consultants, and authors for the original *OEMIW* and in particular my associate editors Abdulaziz Sachedina (University of Virginia), Tamara Sonn (William and Mary), and John O. Voll (Georgetown University) for their remarkable and persistent responsiveness at every stage. Without them, *The Islamic World: Past and Present* would not have been possible.

John L. Esposito

Chronology of
the Islamic World

747–750	*Abbasid family leads revolt against Umayyad dynasty*
750–1258	*Abbasid caliphate*
756	*Abd al-Rahman I ibn Mu'awiyah overthrows government of Andalusia and establishes amirate of Córdoba in Spain*
762	*Baghdad founded as capital of the Abbasid caliphate*
767	*Abu Hanifah, founder of Hanafi school of Islamic law, dies*
786–809	*Harun al-Rashid reigns as caliph; Abbasid power and cultural achievements reach peak*
795	*Malik ibn Anas, founder of Maliki school of Islamic law, dies*
801	*Rabiah al-Adawiyah, Sufi poet, dies*
813–833	*Al-Mamun reigns as caliph, encourages the development of Arabic science and literature*
820	*Muhammad al-Shafi'i, founder of Shafi'i school of Islamic law, dies*
836–892	*Abbasid capital moved from Baghdad to Samarra (Iraq)*
855	*Ahmad ibn Hanbal, founder of Hanbali school of Islamic law, dies*
859	*Islamic mosque-university, Qarawiyin, founded in Fez, Morocco*
874	*Abu al-Qasim Muhammad, son of the eleventh Shi'i imam, goes into hiding; becomes known as the Hidden Imam*
909	*Fatimid dynasty rises to power in Tunisia*
929	*Abd al-Rahman III establishes caliphate in Córdoba, Spain*
969–1171	*Fatimid dynasty conquers Nile Valley, eventually gaining control over Egypt and North Africa, Sicily, Syria, and Iraq; rivals the Abbasid caliphate*
970	*Al-Azhar University founded in Cairo*
977–1186	*Ghaznavid dynasty controls most of Afghanistan, Iran, and the Indus and Ganges Valleys*
1037	*Philosopher Ibn Sina, known in the West as Avicenna, dies*
1038–1194	*Seljuk dynasty rules Iraq, Iran, Syria, and parts of Central Asia; establishes a sultanate in Turkey*
1095	*Pope Urban II calls for a Crusade to take the Holy Land from the Muslims*
1099	*Christian crusaders occupy Jerusalem and establish Latin Kingdom*
1111	*Abu Hamid al-Ghazali, prominent theologian and legal scholar, dies*

1130–1269	*Almohad dynasty conquers North Africa and part of Spain*
1171–1250	*Ayyubid dynasty rules Egypt and Syria*
1187	*Saladin, leader of Ayyubids, defeats crusaders at Battle of Hittin and reconquers Jerusalem*
1198	*Philosopher Ibn Rushd, known as Averröes, dies*
1218	*Mongol ruler Genghis Khan sweeps across Central Asia into Iran*
1250–1517	*Mamluks, former slave soldiers in the Ayyubid army, establish dynasty in Egypt; extend control to Syria and western Arabia*
1258	*Mongols capture and destroy Baghdad, the Abbasid capital*
1273	*Jalal al-Din Rumi, poet and Sufi mystic, dies*
ca. 1300	*Osman I founds Ottoman Empire*
1334–1353	*The Alhambra is built in Granada, Spain*
1369–1405	*Mongol leader Tamerlane (Timur Lang) seizes power and reclaims former Mongol territories*
1406	*Historian Ibn Khaldun dies*
1453	*Ottoman sultan Mehmed II captures Constantinople*
1492	*Spanish monarchs Ferdinand and Isabella conquer Granada, driving Muslims from Spain*
1501	*Shah Ismail establishes Safavid empire in Iran*
1516–1517	*Ottomans conquer Egypt, Syria, and Islamic holy cities of Mecca and Medina*
1520	*Suleyman takes over as Ottoman sultan and brings the empire to peak of power and prosperity*
1526	*Battle of Mohacs brings Hungary under Ottoman control*
1526	*Mughal ruler Babur captures Delhi and establishes Mughal Empire in India*
1529	*Ottomans lay siege to Vienna, Austria*
1556–1605	*Mughal Empire in India reaches its height under the rule of Akbar I*
1571	*European victory at Battle of Lepanto off the coast of Greece stops Ottoman advance*
1588–1629	*Shah Abbas I rules Safavid Empire of Iran*
ca. 1645	*Mughal Shah Jahan completes Taj Mahal at Agra, India*
1658–1707	*Aurangzeb expands Mughal Empire through conquests; costs of military campaigns weaken the state*

1699	Ottoman Empire surrenders control of Hungary to Austria
1722	Afghan rebels capture the Safavid capital of Isfahan, bringing Safavid rule to an end
1750	Religious reformer Muhammad ibn Abd al-Wahhab joins forces with tribal chief Muhammad ibn Saud; the resulting Wahhabi movement conquers and unites tribes of Arabia
1798–1801	French armies led by Napoleon Bonaparte occupy Egypt
1803	British East India Company controls Delhi, seat of the Mughal Empire
1805	Muhammad Ali becomes Ottoman governor of Egypt and attempts to turn Egypt into a modern state
1809	Muslim reformer Usman Dan Fodio defeats Hausa rulers in Nigeria; establishes caliphate of Sokoto
1816	Dutch regain control of Indonesia from British
1821	Ottoman Empire takes control of Sudan
1830	French forces invade Algeria
1836	Ahmad ibn Idris, founder of Idrisi movement, dies
1857	Hindus and Muslims rebel against British rule in India; British depose last Mughal emperor
1869	Suez Canal opened in Egypt
1881	French troops invade and gain control of Tunisia
1882	British occupy Egypt
1885	In Sudan, forces of the Mahdi conquer Khartoum; establish Mahdist state
1898	Anglo-Egyptian invasion brings an end to Mahdist state in Sudan
1908	Young Turks overthrow sultan and restore constitutional government in Ottoman Empire
1914–1918	World War I
1919–1922	Ottoman Empire collapses
1921	Reza Khan seizes power in Iran; becomes Reza Shah Pahlavi in 1925
1922	British grants independence to Egypt but maintains control of foreign affairs
1923	Mustafa Kemal (later called Atatürk) establishes Turkish Republic
1928	Hasan al-Banna establishes Muslim Brotherhood in Egypt

1932   *The territories of Abd al-Aziz ibn Saud proclaimed the Kingdom of Saudi Arabia*

1935   *Persia renamed Iran*

1938   *Political writer Muhammad Iqbal, who led campaign in the Indian subcontinent for a separate Muslim state (Pakistan), dies*

1939–1945   *World War II*

1941   *Muhammad Reza Shah Pahlavi replaces Reza Shah in Iran*

1945   *The Arab League formed*

1947   *Pakistan is founded as a homeland for Indian Muslims*

1948   *The Jewish state of Israel is established*

1952   *Officers under the leadership of Gamal Abdel Nasser seize power in Egypt*

1954   *National Liberation Front (FLN) formed in Algeria and begins war against French rule*

1962   *Algerians win independence*

1964   *Founding of Palestine Liberation Organization (PLO)*

1965   *Malcolm X assassinated*

1966   *Sayyid Qutb, religious thinker and militant Islamic leader of the Muslim Brotherhood, is executed by Egyptian government*

1967   *Israeli victory in Six-Day War between Israel and Egypt, Syria, and Jordan*

1973   *October (Yom Kippur/Ramadan) War between Israel and Egypt and Syria*

1978   *Egyptian president Anwar el-Sadat and Israeli prime minister Menachem Begin sign peace agreement known as the Camp David Accords; peace treaty follows in 1979*

         Coup in Afghanistan brings communist government to power; former Soviet Union occupies the country in 1979

1979   *Ayatollah Ruhollah Khomeini leads coalition of groups in Iranian Revolution, which overthrows the Pahlavi government and drives the shah of Iran into exile*

         Iranians hold a group of Americans hostage at the United States embassy in Tehran

1980   *Hizbullah founded in Lebanon*

1980–1988   *Iran-Iraq War*

1981   *Muslim extremists assassinate Egyptian president Anwar el-Sadat*

1987   *Palestinians launch intifadah (uprising) in protest against Israeli occupation of the West Bank and Gaza*

1988   *Benazir Bhutto becomes prime minister of Pakistan; first female head of state elected in Muslim world*

1989   *Ayatollah Ruhollah Khomeini, head of Islamic Republic of Iran, dies*

1990–1991   *Iraq invades Kuwait, setting off the Persian Gulf War; United States and allies launch Operation Desert Storm against Iraq*

1992   *Resistance fighters (the Mujahidin) in Afghanistan defeat the country's communist government after 10 years of war and begin a battle for control of the country*

1993   *World Trade Center in New York City bombed; Shaykh Umar Abd al-Rahman charged with the attack*

1994   *Taliban fundamentalists take control in Afghanistan*

         In West Bank city of Hebron, Jewish settler (Baruch Goldstein) kills worshippers at Friday prayer in Mosque of the Patriarch, provoking suicide bombings by military wing of Hamas

1997   *Election of Muhammad Khatami as president of Iran opens door to greater liberalization and contact with the West*

1998   *Increasing violence in Kosovo leads to international sanctions against the Yugoslavian (Serbian) government*

2001   *September 11: Members of al-Qaeda terrorist network hijack four American airliners and attack the World Trade Center in New York City and the Pentagon in Washington, D.C., killing about 3,000 people*

2001   *United States heads a military campaign against Afghanistan to destroy the al-Qaeda network and oust the Taliban*

2003   *Charging Iraq with failure to remove weapons of mass destruction, United States leads an invasion of the country and ends Saddam Hussein's regime*

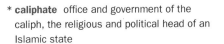

Abbasid Caliphate

The Abbasids were descendants of al-Abbas, an uncle of Muhammad. Abbasid caliphs ruled much of the Muslim world from 750 to 1258. The Abbasids brought an era of strong government, economic prosperity, and a flourishing civilization.

Rise to Power. The Umayyad family had controlled the caliphate* from 661 to 750. The Umayyad reign, however, was a turbulent one, plagued by power struggles and civil war. In the 720s, the Abbasid family began to gather support in the Khurasan province (present-day northeastern Iran). Villagers there resented Umayyad tax policies. In 747 an Abbasid commander named Abu Muslim led a revolt in the province. The rebellion spread, and three years later the Abbasid family took control of the caliphate.

Over the next 100 years, the Abbasids solidified their rule. They faced strong opposition from Umayyad supporters in Syria, and several uprisings erupted in Iraq. The second Abbasid caliph, Abu Jafar al-Mansur, strengthened Abbasid power by establishing a professional army during the first decades of the dynasty*. Caliph Harun al-Rashid further increased the power of the caliphate in the early 800s.

* **caliphate** office and government of the caliph, the religious and political head of an Islamic state

* **dynasty** succession of rulers from the same family or group

Abbasid caliph al-Mutawakkil completed this massive spiral minaret in 848. Known as the Malwiyya, it stands near the rear of the Great Mosque of Samarra (Iraq) and is one of the largest of its kind. As with all minarets, it was from here that Muslims were called to worship. The Malwiyya also represents the great power of the Abbasids.

* **tribute** money or other goods paid to a
dominant power or local government

* **theology** study of the nature and qualities of
God and the understanding of His will

* **medieval** refers to the Middle Ages, a period
roughly between 500 and 1500

* **Shi'i** refers to Muslims who believe that
Muhammad chose Ali ibn Abi Talib and his
descendants as the spiritual-political leaders
of the Muslim community

* **Sunni** refers to the largest branch of the
Muslim community; the name derives from
sunnah, the exemplary behavior of the
Prophet Muhammad

* **Holy Land** refers to Palestine, site of
religious shrines for Muslims, Jews, and
Christians

Iraq became the Abbasids' power base, and al-Mansur established his capital at Baghdad. From there, the family ruled the surrounding provinces, including Mesopotamia, Iran, Egypt, and Syria. Abbasid caliphs appointed a military governor to rule each province. The Abbasid government did not directly rule the distant provinces in its vast empire, though it collected taxes and tributes* from these areas. Local governors usually structured districts according to taxation purposes. The tax collection process depended on the organizational support of landowners, merchants, and money changers. To ensure that no official would become too powerful, the caliph chose different people to head tax collection and the judiciary.

Although Arabs dominated the Abbasid government and military, non-Arab Muslims played important roles in both. Persian influence was especially strong in the caliphate.

A Thriving Civilization. Islamic civilization flourished under Abbasid rule. Growth in industry, agriculture, and commerce brought economic prosperity to the region. Baghdad, with a population close to one-half million residents, became an international center of trade. In the 800s, it was one of the largest cities in the known world.

Abbasid wealth promoted advances in math, science, medicine, architecture, literature, philosophy, and art. Muslim religious leaders became experts in law and theology*. By the 800s, Arabic had displaced local languages throughout most of the empire. Muslim scholars translated classic works of science, literature, and philosophy into Arabic. With Europe going through its so-called Dark Ages, a period of little classical scholarship, Muslim cities became the important centers of learning. Many noted medieval* Christian philosophers and theologians later studied Muslim works.

Islamic scholarship during the Abbasid period included contributions from many foreign sources. Islamic science, for example, combined elements from Persian, Greek, Indian, and Arab studies. Cultural and artistic advances in the Islamic world also reflected outside influences. As the dominant political force, Muslims felt they could borrow from other cultures without losing their own identities. They also believed that cross-cultural exchanges would promote the spread of Islam.

Conflicts and Downfall. Despite great advances in Islamic civilization, the regional, religious, and political differences that divided the empire threatened the stability of the Abbasid caliphate. In the late 800s, local governors in Tunisia, Morocco, Iran, and Syria gained autonomy (self-government) from Abbasid rule. In the 900s, the Fatimid family established an independent Shi'i* dynasty in Egypt. To make matters worse, caliph al-Muqtadir's financial mismanagement weakened Abbasid power in Iraq, and in 945 the Buyids, a Shi'i dynasty from northern Iran, captured Baghdad. They reduced the Abbasids to powerless figureheads.

In the 1000s, Abbasid leader al-Qadir helped rally Sunni* resistance to the Buyids. In 1055 the Seljuk Turks captured Baghdad, where as Sunnis, they accepted the religious leadership of the Abbasid family. In the 1100s, caliph al-Nasir reestablished the family's political power in Iraq as well.

Outside forces finally brought an end to the Abbasid dynasty. Beginning in 1095, Christians invaded the Holy Land* and engaged in fierce battles against Abbasid armies. The Mongols in Asia posed an even greater threat to the caliphate. Sweeping across the continent, Mongol forces captured Baghdad in 1258. They executed the last Abbasid caliph and permanently ended the family's reign.

After the Mongol conquest, a few Abbasid family members reemerged in Cairo as members of the Mamluk court. Retained only to give legitimacy to the sultanate*, these Abbasids had no real power. This last trace of Abbasid status disappeared in 1517 when the Ottomans conquered Egypt. (*See also* **Arabic Language and Literature; Crusades; Mongols; Philosophy; Shi'i Islam; Sunni Islam; Taxation; Trade; Umayyad Caliphate.**)

* **sultanate** government of a sultan, the political and military ruler of a Muslim dynasty or state

Abd al-Qadir

1808–1883
Military leader, scholar, poet

Abd al-Qadir led Algerian resistance to French colonization for nearly two decades. Born in Algeria to a family of Moroccan origin, Abd al-Qadir's ancestors claimed to have descended from the Prophet Muhammad.

Abd al-Qadir was 22 years old when the French invaded Algeria. His father, Sidi Muhyi al-Din, led the resistance and called for a jihad* against the Europeans. Muhyi al-Din became ill, however, and turned over leadership of the resistance to his son in 1832. Three major tribes in Algeria declared Abd al-Qadir "Sultan* of the Arabs." His forces overpowered the French, leading them to call for a truce in 1834. Abd al-Qadir's power and prestige increased rapidly.

* **jihad** literally "striving"; war in defense of Islam

* **sultan** political or military ruler of a Muslim dynasty or state

Fighting resumed again in 1835. After both sides had inflicted heavy losses on each other, the French again sought peace. The Treaty of Tafna divided Algeria between the two sides. France retained the urban areas. Abd al-Qadir controlled the interior areas and the province of Algiers. The treaty brought an uneasy peace that only lasted two years. The French launched an offensive that eventually defeated the Arab tribes. Abd al-Qadir fled to Morocco in 1843, but soon returned to fight for his homeland. By that time, French military power was too great. Abd al-Qadir finally surrendered in 1847 and was imprisoned.

The French released Abd al-Qadir after he had served five years in prison and promised to cease resisting them. He then moved to the Ottoman Empire and settled in Damascus, Syria. There, he prevented Druze* rebels from killing the French consul and thousands of Christians.

A follower of Sufism*, Abd al-Qadir was a leader in the Qadiri order before joining the Naqshbandiyah, a Sufi order characterized by strict adherence to Islamic law. He wrote several major works, which include discussions of Sufi doctrine and collections of mystical poetry. (*See also* **Algeria; Colonialism; Qadiriyah; Sufism.**)

* **Druze** offshoot of Shi'i Islam in Lebanon and Syria

* **Sufism** Islamic mysticism, which seeks to develop spirituality through discipline of the mind and body

Abduh, Muhammad

1849–1905
Egyptian scholar, reformer

Many scholars consider Muhammad Abduh the architect of Islamic modernism. His early years included a traditional education and a commitment to Sufism. As a young adult, Abduh became a disciple of Jamal al-Din al-Afghani and an activist for the Pan-Islamic* movement. Al-Afghani hoped

* **Pan-Islamic** refers to the movement to unify all Islamic peoples

to unite Muslims in opposition to European colonizers. The British exiled both men from Egypt in 1882 for their part in a failed nationalist revolt.

Abduh returned to Egypt six years later. He focused his energies on religious, social, and educational reforms. Abduh perceived that Islam was in decline. He believed passivity and a rigid adherence to tradition had weakened the religion by holding it to outdated practices.

Abduh based his reform agenda on the idea that religion and science were compatible. He believed both were sources of truth and should strengthen one's belief in God. Abduh further sought to ground Islam in reason, rejecting a belief in superstition and blind traditionalism. He expressed many of his theories in *The Theology of Unity*, his most popular book.

Believing in the harmony between reason and revelation, Abduh advocated legal and theological* reform. He called for universal education and modernized the program of study at al-Azhar, the Islamic mosque-university in Egypt. He also encouraged strengthening family life by ending polygyny and divorce. Strong opposition in the legal and academic communities, however, slowed the progress of Abduh's reforms. Nonetheless, Abduh left a lasting legacy. His ideas about a modern Islam influenced thinkers throughout the twentieth century. (*See also* **Afghani, Jamal al-Din al-; Modernism; Science.**)

* **theological** refers to the study of the nature, qualities, and will of God

Ablution

Ablution is the Muslim ritual of purification. Its importance to Islam dates back to the Prophet Muhammad, who stated: "Purity is half the faith." Ablution specifically refers to ritual washing before prayer, which Muslims consider to be a sign of respect for God. By performing acts of purification, believers prepare to present themselves to Allah. Muslims believe ritual physical and spiritual purity is a necessary prerequisite for addressing God in prayer. Ablution is a part of worship and one of the ways to receive forgiveness of sins.

Impurities. Muslims believe people are naturally pure until an impurity disturbs this state. Ablution rituals restore purity by removing any impure agents. Impurities are material substances that defile people or objects. Such substances include blood, urine, feces, semen, and alcohol. People remove real impurities by washing, scrubbing, drying, or another similar action.

See color plate 14, vol. 3.

Partial and Complete Ablution. Islamic law specifies two major purification rituals. Partial ablution (*wudu*) involves washing body parts exposed to dirt and smog with clean water. These areas include the face, lower arms, part of the head, and the feet.

The ablution process begins with a declaration that the performance of the ritual is for the purpose of purity and worship. A Muslim then washes the hands, rinses the mouth, brushes the teeth, and clears the nostrils. He or she then washes the face and the arms. The next step is to cleanse the head, the ears, the neck, and in between the fingers with wet hands. Finally,

Ritual ablution dates back to the time of Muhammad. Performed before prayer, Muslims show respect to God by thoroughly cleansing their bodies. In this photo, an Afghan refugee in a Pakistani camp washes his feet in preparation for prayer.

a Muslim washes the feet, beginning with the right one. Many people conclude ablution with the words: "O God! Place me among the repenters and place me among the pure." Prayers may then begin.

A single ablution can be used for as many prayers as a person wishes. It remains valid until broken, most commonly by bodily discharge of an impure substance. Falling asleep and intoxication from drugs or alcohol also invalidate ablution.

The bath, or *ghusl*, is the second major purification ritual. It is the complete ablution and is necessary after sexual relations, ejaculation, menstruation, and at the end of the bleeding that occurs after giving birth. Shi'i Muslims also require a ritual bath after washing a corpse. Furthermore, both Sunnis and Shi'is recommend a complete bath on special religious days, such as on Fridays, on the days of Muslim festivals, and before entering the holy city of Mecca. Those who have never performed *ghusl* cannot enter a mosque. Muslims believe a person cannot encounter God without maintaining a *ghusl* level of purity.

As with *wudu*, *ghusl* requires clean, odorless water that has not been used for a previous ritual. The bath begins with the declaration of the intention of purity and worship. A Muslim performing complete ablution then washes every part of his or her body. Many use the following order for the ritual: washing the hands, washing the sexual organs, performing the *wudu*, rubbing water into the hair, and pouring water over the entire body. Praising God and asking for guidance finish the bath.

Islam allows for exceptions to the two rituals in certain circumstances. For example, when clean water is not available, dry ablution (*tayammum*) may be substituted for either ritual. After declaring intent, a Muslim begins *tayammum* by placing his or her hands on pure earth or sand and blowing off any excess particles. The person then uses the dust or sand to wipe the face and arms. (*See also* **Pillars of Islam; Prayer; Rites and Rituals.**)

Abortion

* **Qur'an** book of the holy scriptures of Islam

* **fetus** unborn human, usually from three months after conception until birth

* **hadith** reports of the words and deeds of Muhammad (not in the Qur'an, but accepted as guides for Muslim behavior)

Abortion is the deliberate termination of a pregnancy. Because it ends a developing life, abortion raises ethical and legal issues. It is a highly debated issue in cultures throughout the world.

Islam places a high value on preserving life and Muslims view children as divinely created. The Qur'an* teaches that killing will bring punishment in this life and the afterlife. The scripture also maintains that neither poverty nor hunger is a legitimate reason for killing one's offspring. Moreover, in Islam, producing children is an important component of marriage. Based on longstanding traditions, many Muslims reject abortion at any stage of pregnancy.

Islamic legal experts have instituted appropriate punishments for abortion. The gravity of the crime is linked to the status of the fetus* at the time of the abortion. The key issue is "ensoulment," referring to the time when the fetus becomes a human being with a soul. The hadith* contain two important teachings concerning the fetus. The first states that separate organs of the developing human being form 40 days after fertilization. The second tells about an angel coming to write the destiny of the child, around 120 days after conception.

Modern Muslim scholars are divided on the issue of the fetus itself. Some scholars, including Shi'i Muslims, believe that the divine creation of life occurs at fertilization. Some Sunni scholars maintain that a human fetus does not exist until separate organs or characteristics form. The majority of the Sunni, however, believe that human life exists only after the angel's visit—that is, at the end of 120 days.

A clinically induced abortion at any time is a punishable offense. The penalty is usually monetary compensation based on the age of the fetus. Hence, full compensation applies only if the pregnancy has reached full term, or nine months.

The fetus debate takes on an added importance because Islamic law accords certain rights to a fetus. First, the fetus has a right to life (the right to birth and to live as long as God allows). Thus, a pregnant woman cannot receive a death sentence before she has given birth. Muhammad set a precedent for this when he delayed the stoning of an adulterous woman until after she had delivered and weaned her baby. A fetus also has inheritance rights. Executors distribute shares of an inheritance after birth, based on the infant's sex. Finally, a miscarried fetus has a right to a burial, but only if its bones have formed.

Islamic law permits an abortion under special circumstances. Muslims call these therapeutic abortions. An unplanned or unwanted pregnancy is not a legitimate reason for an abortion. Muslims allow for a therapeutic abortion before ensoulment (four months) if the pregnancy threatens the mother's life. In addition, a nursing mother may be allowed an abortion on the grounds that her new pregnancy will reduce her milk supply and threaten the survival of a child she is currently nursing.

The right to life of the fetus creates a dilemma when a pregnancy threatens the life of the mother. Islam resolves such issues by giving priority to the mother's life because she is the one carrying the fetus. Muslims view the fetus as an organ of the mother. More importantly, she is a pillar of the family and has certain responsibilities and duties to other members. (*See also* **Afterlife; Sexuality; Women.**)

Abraham

ca. 2000 B.C.E.
Patriarch of Judaism, Christianity, and Islam

Abraham is considered the patriarch, or founding father, of Judaism, Christianity, and Islam. According to the holy scriptures of Judaism and the Christian Bible, Abram (as he was called) received a call from God to leave his native city of Ur in Mesopotamia (present-day Iraq) and bring his family to another land where he would become the father of a new nation. Abram obeyed, and God later changed his name to Abraham, which means "Father of Many Nations." The writings of Judaism, Christianity, and Islam portray Abraham as a model of faith and monotheism*.

* **monotheism** belief that there is only one God

After receiving God's call, Abraham journeyed with his wife and other family members to Canaan, between Syria and Egypt. God promised him that his children would inherit the land and become as numerous as the stars in the sky. Abraham, however, was already an old man, and his wife Sarah, who was also very old, had been unable to conceive a child. Sarah encouraged Abraham to have sexual relations with her Egyptian servant, Hagar, so that he might have an heir. Abraham agreed, and Hagar gave birth to a son, Ismail. Later, Sarah became pregnant. When Abraham was 100 years old, she bore him a son, Isaac. Jewish and Christian traditions identify with Isaac, while Islamic tradition identifies with Ismail.

After the birth of Isaac, Sarah became jealous of Ismail. As the firstborn son, Ismail would have been the primary recipient of Abraham's inheritance. Sarah, therefore, insisted that Abraham banish Hagar and Ismail. Abraham was reluctant to follow his wife's demand. According to Jewish tradition, he sent them away after God revealed to him that Isaac would be his rightful heir but that Ismail would also become the father of a nation.

See map in Middle East (vol. 2).

Muslims believe that Hagar and Ismail traveled to the desert near Mecca, where they nearly died of thirst. They were saved by a miraculous spring of water that flowed from the sand. When Abraham discovered that they were alive, he joined them in Mecca. To celebrate the miracle in the desert, Abraham and Ismail built (or rebuilt, according to some traditions) the Kaaba, which became Islam's holiest shrine. During the hajj*, Muslims participate in a variety of rituals that commemorate Hagar and Ismail's experiences in the desert.

* **hajj** pilgrimage to Mecca that Muslims are required to make once in their lifetime

The most serious test of Abraham's faith occurred when God commanded him to sacrifice his son. According to the Biblical account, God instructed Abraham to take Isaac to the top of a mountain and sacrifice him as an offering. Abraham went to the appointed spot, constructed an altar, and placed his son on it. He was about to kill Isaac with a knife when God stopped him. Satisfied that Abraham had proved his faith, God provided a ram for the offering instead of the boy. The Qur'an* presents a similar account but does not name the son. Abraham says, "Oh my son! I see in vision that I offer thee in sacrifice." When God sees that Abraham is willing to obey this com-

* **Qur'an** book of the holy scriptures of Islam

mand, he then promises him: "Behold, I make you a leader for the people." Most Muslims, therefore, identify Ismail as the one that Abraham intended to sacrifice.

Abraham died at a very old age—175 years, according to the Bible. He was buried alongside his wife, Sarah, in Hebron's Cave of Machpelah. A Muslim shrine, Haram al-Khalil, now marks the site of the tomb. (*See also* **Hajj; Ismail; Kaaba.**)

Abu Hanifah

699–767
Scholar and jurist

* **Sunni** refers to the largest branch of the Muslim community; the name derives from sunnah, the exemplary behavior of the Prophet Muhammad

* **Qur'an** book of the holy scriptures of Islam

* **hadith** reports of the words and deeds of Muhammad (not in the Qur'an, but accepted as guides for Muslim behavior)

See map in Sunni Islam (vol. 3).

Legal scholar Abu Hanifah is celebrated as the founder of the Hanafi, considered by many to be the most liberal of the four Sunni* schools of law. The other schools are the Maliki, Shafi'i, and Hanbali. The Hanafi school is known for its use of analogy, or comparison, in legal reasoning.

Of Persian heritage, Abu Hanifah was a native of Kufa, a city in what is now Iraq. Kufa, a young city with a diverse population, was a leading center of scholarship and legal thought. Abu Hanifah studied law in Kufa while earning his living as a textile merchant. His academic training and his experience as a merchant enhanced his ability to apply logic to the practical aspects of life.

All schools of Islamic law consult the Qur'an* first for legal and moral instruction. But for matters not specifically addressed in the Qur'an, legal scholars turn next to the sunnah—the actions and sayings of Muhammad as recorded in the hadith*. Scholars differ in their reliance on the hadith. Some follow these teachings strictly, but Abu Hanifah sought to broaden the rules by using analogical reasoning and thoughtful opinion regarding the implications of the Qur'an and the hadith. He relied so heavily on opinion in the formulation of legal rules that his school came to be called the People of Opinion.

The Hanafi school also developed the process of *ijma*, which is the consensus, or agreement, of a group of Islamic legal and religious scholars on a point of law. Once consensus is reached, it is considered to be evidence of the will of God.

Abu Hanifah promoted a degree of respect for personal freedom that is not seen in the other schools of law. The majority of Muslims today follow the teachings of the Hanafi school. (*See also* **Hadith; Ibn Hanbal; Law; Malik ibn Anas; Shafi'i; Sunnah; Sunni Islam.**)

Afghani, Jamal al-Din al-

ca. 1838–1897
Political activist

* **Pan-Islamic** refers to the movement to unify all Islamic peoples

Jamal al-Din al-Afghani was a political activist and writer, perhaps best known for his role in the Pan-Islamic* movement. A controversial figure during his lifetime, al-Afghani became one of the most influential figures in the Muslim world after his death.

Life and Work. Al-Afghani's unusual life was the source of legend, much of it based on his own stories. Although he claimed Afghan origin, evidence suggests that he was actually born in Iran. He began his education in his hometown of Asadabad in northwestern Iran and later traveled to the Shi'i shrine* cities of Iraq to complete his studies in theology* and law. The work al-Afghani did during these years reflects his innovative thinking and unique interpretation of Islamic thought. He borrowed, combined, and developed existing religious themes to create a new system of political and religious thought.

As a young man, al-Afghani traveled to India. Witnessing the effects of colonization on that country probably inspired his lifelong dislike for the British. He became an outspoken critic of Britain and its presence in India, Egypt, and other Islamic countries.

Al-Afghani arrived in Afghanistan in the 1860s and gained access to the amir*. He soon lost this important connection when a change in leadership brought a pro-British ruler to the throne and al-Afghani was expelled from the country. After a brief stay in Cairo, Egypt, al-Afghani left for Istanbul, Turkey. His intelligence and charismatic* personality once again brought him into the circles of power. He lectured at the new university and presented his unorthodox* ideas, which angered the establishment. The university came under attack by the conservative leaders, forcing the head of the university to resign and al-Afghani to leave the country.

From 1871 to 1879, al-Afghani lived in Cairo. A grant from the government enabled him to spend most of his time teaching. With Islamic scholar Muhammad Abduh, he introduced an interpretation of Islam that called for modernization and education while encouraging strict adherence to Islamic principles. He promoted political activism, urging his students to publish political newspapers, while he himself gave speeches and headed a secret society engaged in reformist activities. Several of his followers later became the leaders of Egyptian political and intellectual life. Meanwhile, al-Afghani's fiery speeches against the British soon brought him another expulsion, and he returned to India. Here he did much of his important writing, which consisted mainly of collecting and publishing his speeches. His most famous work, *The Refutation of the Materialists*, includes a defense of Islam against attacks made by Europeans.

In 1886 al-Afghani traveled to Iran and Russia to gather support for a war against Britain. Failing in this endeavor, he accepted an invitation from the Ottoman sultan* to live in Istanbul. Although he lived there in comfort, he was prevented from giving speeches. Al-Afghani died of cancer in 1897. Early biographies (written mostly by his followers before his papers became available in 1963) were based on what he wanted people to believe. In recent years, scholars have found independent documentation of al-Afghani's life and work.

Contributions to Modern Islam. The moving force behind al-Afghani's life and work was his hostility toward British rule in Muslim lands. His anger toward the British was part of a more general anti-imperialism. In keeping with his emphasis on anti-imperialism and his desire to maintain the independence of Muslim countries, al-Afghani emphasized practical aspects of political reform and self-improvement. This included technical and scientific education. When necessary, it also included cooperation with dictatorial rulers.

* **shrine** place that is considered sacred because of its history or the relics contained there

* **theology** study of the nature and qualities of God and the understanding of His will

* **amir** military commander, governor, or prince

* **charismatic** capable of arousing enthusiasm and loyalty

* **unorthodox** contrary to accepted beliefs and practices

* **sultan** political and military ruler of a Muslim dynasty or state

He was not the first to promote these ideas, but he was highly effective at spreading the messages. This was, in part, because he wrote in Arabic, which made his work accessible to more people. Al-Afghani saw nationalism and Pan-Islamism as different but not necessarily contradictory. Both were essentially strategies for Islamic unity and anti-imperialism.

Al-Afghani was one of the first Muslim figures to participate in various forms of political activism. He spoke publicly, wrote for newspapers and encouraged his followers to do so, led opposition groups, and even supported a plot to assassinate the shah* of Iran.

* **shah** king (Persian); ruler of Iran

His use of different arguments for different situations made al-Afghani popular with many groups. His ideas still appeal to those who support political reform and to those who emphasize Islamic principles. He left a legacy of practical, anti-imperialist political activism that continues to be of great importance to the modern Islamic world. (*See also* **Abduh, Muhammad.**)

Afghanistan

Throughout its history, Afghanistan has endured political upheaval and deep social division. Islam serves as one of the few unifying elements in Afghan society. It has flourished since the late 600s as a mainly tolerant force in the region, but political turmoil has complicated the role of Islam. Government takeovers, foreign invasions, and civil war created conditions in which Islamic extremism gained strength in the late twentieth century. Afghan leaders subjected the population to harsh religious law and provided asylum* to suspected international terrorists. In response to the September 11, 2001, attacks on the World Trade Center, the United States launched a military campaign to defeat terrorist forces in Afghanistan. In December 2001, it helped to establish a new Afghan government. This government pledged to rebuild Afghan society and restore human rights to the country.

* **asylum** protection; a safe place to stay

About 99 percent of the Afghan population is Muslim; between 75 and 85 percent are Sunni Muslims, while the rest are Shi'i. Despite their common Islamic heritage, Afghans belong to a variety of ethnic groups that have dominated different regions of the country. The largest group, the Pashtuns, represents about half the population. Other major ethnic groups include the Tajiks, Uzbeks, and Hazaras. Political power in Afghanistan has traditionally belonged to local tribal rulers rather than religious leaders.

 See map in Gulf States (vol. 1).

Early Conflicts. Located on the site of major trade routes in Central Asia, Afghanistan is a landlocked country of some 251,825 square miles. It lies east of Pakistan and west of Iran, bordering China on the northeast, and Turkmenistan, Uzbekistan, and Tajikistan on the north. Its rugged mountains, part of the Himalayan chain, are often impassable in winter and have made it difficult for outside armies to conquer and unify the region. Part of the Persian Empire in ancient times, Afghanistan was conquered by Alexander the Great in the 300s B.C.E.*, and a series of Hellenistic* and Central Asian rulers governed the region. Muslim Arab armies reached the region

* **B.C.E.** before the Common Era, which refers to the same time period as B.C.

* **Hellenistic** refers to the period after Alexander the Great (died 323 B.C.E.) when Greek culture spread throughout the Mediterranean region

by 642 C.E.*, taking over the western areas of Herat and Seistan and bringing Islam to the region. During the 800s, Islam spread to the eastern and northern parts of the region.

* C.E. Common Era, which refers to the same time period as A.D.

By the late 900s, Sultan Mahmud had transformed the city of Ghazni, in northeastern Afghanistan, into one of the most important Islamic capitals in the world. In 1219, however, the Mongol armies of Genghis Khan overran Afghanistan. Tolerant of local religions and customs, the Mongol rulers accepted Islam but governed by military might rather than Islamic principles. After the decline of the Mongol Empire around the mid-1300s, the region reverted to tribal rule, which continued until Afghanistan united under Nadir Shah Afshar and his successor, Ahmad Shah Durrani, in the early 1700s.

Conflicts over succession as well as military and political pressures from Britain and Russia weakened the Durrani empire. Eager to control Afghanistan in order to protect its empire in India, Britain fought two Anglo-Afghan wars (1839–1842 and 1878–1880), but ultimately failed to gain control of the country. After its second defeat in Afghanistan, Britain helped to bring Amir Abd al-Rahman Khan, a descendant of the Durrani dynasty, to power. The Iron Amir, as he was known, became the first Afghan ruler to centralize political power in the name of Islam. He forcibly converted the only remaining non-Muslims in the country and declared himself the ruler of an Islamic state. Islam provided a base for his power and he declared that "whether just or despotic, the king must be obeyed, provided his commands do not violate the *shari'ah**." The Iron Amir used harsh measures against his opponents, instilling fear throughout the country and weakening the power of religious leaders. A strong central state ran contrary to Afghan tradition, and it faced opposition from many Afghans, who continued to depend on village-based structures of authority.

* *shari'ah* Islamic law as established in the Qur'an and the sunnah, the exemplary behavior of the Prophet Muhammad

Emphasizing Islamic Values. New political ideas began to take root in Afghanistan in the early 1900s. King Amanullah introduced the country's first constitution in 1923 and supported the creation of a national philoso-

* **Qur'an** book of the holy scriptures of Islam
* **mullah** Muslim cleric or learned man

* **coup** sudden, and often violent, overthrow of a ruler or government
* **communist** follower of communism, a political and economic system based on the concept of shared ownership of all property

* **mujahidin** literally "warriors of God"; refers to Muslim fighters in proclaimed jihads (holy wars), such as the war against the Soviet invasion of Afghanistan

phy based on ideals shared by all citizens. Conservative spiritual leaders, however, sparked an armed rebellion against him, and drove him into exile in 1929. His successor, Muhammad Nadir Shah, abandoned many of Amanullah's reforms. Muhammad Shah's policies emphasized Islamic values, but unlike the Iron Amir, he did not invoke Islam as the source of his authority. Instead, he affirmed his power through a new political constitution. Muhammad Shah established a Jam'iyatul Ulama, or Supervisory Council of Muslim Scholars, and ordered the country's first printing of the Qur'an*. He also strengthened the power of the mullahs* and reinstated *shari'ah* courts to hear all legal cases.

Marxism and Soviet Invasion. Throughout the rest of the twentieth century, the forces of modernization and conservative Islam often clashed. In the 1950s and 1960s, Marxist and other left-wing parties emerged in the capital city of Kabul. At the same time, students at Kabul University formed the Muslim Youth Movement, an organization dedicated to radical change through the establishment of an Islamic government. In 1978 a coup* led by the People's Democratic Party of Afghanistan brought a communist* government to power. This regime met with strong resistance from most Afghans, and in 1979, the Soviet Union invaded Afghanistan to support the endangered government. To defend their country and Islam, the mullahs launched a popular uprising against the Soviets. Afghans who had fled into exile in Pakistan, as well as thousands of young Muslims from other parts of the Islamic world, rushed to Afghanistan to support the uprising.

The resistance fighters, known as mujahidin*, received military and financial support from the United States and other countries eager to undermine the Soviet Union. In 1989, after a decade of struggle, the mujahidin drove out the Soviet army and took control of most of Afghanistan. The communists, however, still clung to power in Kabul, and the mujahidin continued to fight them.

Finally, in April 1992, the mujahidin defeated the Marxist government and declared Afghanistan an Islamic state. For the first time in Afghan history, religious figures held government power. Yet civil war had devastated the country, and officials found it difficult to rebuild its infrastructure—the public works, such as roads and hospitals, that enable society to function. Huge areas of the countryside contained land mines, posing dangers to refugees and to farmers planting crops. Many men had died in the fighting, leaving wives and children without support, and food shortages plagued the country. Despite these difficulties, Western powers withdrew most of their economic aid, leaving Afghanistan to cope with these challenges on its own.

Rise of the Taliban. In the face of such troubles, the mujahidin failed to create a new Islamic political system, resorting instead to old patterns of tribal-based power that brought them wealth and influence. Bribery, theft, murder, rape, and drug trafficking became common, and private armies competed for power and riches. The mujahidin lost the people's trust when it failed to establish law and order.

Frustrated by these circumstances, a group of religious students led by Mullah Muhammad Omar decided to take control. They called themselves the Taliban, a word meaning "students" in Persian. The Taliban seized power in the region around Kandahar in 1994 and soon controlled most of the country. At first, many Afghans welcomed them because they ended crime and gave citizens a feeling of safety. The Taliban, however, imposed a harsh, puritanical version of Islam that most Afghans found oppressive. They forbade women to hold jobs, attend school, or leave their homes without a male relative. When in public, women had to cover themselves with a long garment called a *burqa*. The Taliban ordered strict punishments for crimes. They amputated a hand and a foot for theft and stoned to death accused adulterers at public executions at the sports stadium in Kabul.

The Taliban had strong ties to non-Afghan fighters who had come to Afghanistan to join the mujahidin against the Soviets. Many of these men stayed in Afghanistan after defeating the communists or returned later to continue the fight for radical Islam. Among them was a Saudi Arabian businessman, Osama bin Laden, who used Afghanistan's remote terrain as a base to train members of his terrorist network al-Qaeda.

On September 11, 2001, members of al-Qaeda attacked the World Trade Center in New York and the Pentagon building in Washington, D.C., killing about 3,000 people. A month later, the United States bombed Taliban and al-Qaeda forces in Afghanistan and began giving military support to anti-Taliban groups such as the Northern Alliance. The Taliban regime fell on November 17, 2001, and Hamid Karzai became the country's new head of state. The following June, Afghanistan called for a *loya jirga*, or traditional council of tribal leaders. This conference led to the creation of a new government and a vote confirming Karzai as head of state.

Post-Taliban Reconstruction. After years of civil war, conflict between Taliban and anti-Taliban forces, and American bombing—which alone resulted in an estimated 3,500 civilian deaths—Afghanistan lay in economic and physical ruin. Hamid Karzai pledged to rebuild the country through peaceful means and took steps to resolve ethnic rivalries, empower women, and unify the region while respecting Islamic traditions and values. However, competing groups continued to threaten Afghanistan's stability. In September 2002, a car bomb intended to assassinate Karzai exploded in Kabul, killing 26 people. The United States and other countries pledged economic support to Afghanistan, but other international events, especially the war with Iraq in 2003, deflected attention away from Afghanistan. (*See also* **Bin Laden, Osama; Loya Jirga; Mujahidin; Qaeda, al-; Taliban.**)

After the Taliban

Afghan women have enjoyed improved conditions since the defeat of the Taliban. Girls have flocked to schools, and women have returned to the workplace. Some have even started their own businesses. Yet, problems continue to plague Afghan women. Maternal health rates remain among the worst in the world. For every 100,000 births in the country, 1,600 mothers die from complications. Although Afghan women may go out in public and dress as they please, many continue to wear the *burqa*, either by choice or because they do not feel safe without it. In addition, some women have been imprisoned—at their families' request—for such actions as refusing to marry their father's choice of a husband. In November 2002, the Afghan government freed 20 women from prison. Some officials, however, have stated that if the government had not imprisoned them for these behaviors, their families would have killed them.

Afterlife

Muslims believe that one's condition in the afterlife is determined by the degree to which that person has accepted the unity and justice of God and therefore acted justly and with mercy toward others. Believers—those who have faith in God's revelations and have lived accordingly—will go to heaven. Nonbelievers and evildoers will be punished in hell.

Qur'anic Teaching. The culture into which Muhammad was born did not generally believe in the afterlife. When Muhammad began to preach about the resurrection* and the accountability of each person at the time of

* **resurrection** coming to life again; rising from the dead

* **Qur'an** book of the holy scriptures of Islam

judgment, he faced scorn and skepticism. Nevertheless, the message of the Qur'an* teaches that God will indeed raise the dead, judge all people based on their deeds during their lifetime, and determine their eternal destiny. The moment of resurrection and judgment represents the final and absolute power of God over human destiny and the crucial nature of responsible human behavior.

The Qur'an provides details about the events that signal the end of time and the coming of the day of resurrection, the judgment process, and the conditions that will be experienced in paradise and in hell. The Qur'an says, for example, that terrifying events will signal the end of the world and that all people will gather for judgment. It describes the crossing of the Sirat bridge (which spans the fires of hell), the possibility of intercession*, and the preparation for one's final entrance into hell or into the gardens of bliss. Surah* 9.19–30 of the Qur'an explains how the circumstances of one's final resting place are indicated in the accounting of one's book of deeds. The person who is given his or her book in the right hand is destined for a blissful eternal rest. But the person who is given the book in the left hand will be seized, bound, and exposed to the burning fire of hell.

* **intercession** act of pleading for another

* **surah** chapter of the Qur'an

The Fire of Hell. The fire of hell—called Jahannam—is often decribed in traditional Islamic literature as having seven gates. Information gathered from several passages in the Qur'an suggests that these gates may be meant for different categories of sinners. The bridge of Sirat stretches over the flames. Those who have lived a good life pass across the bridge easily. But evildoers find the bridge razor-thin and fall into the flames.

The tortures of the fire are fearsome. Roaring flames, fierce boiling waters, scorching wind, and black smoke torment the wretched inhabitants. Their scorched skins are exchanged for new ones so they suffer the pain repeatedly. The sinners drink foul liquids in a hopeless effort to quench their thirst. Boiling water is poured over their heads and iron hooks drag them back if they try to escape.

The Gardens of Paradise. The Qur'an clearly identifies those who are destined for a blissful eternal rest in the gardens of paradise. These fortunate souls do good works and are truthful and obedient. When they fail, they express remorse and seek forgiveness. They feed poor people and orphans, and they have faith in the revelations of God.

Descriptions of life in the garden are as vivid as those of the tortures of the damned. The faithful are peaceful and content. They enjoy gentle speech, pleasant shade, fruits, and meat if they desire. They drink delicious wine from a shining stream and suffer no ill effects. Servants wait on them as they recline in silk robes on beautiful couches. Male inhabitants of the garden enjoy the attentions of the *huris*, beautiful young women with eyes like pearls. The joys of paradise also include choirs of angels singing in Arabic and the ability to eat and drink 100 times more than one could normally hold.

* **theologian** person who studies the nature, qualities, and will of God

* **omniscience** quality of being all-knowing

Religious Issues. Theologians* have addressed a host of issues concerning the reality of human responsibility and of divine judgment. One such question involves the dilemma of individual freedom versus the recognition of divine power and omniscience*. Another is the matter of God's justice balanced with God's mercy. The Qur'an makes it clear that those who are in the fire will remain there forever. Later commentary interprets it to mean that they will remain only as long as the fire lasts, and that God in his mercy will at last bring all souls to paradise.

Throughout Islamic history there have been wide differences in thinking about whether the details of resurrection and judgment should be understood literally or symbolically. Traditionalists believe that for the great mass of the faithful, the descriptions given in the sacred scripture are to be taken at face value. More recently, however, some scholars have come to see the details of the afterlife as metaphors* and symbols.

One of the strong affirmations of traditional Islam has been that those who earn eternal happiness in the garden will have the opportunity to gaze on the face of God. Some Muslims believe that this is to be taken literally. Others interpret this to mean that the ultimate reward of a good life is the supreme pleasure of dwelling in the hereafter in the presence of the divine.

Until recently, most Muslims writing about Islam in the twentieth century have avoided going into detail on the subject of the afterlife. Instead, they have chosen to affirm the reality of human accountability and of the day of judgment without focusing on the specific consequences of that judgment. The great majority of commentators who speculate on the nature of the realities of the afterlife acknowledge that the world to come is beyond clear human understanding. They maintain that all that humans need to know is that the judgment itself is inevitable and that God's justice will prevail.

See Christianity and Islam; Judaism and Islam.

The In-Between Time

Barzakh, which means "interval" or "partition," refers to the time immediately after death and before the resurrection. It is not discussed in the Qur'an, but later writings that deal with the afterlife have suggested several temporary circumstances in the *barzakh* that are affected by the quality of life lived by the deceased. For example, the judgment a person faces at the end of time is predicted by his or her ability to answer correctly the questions posed by two terrifying angels, Munkar and Nakir, immediately after death.

* **metaphor** figure of speech in which one object or idea is directly identified with a different object or idea

Ahl al-Kitab

Ahmadi

Ahmadi refers to a messianic* movement in modern Islam. The Ahmadis have been controversial since their beginnings in British-controlled India in 1889. Nevertheless, they have remained active for more than a century and are known for their zealous dedication to the spreading of their faith. The Ahmadis have established mosques and missionary centers in the Indian subcontinent, the Western world, Africa, and Asia.

The movement was founded by Mirza Ghulam Ahmad, who was born in the late 1830s in India. Ghulam Ahmad's followers claimed he was the Messiah and a prophet. As a result, the Ahmadi movement aroused the fierce opposition of mainstream Sunni* Muslims. In particular, the movement was accused of rejecting the belief that Muhammad was the last prophet. While India was under British rule, this controversy remained an issue among private individuals and religious organizations. When the Ahmadi headquarters moved to the Islamic state of Pakistan in 1947, however, the dispute assumed much greater importance. Religious scholars belonging to the Sunni mainstream demanded the formal exclusion of the Ahmadi movement from the Islamic fold and achieved that goal in Pakistan in 1974.

* **messianic** refers to messiah, the anticipated savior to be sent by God

* **Sunni** refers to the largest branch of the Muslim community; the name derives from sunnah, the exemplary behavior of the Prophet Muhammad

The original religious thought of the Ahmadi movement revolved around Ghulam Ahmad's claim to be a divinely inspired thinker and reformer. The various ways in which he expressed his beliefs, however, enabled both his supporters and his rivals to interpret his claims in contradictory ways.

Ghulam Ahmad based his convictions on the belief that Muslim religion and society had deteriorated to the point where divinely inspired reforms were needed. He claimed to have been chosen by Allah for the task of revitalizing Islam. He maintained that his position was compatible with the Muslim belief that Muhammad was the last prophet by dividing prophets into two categories. He claimed there were legislative prophets, who bring new books of divine law, and nonlegislative prophets, who are sent simply to urge a community to implement laws brought by earlier, legislative prophets. According to Ghulam Ahmad, the belief in the finality of Muhammad's prophethood applied only to legislative prophets.

After Ghulam Ahmad's death in 1908, the movement divided over questions of leadership. The Qadiani faction, the largest of the resulting groups, emphasized Ghulam Ahmad's claim to prophethood. It claimed that the religious authority of Ghulam Ahmad's son Mahmud was no less than his father's had been. The Qadiani faction also considered non-Ahmadi Muslims infidels*. The Lahori faction, on the other hand, held that Ghulam Ahmad never claimed to be more than a renewer of the Islamic faith.

While conflict among Ahmadi factions played a prominent role in the movement's history, one aspect has always remained constant: all Ahmadis consider the peaceful spread of their version of Islam among Muslims and non-Muslims to be of the utmost importance.

* **infidel** unbeliever; person who does not accept a particular faith

Ahmad Khan, Sayyid

1817–1898
Indian writer and political activist

* **regime** government in power

An Indian Islamic writer and reformer, Sayyid Ahmad Khan, defied tradition through his efforts to modernize the interpretation of Islam in British colonial India in the mid-1800s. Ahmad Khan spent his entire professional career in the judicial service of the colonial regime* and as a loyal supporter of the government.

After the mutiny of the Bengal army in 1857, when Indian troops rebelled against their British officers, Ahmad Khan wrote several articles defending the loyalty of Muslim troops. He felt the British had unfairly blamed Muslims for inciting the uprising. He later used this argument to gain British support for Muslim rights in the Indian political system. His efforts also fostered respect and improved understanding between Muslims and Christians.

A visit to London in 1869 convinced Ahmad Khan that Muslim students in India, who traditionally attended orthodox religious schools, could benefit from the modern scientific studies he had observed in Britain. Using Cambridge and Oxford universities as models, he founded the Mohammedan Anglo-Oriental College at Aligarh, a city in northern India, in 1875. Though the college accepted Hindu students, it was primarily a Muslim institution with a bold new purpose: to provide the best elements of modern European education within a distinctly Islamic context. The college, which was renamed

Aligarh Muslim University in 1920, graduated many students who became prominent figures in Indian public life in the early twentieth century.

Ahmad Khan also worked, through the All-India Mohammedan Educational Conference, to promote Muslim nationalism in India. He published two books on religious subjects, *Mahomedan Commentary on the Holy Bible* (in 1862) and *A Series of Essays on the Life of Mohammad* (in 1870). He advocated religious moderation and rational social reforms in Muslim culture—ideas that aroused controversy among conservative thinkers but are now considered a foundation for the modern interpretation of Islam. In 1881 Ahmad Khan received a knighthood from the British government. (*See also* **Colonialism; Education; India.**)

A'ishah

614–678
Third wife of Muhammad

A'ishah was the third and youngest wife of the Prophet Muhammad. Born in Mecca, she was the daughter of Abu Bakr, one of the Prophet's most important supporters. Muhammad married her in 624 after the battle of Badr. A'ishah's intelligence, courage, and personal charm established her as his favorite spouse, and she sometimes accompanied her husband on his travels. When Muhammad died in 632, A'ishah was at his side. Only 18 and without children, she was forbidden to marry again.

A'ishah became an authority on medicine, history, and poetry. She collected and recorded hadith, the words and deeds of Muhammad as reported by his close companions. Historians have traced more than 1,200 of these back to her. She also played a central role in leading prayers for women in the early years of the Muslim community.

A'ishah is best remembered for the active role she played in Muslim political affairs after her husband's death. When disagreement arose over who should succeed Muhammad as caliph*, the majority of Muslims chose her father, Abu Bakr. After his death, Umar succeeded him for 10 years and Uthman for 12. Both men were assassinated. A'ishah remained politically inactive during Umar's caliphate but played a significant role in ending that of Uthman. She gave some support to the opposition movement that ultimately led to his murder.

* **caliph** religious and political leader of an Islamic state

A'ishah also opposed Ali ibn Abi Talib, Muhammad's son-in-law, who was elected caliph after Uthman. A'ishah gathered an army of loyal followers to challenge Ali in battle. Ali defeated her, however, at the Battle of the Camel, named for the animal on which she rode. After capturing A'ishah, Ali freed her on the condition that she abandon politics. A'ishah lived the remainder of her life in Medina. (*See also* **Ali ibn Abi Talib; Caliph; Muhammad.**)

Akbar, Jalaludin Muhammad

1542–1605
Mughal emperor

Jalaludin Muhammad Akbar reigned from 1556 to 1605 and was among the most important of the Mughal (or Mogul) emperors of India. Claiming descent from the Mongol rulers Genghis Khan and Tamerlane, Akbar began his career in 1555 at age 13 when his father, Emperor Humayun, made him governor of the Punjab, a region in northwestern India. When Humayun died the following year, Hemu, a Hindu government minister, tried unsuccessfully to claim the throne. Akbar then assumed rule over Humayun's empire, which at that time included only the Punjab and the region near Delhi. The young emperor immediately began seizing new lands, eventually gaining control of most of India.

With a vast and diverse empire to govern, Akbar made changes that greatly improved the efficiency of his administration. He placed military governors, or *mansabars*, in control of each province, and severely punished any abuses of power. Akbar instituted a tax system that imposed an equal tax on all his subjects and eliminated the *jizyah*, a tax traditionally imposed on non-Muslims. Convinced of the importance of maintaining good relations with the Hindus under his rule, Akbar appointed Hindus to many government posts and, unlike earlier rulers, allowed them to keep their own laws and customs. Finally, to further strengthen political bonds with the numerous princes within his empire, Akbar married their daughters. By the end of his life he had numerous wives, almost all of whom he married for political reasons. His favorite wife was a Hindu, who gave birth to his heir Jahangir.

Although Akbar was unable to read or write, he was an intelligent and creative thinker who enjoyed intellectual debate. His court became an important cultural center. He encouraged communication among the diverse cultures in his domain and ordered that classics of Sanskrit* literature be translated into Persian, the language of his court. He appreciated Western art, and his painters began to use European techniques—such as perspective—in their own work, creating a distinctive Mughal style. A devout Muslim, Akbar convinced his court—despite objections from conservative religious scholars—to accept his authority to interpret Islamic law. He was also interested in other religious teachings and invited Hindus, Christians, and representatives of other religions to discuss theology* with him. From these discussions he hoped to identify universal truths that would be the basis of his new religion, Din-i Ilahi, or "The Divine Religion." Emphasizing the unity of God and God's world, this religion was based primarily on Islamic teaching. Akbar used this new religion to assert the idea of divine kingship*—a notion that Muslim scholars rejected as un-Islamic. Nevertheless, the idea of divine kingship lasted until the end of Mughal rule.

Akbar developed many of his political ideas from the teachings of Abul Fazl, who joined the court in 1574. Abul Fazl believed in the Greek philosopher Plato's concept of the "philosopher king," an ideal type of ruler who would inspire obedience through his wisdom, learning, and wise policies. Indeed, Akbar appeared to consider himself to be such a king. His rule has often been seen as a model of enlightened, strong, and tolerant government. (*See also* **India; Mughal Empire.**)

* **Sanskrit** ancient classical language of India and Hinduism

* **theology** study of the nature and qualities of God and the understanding of His will

* **divine kingship** belief that a ruler's authority comes from God

al-

For names beginning with the Arabic article *al-*, generally see under the following element of the name. For example, for *al-Jazeera*, see *Jazeera, al-*.

Alawi

The Alawi are a minority Muslim sect in northwest Syria and Turkey. Their name comes from the term *Alawiyun*, meaning follower of Ali—Ali ibn Abi Talib, cousin and son-in-law of the Prophet Muhammad. The Alawi believe in a version of Shi'i* faith as inspired by Muhammad ibn Nusayr, a follower of one of the imams*. They are called *ghulat* by other Muslims, which means "exaggerators" or "extremists." The Alawi believe foremost in the oneness of God. They hold that God appeared on earth seven times in human form and that Ali is the last and most perfect manifestation. They believe that God has three personalities: Ali, Muhammad, and Salman al-Farisi, a Persian companion of Muhammad who helped him defend the city of Medina.

The Alawi interpret the Qur'an and Muhammad's teachings allegorically* with good and evil symbolized by light and darkness. Worship of light serves as a major part of their religious system. For Alawis, the sun's light symbolizes the mystery of God. A group of Alawis called the Shamsis believes that Ali lives in the sun; another group, the Qamaris, asserts that Ali lives in the moon, the dark spots of which indicate his presence.

The Alawi also have faith in the existence of countless worlds, the most divine of which is the al-Alam al-Nurani, or World of Light, inhabited by spirits. Humans live in the al-Alam al-Turabi, or Earthly World. The Alawi believe in reincarnation among people, plants, and animals. They hold that, after death, the soul of a faithful Alawi passes into another human body and that the soul of a wicked person passes into the body of an unclean or predatory animal. As a persecuted minority, the Alawi keep their beliefs secret and avoid exposing them to outsiders. They place great importance on rites that initiate them into the mysteries of their religion.

The Alawi celebrate many Muslim festivals, including Eid al-Fitr and Eid al-Adha. Like other Shi'is, they commemorate the martyrdom* of Husayn ibn Ali, whom they consider divine and comparable to Jesus Christ. Alawis also celebrate Persian festivals, especially Nawruz, which marks the beginning of spring. In addition, they participate in some Christian festivals, including the Epiphany, Pentecost, Palm Sunday, and the feast days of the saints John Chrysostom, Barbara, and Mary Magdalene. The Alawi also attend Mass, but instead of believing that the bread and wine are the body and blood of Christ, they view the wine as the manifestation of Ali. (*See also* **Ali ibn Abi Talib; Calendar, Islamic; Shi'i Islam; Syria.**)

* **Shi'i** refers to Muslims who believe that Muhammad chose Ali ibn Abi Talib and his descendants as the spiritual-political leaders of the Muslim community

* **imam** spiritual-political leader in Shi'i Islam, one who is regarded to be directly descended from Muhammad; also, one who leads prayers

* **allegorical** referring to allegory, a literary device in which ideas are expressed through symbolic figures or actions

* **martyrdom** act of dying for one's religious beliefs

Albania

Albania, the only country within the European continent with a majority Muslim population, regained its basic freedoms in 1992 after almost 50 years of communist rule. The regime* of Enver Hoxha, who seized power after World War II, had outlawed religious expression and, in 1967, declared Albania the world's first atheistic* state. When the ban on religion was lifted in 1991, however, Albania's Muslim traditions revived. By early 1992, the

* **regime** government in power

* **atheistic** denying the existence of God

When Albania's ban on religion ended in 1991, the Ethem Bey Mosque in the country's capital of Tirana was able to hold services legally for the first time in 24 years. More than 15,000 Muslims assembled for prayers.

country—in which approximately 70 percent are Muslims or come from traditionally Muslim families, 20 percent are Orthodox Christian, and 10 percent are Roman Catholic—had declared its intention to join the 45-nation Organization of the Islamic Conference (OIC). The OIC is an international group that promotes unity among Muslims of all nations and races.

The Arrival of Islam. Albania's rugged mountain terrain has kept it remote and undeveloped. The country, with an area of about 11,100 square miles, sits on the Balkan Peninsula north of Greece, and also borders Macedonia, Kosovo, and Montenegro. Settled by the ancient Illyrians*, the region was later invaded by the Greeks, Romans, Byzantines, and Ottoman Turks.

The Ottomans brought Islam to Albania when they conquered the region in the 1400s. To crush resistance to colonial rule and to weaken Albanian ties with neighboring Orthodox Christian countries, the Ottomans imposed a heavy tax on Albanian subjects who refused to convert to Islam. As a result, the majority of Albanians became Muslims. Some, however, converted mainly to avoid Turkish discrimination or violence and secretly clung to Christian and pre-Christian beliefs. Sometimes, different branches of the same family practiced different religions. In some areas, men held two names—a Muslim one to use in public, and a Christian one to use at home. British poet Lord Byron once wrote of the Albanians: "The Greeks hardly regard them as Christians, or the Turks as Muslims; and in fact they are a mixture of both, and sometimes neither."

* **Illyrians** people who populated the Balkan Peninsula along the Adriatic coast

Historically tolerant of religious differences, Albania in the 1700s welcomed the Bektashis, a Sufi* order that originated in Turkey in the 1200s. In 1928 when Bektashi leader Salih Dedei was driven out of Turkey, he established himself in the Albanian capital of Tirana. The country today is home to hundreds of Bektashi shrines* and an estimated 800 mosques.

The Roots of Ethnic Conflict. Under Ottoman rule, Albania was relatively isolated. In 1912, however, patriot Ismail Kemal declared Albanian independence. But freedom was short-lived. In 1913 the Great Powers of Europe—Britain, Germany, Russia, Austria-Hungary, France, and Italy—redrew Albania's borders, giving more than half of its land and population to neighboring states. This redistribution later contributed to bloody conflicts in the region. Through the 1990s, many Balkan states and provinces experienced civil strife rooted in ethnic* divisions. In the late 1990s, Christian Serbs targeted Albanian Muslims living in the Serbian province of Kosovo for brutal forced removal, or "ethnic cleansing." NATO (North Atlantic Treaty Organization) and United Nations troops occupied the province to protect Kosovo's Albanian population from forced deportation and violence.

Religious Repression. From 1925 to the communist takeover in 1944, kings ruled Albania. When the Nazis occupied the country during World War II, Albania refused to hand over its 300 Jews to the Germans; only five Albanian Jews perished in the Holocaust*. Hoxha assumed control of the country in 1944 and imposed a strict dictatorship, closing Albania's borders and suppressing religious life. Hoxha imprisoned as many as 200 priests and Muslim clerics, several of whom disappeared and are assumed to have been executed. After Hoxha declared his country officially atheist in 1967, some 2,169 mosques, churches, monasteries, and other places of worship were closed, destroyed, or converted to other uses. Individuals caught wearing religious symbols could be imprisoned for up to ten years.

Return to Religious Freedom. After Hoxha's death in 1985, Albania struggled to achieve democratic reforms. In 1990 massive student demonstrations forced Hoxha's handpicked successor, Ramiz Alia, to reverse the country's ban on religion. The following year, more than 15,000 people in Tirana attended Albania's first legal Muslim service in 24 years at the Ethem Bey Mosque. Since then, crowds have celebrated the rededication of mosques and the restoration of precious Islamic artworks. Much of the interest in Albanian Islamic revival has come from the country's youth, who have grown up without much religious instruction but who are eager to embrace their traditions. To this end, several Islamic countries have sent religious teachers to Albania—which, in the 1990s, had only about 200 practicing imams*. They have established charities in the country. Christian evangelical* sects have also established Albanian missions. The new Albanian constitution guarantees freedom of religion.

Islamic countries have also begun investing in Albania's economy, which remains the poorest in Europe. The Arab-Albanian Islamic Bank, established in 1993 with the help of investors from Saudi Arabia and Bahrain, promotes investment within the guidelines of Islamic banking principles. (*See also* **Art; Banks and Banking; Christianity and Islam; Imam; Kosovo; Ottoman Empire; Saudi Arabia; Sufism; Sunni Islam.**)

* **Sufi** refers to Sufism, which seeks to develop spirituality through discipline of the mind and body

* **shrine** place that is considered sacred because of its history or the relics contained there

* **ethnic** relating to groups of people who share a common racial, national, tribal, religious, linguistic, or cultural background

Albanian Mosques

Albania's first mosque was built in Berat in 1380, at the beginning of the Ottoman invasion; the second oldest mosque, Ilias Mirahori, was constructed in 1484 in Korce. One of the most important examples of Islamic architecture in Albania, the Abdurrahman Pashi Mosque, was built near Peqini in 1822.

Berat is known for several other mosques, among them the Alveti Tekke (a small shrine for Bektashi worship) constructed in 1790; the ornately decorated Bachelor's Mosque, built in 1827; and the Leaden Mosque, built in 1955 and named for its lead-covered cupola.

* **Holocaust** refers to the systematic mass murder of Jews and other European civilians by the Nazis during World War II

* **imam** spiritual-political leader in Shi'i Islam, one who is regarded to be directly descended from Muhammad; also, one who leads prayers

* **evangelical** characterized by religious zeal and dedication to the spread of religion, usually Christian

Alchemy

* **medieval** refers to the Middle Ages, a period roughly between 500 and 1500

The term *alchemy* refers to certain "scientific" ideas and practices of the medieval* world. Alchemists believed it was possible to change common metals such as lead or iron into gold, and they experimented with various substances in an effort to achieve this. Alchemy has often been associated with magic. However, it actually represented the most serious scientific scholarship of its time and is now credited as a foundation of modern chemistry. Some basic roots of alchemy have been traced to ancient Egypt, India, and China, but the science reached its full development in the Islamic world of the Middle Ages.

Islamic alchemists accepted the idea of Aristotle, the ancient Greek philosopher, that all matter is composed of four primary elements: earth, water, fire, and air. Unlike Aristotle and the other Greek philosophers, however, some Muslim alchemists believed that the four primary qualities (hot, cold, moist, and dry) existed as independent entities. Thus, Islamic alchemists developed a unique theory of the elements. According to this theory, all metals belonged to the same category and possessed different properties only because of natural "accidents." Therefore, alchemists believed, the transmutation* of one metal to another was a process that occurred slowly in nature. Trying to change a base metal into gold, then, would not be an act of magic but simply a way of advancing a natural process. Another important theme in Islamic alchemy was the belief in an elixir* that could prolong human life. This became a repeated theme in the early history of medicine.

* **transmutation** act of changing one substance into another

* **elixir** substance believed to have special properties, such as the ability to prolong life; medicinal mixture

Muslim alchemists influenced scholars throughout medieval Europe and made lasting contributions to the advancement of science. They developed the theory that all metals are composed of sulphur and mercury, and they introduced sal ammoniac, a substance central to the development of modern chemistry. Muslim alchemists were among the first to practice the scientific method. They made careful observations and kept precise recordings of their experiments, providing an important model for later scientists to follow. (*See also* **Cosmology; Medicine; Science.**)

Algeria

Algeria, the second largest country in Africa, has been predominantly Muslim since Arabs conquered the region almost 1,400 years ago. Since the 1960s when Algeria gained independence from France, however, ideological differences have transformed the country into a battlefield. The opposing sides consist of two groups: those who favor a secular* nation with ties to France and those who seek to form an independent Islamic state.

* **secular** separate from religion in human life and society; connected to everyday life

Geography and History. Algeria covers more than 900,000 square miles, most of which lies in the Sahara. The nation's major cities are located in the north, near its Mediterranean coast. Algeria shares borders with Libya, Mali, Mauritania, Morocco, Niger, Tunisia, and Western Sahara.

Algerians gather at an outdoor market, or souk, in the desert town of Ghardaía, about 300 miles south of Algiers.

* **indigenous** refers to the original inhabitants of a place

* **dynasty** succession of rulers from the same family or group

In ancient times, North Africa served as a transfer point for people traveling to Europe and the Middle East. This contact with various languages and cultures influenced the development of the Berbers, the indigenous* peoples who lived in the region. Despite invasions by the Carthaginians, Romans, and Byzantines, the Berbers controlled what is now known as Algeria until Arabs arrived in 642. By 711 the Arabs had conquered all of North Africa and converted most of its inhabitants to Islam. Arab dynasties* ruled Algeria for centuries.

From the 1500s to the 1800s, Ottoman Turks officially controlled the northern part of the country, but they allowed local leaders to govern on their behalf. During this period, piracy flourished in the Mediterranean Sea and became a major source of income for the merchants and rulers of the port city of Algiers. Muslim merchant vessels often attacked European ships sailing in the Mediterranean. In 1827, after a period of skirmishes and minor diplomatic disagreements, France imposed a three-year blockade on Algiers, leading to a full-scale invasion of Algeria in 1830. After several decades of warfare, France gained control of the entire country. Algeria remained a French colony until winning its independence in 1962.

Colonial Rule. The French destroyed Algeria's economy and social structure. By the end of the 1800s, French authorities had seized almost 40 per-

See map in Ottoman Empire (vol. 2).

* **radical** favoring extreme change or reform, especially in existing political and social institutions

* **Qu'ran** book of the holy scriptures of Islam

* **hadith** reports of the words and deeds of Muhammad (not in the Qur'an, but accepted as guides for Muslim behavior)

* **guerrilla** member of a group of fighters, outside the regular army, who engages in unconventional warfare

cent of the country's agricultural land and made it available to European commercial farmers. Hundreds of thousands of European immigrants displaced the traditionally rural population. Eventually, the village economies collapsed, and many Algerians migrated to the cities to find work. French became the official language, and the government closed many traditional Muslim schools. Only a small minority of Algerians attended the new French schools. Under the colonial government, native Algerians suffered discrimination in the form of laws, taxes, and limitations on their voting rights.

French policies, which seriously damaged traditional Algerian society, also inspired a strong resistance movement. An emerging class of educated Algerian men formed new political organizations. Some, such as the Young Algerians, advocated moderate change and hoped to secure equal rights for Muslims without severing ties with France. Other organizations were more radical* and nationalist. The L'Etoile Nord Africaine (ENA), a leftist group, demanded Algerian independence. Its leader, Messali al-Hajj, combined French-style radicalism with the recognition of Islam's role in Algeria. The Muslim reform movement, led by Ben Badis, stressed that the Qur'an* and hadith* should guide Muslim belief and practice. The reform movement sponsored preachers, publications, and schools, giving shape to an Algerian national identity. By the 1930s, demands for independence grew stronger. During World War II, some nationalists began to consider violence as a means of achieving their goals. On November 1, 1954, a group called the National Liberation Front (known by its French initials FLN) was formed. The FLN launched a series of nationwide guerrilla* attacks that began the Algerian war for independence.

Revolution and Independence. The French considered Algeria to be an integral part of France itself, not simply a colony. As a result, it suppressed the independence movement with extreme force. A bloody pattern of repression, terrorist actions, and retaliation began. In August 1955, at Philippeville, an FLN-led mob killed Europeans and their moderate Muslim allies. The French army slaughtered more than 1,000 Muslims in response. Violence continued to escalate, and in 1958, the French army in Algiers revolted. General Charles de Gaulle took control and presided over negotiations that finally resulted in peace talks in 1961. After great loss of life—including as many as 6,000 French civilian casualties and an estimated 300,000 to 1.5 million Algerian casualties—Algeria formally won its independence in July 1962.

After almost a decade of civil war, the country faced enormous challenges. Algeria's economy was in ruins: unemployment in urban areas reached 75 percent and poverty was widespread. The FLN considered Muslim Algerians who had served in the French army to be traitors, and after the war, massacred thousands of people, including entire families.

* **socialist** refers to socialism, the economic system in which the government owns and operates the means of production and the distribution of goods

Independent Algeria became a socialist* state with one political party, the FLN. Ahmed Ben Bella headed the nation's first government, but he was overthrown in a coup led by Colonel Houari Boumédienne. By 1967 Boumédienne's government had begun to implement substantial economic and social reforms. Until 1988 Algeria remained a one-party state controlled by the FLN.

Islam and Politics. Algeria's new leaders wanted to modernize the country while strengthening its Arab and Muslim identity. They recognized that Islam could play a role in achieving this goal and made it the state religion. Before the independence movement began, Islam in Algeria was largely a folk tradition based on a belief in saints who performed miracles. Because the literacy rate was low, people were not familiar with the actual words of the Qur'an. Reformist Muslims, who had received a more modern education, rejected this version of Islam. They believed that Muslims in Algeria should conform to the Qur'an and practice Islam the way other Muslims did. In 1976 "saintly" Islam was officially rejected in the country's new constitution.

Under the FLN, the Algerian government controlled Muslim teaching and practice. The government appointed imams*, monitored sermons, and required that all religious services be held in approved mosques. By the 1980s, however, opposition to this stringent control began to grow. Fundamentalists*, influenced in part by the religious revolution in Iran in 1979, criticized Algeria's socialist government and demanded the formation of an Islamic republic. These religious activists, also known as Islamists, rejected Western cultural and political dominance and opposed attempts to secularize the government.

* **imam** spiritual-political leader in Shi'i Islam, one who is regarded to be directly descended from Muhammad; also, one who leads prayers

* **fundamentalist** person who believes in a literal interpretation of scripture; Muslim who accepts Islam as a comprehensive belief system that can be applied to modern times

During the early 1980s, President Chadli Benjedid implemented a series of reforms designed to shift the Algerian economy away from socialism. Unfortunately, these changes did not ease the country's shortage of jobs, food, and housing. In 1988 army troops opened fire on demonstrators protesting economic conditions. Public anger toward the government grew, and the appeal of the religious opposition increased. The government attempted to improve the situation by introducing more political freedom. In 1989 Benjedid replaced the single-party rule of the FLN with a multiparty system. The Islamic Salvation Front (known by its French initials FIS), the strongest opposition party, demanded the establishment of an Islamic state and the privatization of the economy. In 1991 the FIS won a number of local elections and fared well in the first round of national elections. The Algerian army, whose leadership was secularist, felt threatened by the possibility that the FIS would take control of the country. Consequently, the military overthrew the government, banned the FIS, and sent many Islamists to prison camps in the Sahara.

This crackdown, which suspended the democratic process, outraged the Islamists. The country plunged into a bloody civil war. Several new militant Islamic organizations emerged. They began to carry out terrorist actions, such as bombings and assassinations. The government responded with extreme force. Through the end of the 1990s, Algeria remained unstable. The killings of unveiled women prompted the formation of anti-Islamist groups. Radical Islamists continued to create new organizations, such as the Armed Islamic Group (GIA) and the Islamic Salvation Army (AIS). In 1999 Abdelaziz Bouteflika assumed power of the government and pledged to end the violence. At the beginning of the following year, the AIS and other militant groups surrendered under a partial government pardon. Within six months, however, violence again erupted near Algiers. It is estimated that by the beginning of 2000, the civil war had claimed the lives of 100,000 civilians. (*See also* **Colonialism; Fundamentalism; North Africa.**)

Saintly Islam

Most of Algeria's 32 million people are Sunni Muslims. A distinctive feature of Islam in North Africa is the role of the *marabouts,* or saints. Followers of *marabouts* believe that these holy men and women possess the ability to perform miracles, such as exorcism or healing. Over the centuries, Algeria acquired hundreds of saints whose tombs became the sites of festivals and pilgrimages. Historically, Islamic reformers and government leaders have viewed *marabouts* as a threat to established authority and have tried to limit their influence.

Ali ibn Abi Talib

ca. 597–661
Cousin and successor
of Muhammad

* **Shi'i** refers to Muslims who believe that Muhammad chose Ali ibn Abi Talib and his descendants as the spiritual-political leaders of the Muslim community

* **Sunni** refers to the largest branch of the Muslim community; the name derives from sunnah, the exemplary behavior of the Prophet Muhammad

* **caliph** religious and political leader of an Islamic state

* **imam** spiritual-political leader in Shi'i Islam, one who is regarded as directly descended from Muhammad; also, one who leads prayers

* **arbitration** settlement of a dispute by a person whose decision the conflicting parties agree to accept

Ali ibn Abi Talib was the first cousin of Muhammad and husband of the Prophet's daughter, Fatimah. Ali's close relationship to the Prophet inspired some Muslims to accept him as their leader after Muhammad's death. Others, however, did not consider the family relationship to be of primary importance and initially rejected him in favor of more senior members of the community. The difference of opinion over the method of choosing the leader of the Muslim community ultimately resulted in the division of Muslims into two major groups—Shi'i* and Sunni*.

Ali grew up in Muhammad's household and embraced Islam when he was about ten years old, making him the Prophet's first male follower. When Muhammad left Mecca for Medina in 622, Ali joined him and married Fatimah. The marriage produced four children—two sons and two daughters. Ali participated in most of Muhammad's expeditions and became widely admired for his bravery. He also gained respect as a fair and compassionate judge. The Prophet often referred to Ali as "brother" and "heir."

When Muhammad died in 632, his followers argued about who should become their new leader. Some believed that Ali should rightly assume this role. A majority, however, chose to follow Abu Bakr, who became the first caliph* after Muhammad. Ali became the first imam* of the Shi'is and the fourth of the Rashidun, or "rightly guided," caliphs of the Sunnis.

Umar ibn al-Khattab, the second caliph, succeeded Abu Bakr in 634. Ten years later, when Umar died, Uthman ibn Affan became the third caliph. Uthman's assassination in 656 seriously threatened Muslim unity and pressure mounted for Ali to take control. Although elected fourth caliph, Ali did not have wide political support. Uthman's family believed that Ali should avenge Uthman's death and punish those responsible. But Ali's supporters insisted that Uthman had died deservedly because he had ruled unjustly. In order to retain power and keep his followers unified, Ali had to satisfy both sides.

Establishing a stronghold in the Iraqi city of Kufa, Ali marched on his enemies in Basra and defeated them. Yet his failure to condemn Uthman's murder weakened his support among his followers. The Umayyads, who ruled in Syria and who were related to the slain caliph, felt it was their duty to avenge Uthman's death and rose up against Ali. A battle on the upper Euphrates River proved inconclusive and the leaders agreed to settle their differences through arbitration*. Some of Ali's followers felt betrayed by this move. To them, a compromise based on human judgment would be a challenge to God's will, and therefore against Islamic principles. They abandoned Ali for a new commander. Despite Ali's attempts to eliminate these rebels, known as the Kharijis, their movement spread. In 660 a Kharijite assassin fatally wounded Ali while he was worshipping in the mosque of Kufa. He died two days later, and his tomb in nearby Najaf became an important holy site for Shi'i pilgrimages.

Many Shi'i Muslims honor Ali for his teachings concerning social justice, which were collected and published in the 1200s in *The Peak of Eloquence.* One of Shi'i Islam's most important holy days, the Festival of Ghadir, commemorates the day on which Muhammad named Ali as his successor. (*See also* **Fatimah; Imam; Karbala and Najaf; Khariji; Muhammad; Shi'i Islam; Sunni Islam; Umayyad Caliphate.**)

Alim

See *Religious Scholars*.

al-Jazeera

See *Jazeera, al-*.

Allah

The Arabic word for God is Allah. It is the term used by both Muslims and Arabic Christians to describe their supreme deity. This one all-powerful God, Muslims believe, is the same deity worshipped by Jews and Christians. As the Qur'an describes Allah in the famous "Throne Verse" (surah 2.255):

> God! There is no god but He, the Living, the Self-Subsistent. Slumber seizes Him not, nor sleep. To Him belong all that is in the heavens and upon the earth. Who is there who intercedes with Him except with His permission? He knows what has appeared as past and as yet to come, and there is no share in His knowledge except by His will. His throne extends over the heavens and the earth, and their preservation wearies Him not. He is the All-sublime, the All-glorious.

The word *Allah* is a contraction of the Arabic *al-ilah*, which means simply "the god." Arab tribes before Muhammad's time already worshipped a god called Allah. Indeed, Muhammad's father was named Abd Allah, or "Servant of Allah." Allah may have been their highest god, but they also worshipped many other gods, including the goddesses Manat, al-Lat, and al-Uzzah. Muhammad's teachings did not introduce a new deity to the Arab tribes, but simply urged them to reject their pagan belief in many gods and accept Allah as the one and only deity. The meaning of the term *Islam* is "surrender to Allah," and the most important Muslim virtue is total trust and reliance on God.

Though Muhammad's people were already familiar with Allah, the Prophet's teaching reflected a bold new understanding of the deity. No longer the Allah of the pagan tribes, Allah became the all-powerful supreme deity whom Muhammed called "Lord" and "Rahman," or "Merciful One."

The Qur'an emphasizes several basic attributes of Allah: He is creator and judge of all things, He is unique (*wahid*) and one (*ahad*), and He is all-powerful and all-merciful. As the Qur'an states: "Say He is Allah the One, Allah the Eternal. He never begot, nor was begotten. There is none comparable to Him." Similarly, it is written in the Qur'an that "He is the First (*al-Awwal*) and the Last (*al-Akhir*); the Outward (*as-Zahir*) and the Inward (*al-Batin*); He is the Knower of All Things." Muslims believe that Allah directs all things in the universe and has guided human history through his prophets—Abraham, Moses, Jesus, and Muhammad. Through them, Allah founded his chosen communities, the People of the Book, who accept His revelation as recorded in sacred scripture.

The Islamic profession of faith requires the believer to acknowledge that there is no god but Allah and that Muhammad is His messenger. Muslims believe that everything that happens is the will of Allah. They often inject the saying "*insha' a Allah*," or "if God wills," into their daily activities. The

Beautiful Names of Allah

The Qur'an refers to Allah in many poetic ways. Muhammad identified 99 beautiful names of God—an odd number, to signify God's uniqueness—and taught that Muslims who memorized the 99 beautiful names of Allah would enter paradise. Among these names are: The One and Only, the King, the Living One, the Bestower of Peace, the Most Compassionate, the Most Holy, the Provider, the Protector, the Mighty, the Bestower of Form, the All-Hearing, the All-Seeing, the Witness, the Eternally Besought, the Causer of Death, the Restorer to Life, the Most Exalted, the Sustainer, the Avenger, the Owner of the Kingdom, the Everlasting, the Constant Forgiver. Many Muslims recite the beautiful names of Allah as a type of prayer.

first verses of the Qur'an present the basic Muslim view of God: "Praise be to Allah, the Lord of the Worlds, the Merciful, the Compassionate, the Sovereign of the Day of Judgment. Truly, it is You we worship and You whose aid we seek." (*See also* **Muhammad; Qur'an.**)

al-Qaeda

See *Qaeda, al-*.

Amir

From the Arabic root *amara*, which means "to command," amir (also spelled emir) is traditionally defined as military commander, leader, governor, or prince. The term *amir* may have been adapted from the passage from the Qur'an (surah 4.59, 83) that states: "Obey God and obey the Apostle and those invested with command (*ulu al-amr*) among you."

Historians trace the use of the term back to the caliphs*, specifically to Umar ibn al-Khattab, the second caliph. Umar considered himself the *amir al-mu'minin,* meaning "commander of the faithful." Throughout Islamic history, numerous leaders have adopted the title, combining political as well as religious leadership.

Occasionally, the title of amir was given to people who had earned special honor and respect. For example, the title *amir al-hajj* (leader of the hajj) might be given to one who led the annual pilgrimage* to Mecca. The *amir al-umara* (commander-in-chief) led the caliph's army. Caliphs often bestowed the title of amir on army commanders, especially conquering generals. These military heroes became governors in the provinces they had conquered for the caliph.

The duties of the amirate* (also spelled emirate) eventually expanded to include administrative and financial responsibilities, such as concluding official agreements, distributing pay, levying taxes, leading prayers, and building mosques and other public works. The power that came with these additional tasks enabled many amirs to amass great fortunes and to establish dynasties*. In time, the amir's loyalty to the caliph lessened, reducing the relationship to merely reciting the caliph's name in the Friday *khutba* (sermon).

Use of the title decreased with the rise of Ottoman dominance in the 1200s, except in West Africa, where Muslims continued to call their leaders amir as late as the 1800s. More recently, some Muslim countries, such as Saudi Arabia and Brunei, use the title amir to mean prince, referring to a member of the ruling family. Curiously, the rulers of the United Arab Emirates* are not called amirs, but shaykhs*.

* **caliph** religious and political leader of an Islamic state

* **pilgrimage** journey to a shrine or sacred place

* **amirate** office or realm of authority of an amir

* **dynasty** succession of rulers from the same family or group

* **United Arab Emirates** union of seven small states located on the Arabian Peninsula

* **shaykh** tribal elder; also, title of honor given to those who are considered especially learned and pious

Andalusia

Andalusia, the southernmost region of Spain, was for several centuries the jewel of the Muslim empire in the west. A center of commerce, art, and learning, medieval* Andalusia supported a thriving and diverse community and became a symbol of the most renowned aspects of Muslim culture. Mus-

* **medieval** refers to the Middle Ages, a period roughly between 500 and 1500

Built by Spanish Muslims in 1232, the majestic Alhambra palace of Andalusia sits on a plateau overlooking Granada. Perhaps the best example of Islamic architecture in Europe, it remains one of the area's main tourist attractions.

The Alhambra

The spectacular fortified palace known as the Alhambra is an impressive reminder of the golden age of Islam in Andalusia. The complex, begun by Ibn al-Ahmar in 1238 and completed in 1358, is actually a network of linked buildings that included residential quarters, court chambers, a bath, and a mosque. The Alcazaba, or citadel, is the oldest portion of the complex; only its outer walls, towers, and ramparts have survived. The Alhambra's lovely archways, fountains, and light-reflecting water basins, especially in the Lion Court, were laid out according to descriptions of paradise in Islamic poetry. After the Reconquest, much of the Alhambra was destroyed. Charles V rebuilt portions of the complex in the Renaissance style. Since 1828 the Alhambra has been under extensive restoration.

lims still consider the loss of Andalusia—to Christian armies between the 1200s and 1400s—to be a deep historical injustice.

Golden Age of Islam. Present-day Andalusia comprises the provinces of Huelva, Cádiz, Seville, Málaga, Córdoba, Jaén, Granada, and Almería, a total area of more than 30,000 square miles. The region is surrounded by the Mediterranean Sea, the Atlantic Ocean, and Portugal. Muslims once referred to the entire Iberian Peninsula as *al-Andalus*, which probably means "country of the Vandals." Christians later used the term *al-Andalus* (or Andalucía in Spanish) to identify only those parts of the region that were still under Muslim control.

In ancient times, Phoenicians, Carthaginians, and Greeks established colonies in Andalusia. It became part of the Roman Empire in 206 B.C.E.*, and Roman rule lasted until the Vandals and the Visigoths invaded in the 400s C.E.*.

In 711 Muslim armies under Tariq ibn Ziyad entered Andalusia by crossing the Strait of Gibraltar from Tangier (in present-day Morocco). Quickly

* **B.C.E.** before the Common Era, which refers to the same time period as B.C.

* **C.E.** Common Era, which refers to the same time period as A.D.

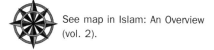

See map in Islam: An Overview (vol. 2).

See color plate 12, vol. 2.

defeating the Visigoths, the Muslims conquered the Iberian Peninsula, spreading Islam and the Arabic language. In 929 Abd al-Rahman III took the title of caliph*, with the city of Córdoba as his capital. Other important cities included Granada and Seville. Under the reign of Abd al-Rahman, Córdoba became a great urban center. Described as "the ornament of the world," the city boasted 1,600 mosques*, 900 public baths, lighted streets, beautiful villas, and numerous libraries. Abd al-Rahman's library alone contained some 400,000 volumes. Andalusia attracted the leading scientists and scholars of the day. They made significant contributions to the fields of chemistry, medicine and surgery, mathematics, and philosophy.

This thriving region supported a diverse population made up of Arab and Berber* Muslims, Spanish Christians, and Jews. Islam became the dominant faith, but Christians and Jews who accepted Muslim rule were allowed to practice their own religions.

While commerce and the arts flourished in Andalusia, military strength also increased. Abu Amir al-Mansur, who served as chief minister under the caliph Hisham II in the late 900s, conducted more than 50 raids against Christian targets in northern Spain. His army consisted largely of hired soldiers from Berber tribes in North Africa. One of al-Mansur's most daring exploits was the sacking of the Christian shrine of Santiago de Compostela, an important pilgrimage site. He destroyed the church there and took the church bells back to Córdoba, where he ordered that they be placed in the Great Mosque. Al-Mansur died in 1002, while returning to Córdoba from a battle in La Rioja.

Reconquest. By the early 1000s, political conflicts between the Arabs and the Berbers had eroded the unity of Andalusia, and the region was divided into smaller kingdoms, or *taifas*. Because these kingdoms were often at war with one another, Andalusia became vulnerable to Christian armies and other foes. Hired soldiers from Catalan attacked Córdoba in 1010. Three years later, Berber soldiers killed many of city's scholars and destroyed many homes. In 1064 Christian forces slaughtered thousands of Muslims in Barbastro after the two groups had signed a peace treaty. Alfonso VI, king of Castile-León, captured Toledo in 1085. Alarmed by the fall of Toledo, the rulers of the other *taifas* sought help from the Almoravids of Morocco, a group of zealous Berbers. The Almoravids defeated Alfonso's army in 1086 and reunited Islamic Spain.

Almoravid rule lasted until 1147, when the Almohads from Morocco toppled the empire. Neither the Almoravids nor the Almohads were able to hold off the advancing Christian armies, however. In 1212 Alfonso VIII defeated the Almohads at the battle of Las Navas de Tolosa.

After this defeat, the remaining Muslim states in Andalusia were too weak to mount an effective resistance. Within less than 50 years, Christian rulers successfully reconquered most of Spain. In 1236 Córdoba fell to King Ferdinand III of Castile-León, who ordered the city's Great Mosque to be set aside for Christian worship. It was renamed the Cathedral de Santa Maria. Victories at Murcia, Jaén, and Seville soon followed. By 1251 Ferdinand III controlled all of Andalusia except for the Muslim kingdom of Granada, which finally fell to King Ferdinand and Queen Isabella's forces in 1492. With the Reconquest complete, all of Andalusia became part of the Christian kingdom of Castile.

The new rulers gave the Muslims who remained in Andalusia a choice—convert to Christianity or be expelled. By 1614 the last of about three million Spanish Muslims had been forced out of the country. These exiles went on to spread Andalusian culture through much of the Mediterranean and the Middle East. Many displaced Muslims settled in North Africa, with Morocco in particular attracting large numbers. To this day, some Moroccans keep the keys to homes in Andalusia that their ancestors lost. For many Muslims, the Reconquest became a symbol of Christian persecution that is as painful today as it was 500 years ago.

Modern Andalusia still shows traces of its distinguished Islamic heritage. Many words in the Andalusian dialect are Arabic, and the names of geographic features often begin with the prefix *al*, Arabic for "the," or *guad*, Arabic for "river." Buildings in Andalusia reflect the style of Muslim architecture that dominated the region in the Middle Ages. The Alhambra, a fortress and palace built in Granada in 1238 and later enlarged by successive Muslim rulers, remains one of the area's greatest tourist attractions and is possibly the best-known example of Islamic architecture in Europe. Many Andalusians consider themselves culturally distinct from the majority population in Spain, and the Andalusian Muslim League has revived pride in the region's Islamic history. (*See also* **Architecture; Art; Libraries; Literature.**)

Arabic Language and Literature

Arabic, which is the first language of about 181 million people today, ranks fifth worldwide in number of primary speakers. The spread of Arabic, which has influenced many languages and literatures in Africa, the Middle East, and Asia, is closely linked to the spread of Islam. Arabic became the official language of the vast Islamic empire and was the universal language of learning during the early Middle Ages. Arabic is the language of the Qur'an* and is still today the common language of worship for Muslims throughout the world. It is also, of course, the living language of the Arab peoples.

* **Qur'an** book of the holy scriptures of Islam

Language

Arabic, a language from the Semitic* branch of the Afro-Asiatic language family, originated in the Arabian Peninsula as early as the 400s B.C.E.* It remained a relatively localized language, however, until the spread of Islam in the 600s C.E.* As Muslim armies conquered new territories, they brought their language with them. Inhabitants of the regions closest to Arabia whose languages were originally Semitic, as in Mesopotamia (present-day Iraq) and Syria, became Arabic speakers. So did those in Egypt and North Africa whose languages were originally Hamitic*. In other regions, such as Persia (present-day Iran) and India, populations who became Muslim kept their original languages, but adopted many words from Arabic and often used the Arabic writing system.

By the mid-700s, the Muslim empire reached from present-day Afghanistan through the Middle East into North Africa and Spain. While Per-

* **Semitic** refers to a subfamily of languages that includes Hebrew, Aramaic, Arabic, and Amharic

* **B.C.E.** before the Common Era, which refers to the same time period as B.C.

* **C.E.** Common Era, which refers to the same time period as A.D.

* **Hamitic** refers to subfamily of Afro-Asiatic languages that includes Berber, Egyptian, and Cushitic

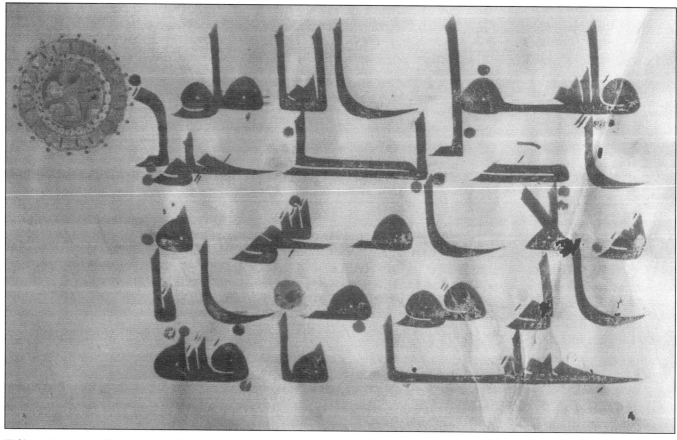

Characterized by its bold, angular script, scribes often used the Kufic style of Arabic writing in ornamental carvings on stone or metal. It rarely appeared in manuscripts, except for special copies of the Qur'an, as shown here.

* **treatise** long, detailed essay on a particular subject

* **Sanskrit** ancient classical language of India and Hinduism

sian became the dominant literary language in the eastern part of the empire, Arabic became the language of government, law, and religion throughout the western portions of the empire. It was also widely used in trade and commerce in these regions. The leading philosophers, historians, scientists, and physicians of the day wrote their books and treatises* in Arabic. Muslim scholars also translated works from other cultures into Arabic. Among these were the works of Greek philosophers, including Plato and Aristotle, as well as writings in Sanskrit*, Hebrew, and other languages. Indeed, many European scholars advanced their own learning by studying works written in Arabic. This was especially important in the late Middle Ages, when Arabic translations of these texts passed through Muslim Spain to western Europe and were thus preserved for future generations.

System of Writing. Before the Muslim conquests, Arabic was primarily a spoken language with various local dialects, although a simple system of writing had developed, probably during the 300s. The earliest surviving example of Arabic writing dates from 512, and is part of an inscription in three languages—Greek, Syriac, and Arabic. Early in the Muslim era, two different types of Arabic writing developed. The Kufic style, noted for its distinctive angular script, appeared in the late 600s. Especially well suited for writing or carving on stone and metal, scribes decorated the walls of mosques with elegantly handwritten religious inscriptions. Although Kufic writing was not often used on paper, it was used for precious manuscript copies of the Qur'an. Today, the Kufic style is obsolete. Modern Arabic writing derives from the *naskhi* style, which was a more cursive type of writing suitable for use on papyrus* or paper.

As in other Semitic writing systems, Arabic is written from right to left. The Arabic alphabet, which probably derives from Aramaic* and Nabataean* scripts, contains 28 consonants. The letters *alif*, *waw*, and *ya* represent the long vowels a, u, and i. The shapes of letters depend on whether they are placed at the beginning, middle, or end of a word. Another form is used for each letter when it is written alone. After the Latin alphabet, the Arabic script is the most widely used writing system in the world. It has been adapted to such diverse languages as Persian, Turkish, Spanish, Hebrew, Urdu, Berber, Malay, and Swahili.

Classical Arabic. Because so many diverse peoples adopted Arabic after the Muslim conquest, the spoken language evolved rapidly. Dialects differed significantly from place to place. Concerned that Arabic might shift too far away from the original language of the Qur'an, scholars in Basra (in present-day Iraq) in the 700s, began to codify* the language. They studied the pure Arabic that had originated with the tribes in the Arabian desert and worked out the derivations from root words, compiled vocabularies, and established grammatical rules for the language. The scholar Sibawayh used this information to create a comprehensive work of Arabic grammar. Around the same time, scholars compiled Arabic dictionaries. These works helped to establish what is considered classical or pure Arabic.

Although Arab countries today retain distinctive spoken dialects, they conduct formal spoken and written communication in modern standard Arabic. Based on classical Arabic, this language has added words and phrases that reflect adaptations to the modern age. In some cases, modern standard Arabic has borrowed from Western languages to create words relating to new technologies, such as *tilifun* (telephone) and *tilifizyun* (television). Often, however, Arabs today have used existing Arabic roots to form new words. For example, the word *thallajah*, which means "refrigerator," comes from the noun *thalj* (snow, ice). The word *matar* (airport) derives from the verb *tara* (to fly).

In general, modern standard Arabic has kept the basic characteristics of classical Arabic. Though some reformers have suggested that Arabic speakers should modify the Arabic script or use the Latin alphabet, in which English and other Western languages are written, this idea has met with great resistance. Arabs wish to maintain their cultural unity by preserving the language of the Qur'an and all the Islamic culture that has flowed from it.

Literature

The first book written in Arabic was the Qur'an. Because Muslim scholars had worked to preserve the original language of that sacred work, they played a central role in the development of Arabic literature. Scholars in the 700s, beginning to research the origins of the language, wrote down the oral traditions of the Arab tribes. These included poems as well as stories of the Prophet Muhammad and the early Muslim leaders. In this way, the classical poetry of the desert was preserved.

This poetry began in pre-Islamic times, when Bedouin* poets served as oracles* for their tribes. The predominant poetic form was the *qasidah*, or

* **papyrus** writing material made from the stem of the papyrus plant

* **Aramaic** ancient Semitic language

* **Nabataean** ancient Semitic language

* **codify** to create a system of rules

See color plate 3, vol. 2.

* **Bedouin** nomad of the desert, especially in North Africa, Syria, and Arabia

* **oracle** religious figure through whom God is believed to speak

ode. A poet discovering traces of an abandoned camp might be inspired to compose an ode about it. Poetry was always highly valued by Arab peoples, and both men and women composed poems in the pre-Islamic period. For example, al-Khansa's poems commemorating her deceased brother have become part of the rich Arabic literary heritage.

Classical Period. With the rise of Islam, the Qur'an became a model for poetic style. Its rich imagery and repeated rhythmic patterns, as well as its religious message, influenced Arabic literary traditions. At the same time, the styles and ideas from the diverse cultures that were incorporated into the Muslim empire also enriched Arabic literature. By the late 700s, al-Khalil, the creator of the first Arabic dictionary, had codified a detailed metrical system for Arabic poetry. The panegyric* became a highly refined art form, as did the *ghazal*, or shorter ode. In the 800s, the works of poets Abu Tammam (died 845) and al-Buhturi (died 897) became well known, as did the works of the more satirical Abu Nuwas (died 815). The most important poets of the following two centuries were al-Mutanabbi (died 965) and Abu al-Ala al-Ma'arri (died 1057). Sufi* poets from this period used images of intoxication, as with wine or romantic love, to describe the ecstasy of religious experience.

In addition to traditional poetry, new literary forms emerged during the classical period. Among these was the *adab*, a short narrative meant to both teach and entertain. Writers used many types of stock characters, ranging from rulers and judges to misers and party-crashers. The *adab* might include verses from the Qur'an, hadith*, and poetry, and often contained adaptations from Persian and Indian traditions as well. Indeed, Persian literature became a significant influence in Arabic writing. The master of the *adab* was al-Jahiz (died 869), whose *Book of Misers* blends Persian and Arabic elements. Another literary form that emerged this period was the *maqamah*, invented by Badi al-Zaman al-Hamadhani (died 1008). The *maqamah* was a rhymed prose form featuring a roguish hero who uses his wits to outsmart his rivals. This form was popular in Andalusia (Islamic Spain), where author Ali ibn Hazm (died 1064) wrote his treatise on the psychology of love, *The Dove's Neckring*. The theme of courtly love frequently appeared in Andalusian literature, and has often been linked to the rise of the troubadours*. The *Maqamat* of al-Hariri (died 1122), one of the most impressive examples of the form, became a model for writers in the 1800s who were eager to reenergize Arabic literature.

Mystical works from this period include the great allegory, *Alive Son of Awake*, by Ibn Tufayl (died 1185 or 1186). In this masterpiece of the Arabic-Islamic philosophical tradition, an abandoned infant grows up alone on an island and discovers science and mysticism on his own. He meets another young man seeking shelter from society, and after an unsuccessful attempt to correct societal problems, the two live happily on their island.

Writers also began to experiment with the autobiographical form during this time. *The Deliverer from Error* by Abu Hamid al-Ghazali (died 1111) recounts a spiritual quest and has been compared to the autobiography of St. Augustine, an early Christian philosopher. More common, however, were accounts of adventurous lives, such as that of warrior Usamah ibn Munqidh, whose writings describe the fighting between Arab and Christian armies during the Crusades.

* **panegyric** poem of elaborate praise

* **Sufi** refers to Sufism, which seeks to develop spirituality through discipline of the mind and body

* **hadith** reports of the words and deeds of Muhammad (not in the Qur'an, but accepted as guides for Muslim behavior)

* **troubadour** poet-musician who flourished in southern France and Italy from the 1000s to the 1200s

Letter writing, secretarial correspondence, and works of history and philosophy flourished in the classical period. Arabic writers developed a literary tradition that emphasized formal and technical skill in the creation of intricate patterns of rhymed prose. Stylistic experimentation and thematic novelty were not considered desirable qualities.

Perhaps the best-known work from classical Arabic literature is *The Thousand and One Nights*. This work includes stories that were collected over several centuries. Its framing narrative explains how King Shahryar has each of his wives killed before they can fall out of love with him. His new bride, Shahrazad, is able to postpone her own death each day by promising to tell her husband a new tale that night. Among these tales of adventure, fantasy, magic, and romance are the well known "Voyage of Sinbad," "Aladdin and the Magic Lamp," and "Ali Baba and the Forty Thieves." Readers throughout the world have enjoyed the book's tales of flying carpets, hidden treasures, and spirits who grant wishes. Many of the story cycles from *The Thousand and One Nights* reappear in updated form in Arabic literature of the twentieth century.

Modern Era. In the 1800s, as the Arab empire declined and European powers took control of Muslim territories, Islamic writers reacted to European influences in several ways. Writers such as Muhammad al-Muwaylihi (died 1930), Ahmad Shawqi (died 1932) and Hafiz Ibrahim (died 1932) used the *maqamah* form to express their opinions on social issues. Free verse developed in Arabic poetry and came to dominate it in the works of the poets Salah Abd al-Sabur (died 1981), Adonis, Mahmud Darwish, and Ahmad Abd al-Mu'ti Hijazi. Drama appeared as an independent form. One of the central works of Arabic literature from this period is *The Days*, the autobiography of Egyptian scholar and writer Taha Husayn (died 1973). The book recounts how Husayn, a blind boy, overcame social and educational barriers, studied in France, and became a professor at the modern university in Cairo. The book is admired for the drama of its story and for its descriptions of cultural differences between Arab and Western cultures.

The first Arabic novel, *Zaynab*, was written by Egyptian writer Muhammad Husayn Haykal and published in 1913. The author's reading of French literature from the 1800s inspired this highly romantic work. Naguib Mahfouz (born 1911), a native of Cairo, began his career in journalism and also wrote historical novels, but soon he turned to writing works with modern Egyptian themes. The novellas in his *Cairo Trilogy* follow three generations of an Egyptian family in the early twentieth century and explore issues of social change. His more recent fiction criticizes the old Egyptian monarchy, British colonialism, attitudes toward women and family, and social class. Many of Mahfouz's characters search in vain for an absent father figure—a symbol for the god who seems to no longer exist in their lives. Winner of the Nobel Prize in Literature in 1988, Mahfouz is the first Arabic writer to achieve this honor.

Another Egyptian writer, Nawal al-Sadawi (born 1931), has received both censure and acclaim for her harsh criticism of the position of women in Arab society. A physician, al-Sadawi has written both fiction and nonfiction. Her first book to be translated into English, *The Hidden Face of Eve: Women in the Arab World*, begins with a description of how, at age six, she was taken

Arabic Enhances English

Though Arabic sentence structure and sound patterns are very different from those in English, many words in English derive from Arabic roots. Words that begin with the prefix *al*, for example, such as alcohol, alchemy, and algebra, are of Arabic origin. Sometimes, the literal translations of Arabic root words in English are richly descriptive. The word *arsenal*, for example, derives from the phrase *dar as sina'ah*, which means "house of making," or in other words, a factory. Many English words, such as coffee, cotton, giraffe, and jar, come from Arabic words. Sometimes, Arabic terms entered the English language through French, Spanish, Italian, or other languages. The word *orange*, for example, came to English by way of Sanskrit, while the word *talisman* came via Greek. From admiral (*amir al-bahr*, meaning "ruler of the seas") to zero (*sifr*, meaning "empty"), Arabic terms have enriched the English language.

out of her bed in the middle of the night and brought to the bathroom. There, with no anesthesia, she was subjected to ritual female circumcision, in which a part of her sex organs was removed. Later, as a doctor, al-Sadawi saw how such experiences had physically and emotionally scarred many women in the Muslim world. Her novel, *The Circling Song*, is also about the physical and political degradation of women. For her strong advocacy of women's rights, al-Sadawi served a two-month prison term in 1981. She received death threats from religious extremists after the publication of her novel *Fall of the Imam*, which satirizes political hypocrisy.

In recent decades, postmodern elements have made their way into Arabic novels. Contemporary Muslim writers have responded to this development by returning to classical traditions and redefining them for a new audience. Among these experimental writers is Egyptian novelist Jamal al-Ghitani, who draws on the rich Arab-Islamic textual heritage, including historical, biographical, and mystical writings, to create contemporary narratives. Palestinian writer Emile Habibi and Tunisian writer al-Misadi have also received praise for their similarly innovative approaches to fiction.

Another recent development is the return to morally instructive literature. Works such as *Days from My Life*, which describes the imprisonment and torture of Egyptian political activist and author Zaynab al-Ghazali in the 1960s, and the books of Iraqi writer Bint al-Huda convey the author's views of proper behavior for Muslim women. According to Bint al-Huda (a woman), Muslim women should reject Western values, embrace domestic life, and wear the veil in public, but not be subservient to men. They should even bear arms if the Islamic mission requires it.

Overtly political themes also dominate the work of Palestinian poet Mahmoud Darwish (born 1942). His poems, influenced by the work of Chilean poet Pablo Neruda and Spanish poet Federico Garcia Lorca, as well as Marxist* theory, deal with the anger and pain of the Palestinian people under Israeli occupation. The Israeli government imprisoned Darwish after the publication of each of his books and also placed him under house arrest between his jail sentences. While his early work is descriptive, his later poems communicate a more sophisticated understanding of political realities. Many of these later works criticize Arab regimes and describe their failure to deal effectively with the Arab-Israeli conflict.

Today Arabic literature is a major cultural force in the Middle East, both in its secular and religious forms. Through its relations with other contemporary literary traditions, especially Western ones, Arabic literature is part of an emerging world literary culture. At the same time, it acknowledges its own unique Arab and Islamic heritage. (*See also* **Literature; Qur'an; Women and Reform.**)

* **Marxist** refers to a political philosophy that rejects capitalism and advocates a classless society

Arab-Israeli Conflict

The conflict pitting Palestinian Arabs against Israelis has been simmering, and often boiling over, for nearly a century. It is a conflict that has political-historical, socio-economic, and psychological dimensions. Jewish communities have existed throughout the Mediterranean world since the days of the

All Palestinians in the Israeli-occupied West Bank and Gaza Strip must pass through checkpoints established along the Israeli border. Here, Palestinian workers wait to enter Israel at a checkpoint in the Gaza Strip.

* **medieval** refers to the Middle Ages, a period roughly between 500 and 1500

Roman Empire. In medieval* times, large communities of Jews emerged in Muslim societies and in European countries. In Europe, the Jews lived mainly in ghettos and were subject to persecution and discrimination. In the 1800s, with the development of movements for national self-determination, some European Jewish intellectuals and activists decided that the time had come to establish a homeland for the Jews. Disagreement existed concerning the location of a Jewish state, but many eastern European Jews favored the establishment of a Jewish state (Israel) in Palestine, their historic homeland. The movement to establish a Jewish state is called Zionism.

The Arrival of Settlers. Jewish settlers began to arrive in Palestine in the late 1800s. In 1917 British foreign secretary Arthur Balfour issued a statement favoring the creation "of a national home for the Jewish people" in Palestine. Although their leaders welcomed the Jews as refugees, many Palestinians (the indigenous Arab population of Palestine) viewed the arrival of Jewish settlers as a threat to their security and to their land. To justify the creation of Israel, Zionist leaders convinced the British government that

See map in Israel (vol. 2).

Palestine was "a land without people" for the Jews to settle, serving both Zionist aims and British imperial* interests.

During World War II (1939–1945), Jews had been the main victims of Nazi genocidal* policies and more than six million had perished in the concentration camps of central Europe. This tragic annihilation of European Jewry, referred to as the Holocaust, led to the acceleration of Jewish immigration to Palestine. This, in turn, provoked clashes with the local Palestinian population. British forces armed both sides—Arabs and Jews. For the Palestinians, the British had betrayed the promises they made to the Arabs after World War I (1914–1918) to create an independent confederation* of Arab states.

Opposition to Statehood. By the end of World War II, Israeli statehood was gradually becoming a reality. In fact, in November 1947, the United Nations General Assembly adopted U.N. Resolution 181 to partition Palestine and establish a Jewish state on 55 percent of the territory belonging to Palestinians. At the time, the Jews represented only one-third of the population in Palestine and owned only 6 percent of the land. The Arab countries and the Palestinians rejected the U.N. resolution and war erupted between Palestinians and Arab armies on one side and Israeli forces on the other. Britain declared its intention of withdrawing from the region in April 1948. A month later, on May 14, 1948, David Ben-Gurion (one of Israel's founders and the country's first prime minister) announced the establishment of the Jewish state of Israel. The following day, the combined forces of Egypt, Syria, Jordan, Iraq, Lebanon, Saudi Arabia, and Yemen attacked the new nation.

Despite overwhelming odds, Israel prevailed and by January 1949, Israeli forces controlled about 20,000 square miles of Palestinian land. The remaining portions—the West Bank and Gaza Strip—came under the control of Jordan and Egypt. Hundreds of thousands of Palestinians fled or were forced to leave their homes by Israeli forces. A significant number, however, stayed behind in Galilee, a hilly region in northern Israel, and were absorbed into the Israeli state. These Palestinian Israelis constitute 17 percent of the Israeli population.

Refugee Problem Begins. The Arab-Israeli war marked the beginning of a Palestinian refugee problem. Those who left their homes became refugees in neighboring countries, such as Jordan, Syria, and Lebanon, and in the West Bank and Gaza Strip, where they were treated as foreigners and confined to refugee camps along the borders.

The loss of Palestine, a critical event in Arab-Palestinian history, led to several armed conflicts between Arab and Israeli military forces. Between the wars, a pattern of guerrilla* attacks began. With the help of Egypt and other Arab governments, the Palestinians trained and armed themselves to harass the Israeli military, which they regarded as the occupier of land that legitimately belonged to them. The Arab defeat also inspired Palestinians to take their fate into their own hands, and in 1964 they founded the Palestinian Liberation Organization (PLO). Headed after 1969 by Yasir Arafat, the PLO asserted itself as an independent organization focused on Palestinian nationalism, rather than on Arab nationalism.

Nearly a decade after the first major Arab-Israeli conflict, President Gamal Abdel Nasser of Egypt took control of the Suez Canal, which had been under joint French-British administration. With the support of Israeli troops, France and Britain invaded Egypt in October 1956. President Dwight Eisenhower of the United States pressured France, Britain, and Israel to withdraw their troops from Egypt. Israelis and Palestinians, involved in attacks and counterattacks, kept tensions high in the Middle East. Then in 1967, the Israeli Defense Forces (IDF) launched a preemptive strike against the armies of Egypt, Syria, and Jordan. In just few days, Israeli forces had destroyed the air power of the three Arab countries. This third Arab-Israeli war, known as the Six-Day War, resulted in the Israeli occupation of the West Bank and East Jerusalem (under Jordanian control) and the Gaza Strip (under Egyptian control). In addition, Israeli troops occupied the Golan Heights, which belonged to Syria, and more Palestinians (around 250,000) became refugees.

On November 22, 1967, the United Nations Security Council adopted Resolution 242, which emphasized the "inadmissibility of the acquisition of territory by war" and called for the "withdrawal of Israeli armed forces from territories occupied in the recent conflict" and for the "acknowledgement of the sovereignty . . . of every state in the area and their right to live in peace within secure and recognized boundaries." This resolution became the basis of several diplomatic efforts based on the premise of "land for peace." Israel would have to withdraw from the land it occupied in 1967 and in exchange the Arabs and the Palestinians would establish peaceful relations with the Jewish state.

Peace Process Begins. Peace did not last, and in 1973, another war broke out between Israel and its Arab neighbors. Known as the October War (or the Yom Kippur War in Israel because it began on Judaism's most important holiday), Egypt and Syria mounted a surprise military attack against Israeli forces occupying Egyptian and Syrian territories. The early stages of the war went well for the Arab armies, but Israel rallied and ultimately defeated them. Although both sides suffered heavy losses, the October War paved the way for the beginning of a peace process in the Middle East. Egyptian president Anwar el-Sadat realized that the conflict with Israel was taking its toll on his country's economy. With support and encouragement from the United States, Sadat initiated a dialogue with his Israeli counterparts that eventually led to normalization of relations. In 1977 Sadat took the dramatic and unprecedented step of traveling to Israel where he addressed the Israeli people.

The trip was a major breakthrough, but further peace talks reached an impasse in 1978. To break the stalemate, U.S. president Jimmy Carter invited Sadat and Israeli prime minister Menachem Begin to Camp David, the presidential retreat in Maryland. After arguing for nearly two weeks, both sides reached an agreement known as the Camp David Accords on September 17, 1978. For this historic agreement, both Sadat and Begin were awarded the Nobel Peace Prize. But peace was still elusive. Arab demands for the return of the occupied territories and for the creation of a Palestinian homeland remained unmet.

Beyond the Peace Process. Arabs generally opposed the Camp David Accords, which they perceived to be a sell-out of Palestinian rights in Israel. The PLO had established bases in southern Lebanon, from which it conducted attacks against Israel. These attacks led to the Israeli invasion of

The *Intifadah*

After years of discrimination, the confiscation of their land, and the building of Jewish settlements in the heart of Arab communities, the Palestinians began an *intifadah* (uprising) against Israeli occupation in 1987. The *intifadah* demonstrated the leadership of the PLO and Arafat, and provided an indication of the will of the Palestinians to have their own country.

Despite the energy and determination with which the *intifadah* began, repeated failures to reach a solution to the Arab-Israeli conflict has led to Arafat's loss of credibility and a decline in the ability of the Palestinians to withstand the pressure of the occupation. Daily clashes between the Israeli army and the Palestinians continue.

Lebanon in 1982. The aim of the invasion, under the leadership of Defense Minister Ariel Sharon, was to destroy PLO bases in southern Lebanon, defeat the Syrian army (which had entered Lebanon in 1976), and install a pro-Israeli government in Lebanon. Israel achieved only its first objective and the Israeli army remained in southern Lebanon until 2000.

Following this latest military action in the Middle East, peace efforts between Arabs and Israelis resumed under the guidance and supervision of the United States. A major boost to the peacemaking efforts occurred in the aftermath of the Gulf War (1990–1991), which began when Iraqi dictator Saddam Hussein invaded Kuwait. U.S. president George H. W. Bush had formed a coalition of countries that included some Arab countries to defeat Saddam Hussein's troops. Following that war, the United States and Russia sponsored an international conference in Madrid, Spain, to bring a permanent peace to the Middle East.

Meanwhile, some Palestinians and Israelis were holding secret meetings in Oslo, Norway, where they reached an agreement on some principles for the first stage of conflict resolution. Israel's prime minister, Yitzhak Rabin, and PLO chairman, Yasir Arafat, signed the agreement in Washington, D.C., on September 13, 1993. One of the issues to be decided was, and still is, the status of Jerusalem, the spiritual capital of both Palestinians (Muslims and Christians) and Israelis. One solution, which has been part of previous peace plans, has been to internationalize the holy city, providing equal access to the holy sites for Muslims, Jews, and Christians.

Political or Religious Struggle. Although the Arab-Israeli conflict has generally been viewed as a national struggle, religion and politics cannot be entirely separated. The majority of people in the region continue to see the situation as a dispute over territory and self-determination. But as the political leadership fails to bring a just and lasting peace to the region, many have turned to their religious authorities for a solution to the conflict. (*See also* **Israel; Palestine; Palestine Liberation Organization.**)

Arab League

The Arab League, an organization to promote unity and cooperation among Arab states, formed in Cairo, Egypt in 1945. It emerged as a means through which Arab states could protect their interests after Ottoman, British, and French colonial rule ended in the Middle East. The founding members of the Arab League were Egypt, Syria, Lebanon, Iraq, Transjordan (now Jordan), Saudi Arabia, and Yemen. Libya joined in 1953, followed by Sudan in 1956, Tunisia and Morocco in 1958, Kuwait in 1961, Algeria in 1962, South Yemen in 1967, and Bahrain, Qatar, Oman, and the United Arab Emirates in 1971. Mauritania joined the league in 1973, followed by Somalia in 1974, Palestine in 1976, Djibouti in 1977, and the Comoros Islands in 1993. Each league member has one vote, and decisions are binding only among those states that accept them. Arab League headquarters are located in Cairo.

In its first decades, the Arab League focused on economic, cultural, and social issues. These included such joint business ventures as the Arab Potash

Company, the Arab Maritime Companies, the Arab Satellite Communications Organization, the Arab Monetary Fund, and the Arab Fund for Economic and Social Development. The Arab League held the first Arab petroleum congress in 1959, and established the Arab League Educational, Cultural, and Scientific Organization in 1964. Since the 1970s, the league has increasingly emphasized political engagement, sometimes leading to disagreements within the organization. One of the organization's early actions was to declare a boycott against Israel, protesting the creation of a Jewish state in Palestine. Although the boycott was effective at first, it was not consistently enforced and, by the 1990s, many member countries had abandoned it. In 2001 the Arab League convened to consider a renewal of the boycott, but several members, including Egypt, Jordan, Morocco, and Qatar, failed to attend.

Attitudes toward the use of force have also caused rifts within the organization. When Egypt signed a peace treaty with Israel in 1979, it was expelled from the league and not readmitted until 1987. The league was further divided about whether to support or punish Iraq after it declared war on Iran in 1980. In 1990 Iraq's invasion of Kuwait, which led to a military response by the United States and its allies, further shattered the league's unity. Saudi Arabia, Egypt, Syria, Morocco, Qatar, Bahrain, Kuwait, United Arab Emirates, Lebanon, Djibouti, and Somalia voted to allow U.S. troops to use Saudi Arabia as a base for defending Kuwait. The other members, however, strongly objected to this measure. In the late 1990s, renewed violence between Israelis and Palestinians prompted a more unified response from the members. At the 2002 Arab League summit meeting in Beirut, Crown Prince Abdullah of Saudi Arabia presented a peace plan that called for the withdrawal of Israeli forces from Arab territories and an end to military engagement in the region.

In early 2003, a military coalition led by the United States invaded Iraq, claiming that Iraqi president Saddam Hussein had failed to comply with a United Nations resolution on arms inspection. The coalition forces gained control of the country in a few weeks and ended Saddam Hussein's regime. Many members of the Arab League denounced the attack. Qatar, however, permitted American and coalition forces to use military bases in its territory.

Although the Arab League has succeeded in promoting many Arab causes, divisions among its member states continue to threaten its effectiveness on political issues. The league has made its most significant contributions in the areas of cultural preservation and education. (*See also* **Arab-Israeli Conflict; Egypt.**)

Architecture

Architecture refers to the design and construction of buildings and other structures, such as tombs and gardens. It may characterize a particular time and place in history. Architecture not only defines functional spaces in which people can live, work, study, and worship, it also reflects their ties with particular religions, cultures, or dynasties*. Traditional architecture provides images of the past, enhancing a community's understanding of its origins.

* **dynasty** succession of rulers from the same family or group

Built in the early 1900s, the Ubudiah Mosque of Kuala Kangsar, Malaysia, boasts a large golden dome. Towering minarets, from which the faithful are called to prayer, surround the mosque.

See color plate 7, vol. 2.

Contemporary architecture, on the other hand, reflects the present, expressing cultural changes or a break with the past. These roles of architecture are apparent throughout the Islamic world. Contemporary Islamic architecture reflects changes that have occurred in the Muslim world over the past two centuries.

Traditional Islamic Architecture

In many ways, traditional Islamic architecture provides a visual overview of Islamic history. Master builders, rather than professional architects, designed and built the earliest Muslim structures. The most distinctive type of building was the mosque*. Other traditional types of structures included grave markers, bathhouses, commercial buildings, and homes.

* **mosque** Muslim place of worship

Mosques, Domes, and Minarets. The form of the mosque generally follows one of three models. From the beginning of Islam in the 600s to about 1000, mosques were large enclosed areas that combined a flat-roofed room for worship with an open courtyard. Mosques of this type were built in the western Islamic world, from Spain to Central Asia. In the 1000s, a new style of mosque appeared. It had balconies on two or more sides of an unroofed central courtyard. This type was built from Egypt and Turkey eastward to India and Pakistan. A third model developed with the expansion of the Ottoman Empire, beginning in the 1400s. Built in places from the Balkans to Saudi Arabia, it had a dome-covered central prayer space and a courtyard.

Today, as in the past, domes and minarets* characteristically adorn mosques. Domes signal to the public a place of prayer and Islamic learning. Minarets are used to call the faithful to prayers. Both structures differ in shape, building materials, and other features depending on when and where they were built.

Domes throughout the Islamic world vary in style, according to the different ethnic or national identities they represent. Mamluk-style domes, for example, are associated with the dynasty that ruled Egypt in the 1300s and 1400s. They are still common throughout the country and are easily recognizable by their high sides, pointed top, and patterned surfaces. Originally made of stone, Mamluk-style domes are constructed today of reinforced concrete. Similar in style to the original domes, they provide a visual link with Egypt's past. Many Muslim communities in the United States and elsewhere have adopted Mamluk-style domes, perhaps reflecting Egypt's role as a major center of Islamic learning.

Another style of dome, which originated farther to the east in Uzbekistan, spread throughout much of the eastern Islamic world. Associated with the Timurid dynasty, which began in the 1300s, this dome has high sides, a rounded top slightly wider than the sides, and glazed tile surfaces. The Timurid-style dome can be seen as far south as India. Timurid-style domes adorn the world-famous Taj Mahal, built in Agra, India, in the 1600s.

The minaret is one of the most widespread symbols of Islam throughout the world. As with the dome, specific details of the minaret have come to reflect the architectural preferences of different dynasties and different regions. The most common and basic form of the minaret is a tapering, rounded shaft, found throughout Turkey, Iraq, and Iran.

Various ruling dynasties modified the basic form of the minaret to reflect their own architectural style. One widespread modification is associated with the Ottoman Empire, which took over much of the central Islamic world starting in the mid-1400s and continued through the early 1900s. The Ottoman-style minaret is taller and more tapered than the basic form and has a cone-shaped top. As the Ottoman Turks expanded into areas that were predominantly Christian or ruled by other Muslim groups, the distinctive cone-topped minaret on the skyline clearly indicated the Ottoman presence in the region.

Mimar Koca Sinan was perhaps the greatest of the Ottoman architects. During his 50-year career, Sinan built or supervised more than 300 structures in Istanbul alone, including mosques, palaces, tombs, schools, and hospitals. His crowning achievement is the immense domed Selimiye Mosque at Edirne, in western Turkey.

* **minaret** tall, slender tower of a Muslim mosque from which the faithful are called to prayer

See color plate 9, vol. 2.

Grave Markers. Throughout the history of Islam, Muslims have marked the graves of their dead in various ways. As early as the mid-600s, tombstones became commonplace in Egypt and soon thereafter throughout the Islamic world. Masonry screens first shielded burial sites in the 700s. By the 1200s, they were made of wood, and today ornate metal screens often mark gravesites.

The most elaborate form of grave marker is the mausoleum, a small building-like structure where the remains of a person or family of special status were buried. In Islamic countries, it is a domed structure that stands alone in a cemetery outside the city, or it is part of a mosque or other palace within a city. Construction materials varied from mud bricks to marble, depending on the importance of the deceased. The shape of the mausoleum's dome and inner chamber reflect the time and place it was built. For example, the chamber of a Mamluk mausoleum was square; that of an Ottoman mausoleum was round or octagonal.

Bathhouses. Prior to the 1900s, bathhouses were often constructed near mosques so that worshippers could cleanse themselves before prayers. A bathhouse usually contained changing rooms, chambers with hot and warm water, and a steam room. Steam, generated by heating water, flowed into the room through holes in the walls. The room was covered by a dome, which allowed the hot, moist air to circulate. Small windows in the dome let in daylight. Unless there were two separate bathhouses in a community, men and women used the same facility, but at different times.

See color plate 8, vol. 2.

Commercial Buildings. Two types of commercial buildings were common in early Islamic architecture—structures for storage and lodging (such as the caravansary) and covered marketplaces. Caravansaries, usually a two-story structure, provided temporary lodging for traveling merchants and their animals. Travelers stabled their animals on the ground floor and slept and stored their goods on the second floor.

Most covered marketplaces consisted of shops that sold expensive goods, such as precious metals, silks, and jewels. The market had a formal entrance that could be closed at night and locked for security. Many Islamic cities have incorporated traditional marketplace features into today's modern shopping districts.

Houses. Traditional Islamic houses included separate spaces for public and private functions. Men generally occupied the public space, while women and children used the private space. Large homes not only had separate rooms for men and for women, but separate entrances as well. In small houses, people hung curtains to separate the spaces used by the men and the women in the family. Sometimes men and women used the same space. The men used the space for one part of the day, the women for another.

Contemporary Islamic Architecture

Beginning in the 1800s, professional architects gradually replaced traditional master builders in the Islamic world. The earliest professional architects to practice there were Westerners, primarily from Europe. Eventually, European-trained Muslim architects began to practice in Islamic countries, followed by locally trained Muslim architects.

Influence of the West. In the 1800s and early 1900s, Western architects traveled to Islamic countries to work either for the local rulers or for colonial powers. Many of these architects influenced the architectural development of the regions in which they worked. For example, more than 120 French architects worked in Morocco during the 1920s when the country was a French protectorate*. They were, in large part, responsible for the growth of modern Moroccan cities. Western architects also left their mark on the architecture of Egypt, Turkey, Iraq, India, Indonesia, and Afghanistan, where they designed palaces and mosques, as well as commercial and government buildings.

* **protectorate** country under the protection and control of a stronger nation

Development of Local Architecture in Islamic Countries. Mehmet Vedad and Ahmet Kemalettin, among the earliest professional Islamic architects, came from Turkey. After studying architecture in Europe, they returned home to design numerous buildings for the Ottoman rulers during the early 1900s. Their work incorporated both European and traditional Ottoman elements and evolved into Turkey's first "national style."

Another early professional architect was Sayyid Kurayyim, an Egyptian who trained in Switzerland. In the mid-1900s, he was the busiest architect in the Islamic world and founder of the first architecture journal in the Islamic world. The Muslim architect who received the most international recognition, Hassan Fathy, also came from Egypt. Fathy rejected Western architectural styles, favoring the use of traditional rural Egyptian architectural elements in his designs.

See color plate 11, vol. 2.

By the late 1900s, Islamic architects had begun to develop their own architectural styles and established design schools in their home countries. By the mid-1980s, more than 60 architecture schools existed in the Islamic world. More journals were being published and awards for architectural design had been established. The best known honor is the Aga Khan Award for Architecture, which was established to enhance the understanding and appreciation of Islamic culture as expressed through architecture. Judges award up to $500,000, the largest architectural award in the world, for architectural excellence that reflects contemporary design, community improvement, and a concern for environmental issues.

New Building Types and Styles. Recent developments in Islamic architecture include the construction of nontraditional types of buildings and facilities. These include airports, museums, banks, university campuses, and apartment buildings. Large national mosques also have been built in countries such as Malaysia, Morocco, Jordan, Saudi Arabia, Kuwait, and Pakistan.

Architectural styles have changed as well. During the colonial period, Western architects brought elements of classical and neo-Renaissance revivals to the structures they designed in Islamic regions. Based on much earlier styles of architecture, these revivals were eventually replaced by a return to a more traditional Islamic style.

By the 1950s, many Western architects and Western-trained Muslim architects had adopted the Modernist style, which emphasized technology over tradition. Modernist architects incorporated large expanses of concrete and glass into their designs. By the late 1900s, Islamic architects had again returned to traditional Islamic architecture for inspiration, due in large part to the rise in religious sentiment at that time.

Islamic Architecture: Walt Disney Style

Designed by government officials, the Moroccan Exhibition at Epcot Center in Orlando, Florida, provides a visual overview of the architectural history of Morocco. The minaret on the structure is an exact replica of the minaret on a mosque in Marrakesh that dates from the 1100s. Next to the minaret is a courtyard pavilion, similar to one in Fez, built in the 1500s. The exhibit also features a replica of the type of house built by Berbers before the 1900s.

Gardens

Since the 1400s, Islamic gardens from India to Morocco have fascinated artists, historians, poets, and travelers. Gardens in courtyards, plantings along walkways, and landscaped parks and hunting preserves once enhanced the landscape of Muslim communities. With modern urban sprawl and explosive increases in population, especially in such large cities as Cairo, Tehran, and Istanbul, the space left for gardens has all but disappeared. Although the gardens that remain contain different plants, a sense of the original gardens can be felt in the layout of walkways leading to ornamental pools and fountains.

The use of water is one of the most striking elements of traditional Islamic gardens. Pools of water were strategically placed to reflect adjacent structures, such as pavilions. Often conducted from one pool to another, water ran in narrow channels alongside paved walkways.

The traditional Islamic garden layout usually followed one of two designs—linear or cross-axial. The linear plan probably originated in ancient Rome. It consists of a rectangular plot with two long, parallel walkways that run from one end of the garden to the other. The cross-axial plan may have come from ancient Persia. It is a rectangular plot with two perpendicular walkways, leading in four cardinal directions and intersecting at the center of the garden.

Architects used the linear garden plan more often in the eastern section of the Islamic world, the cross-axial plan more commonly in the western part. In many places, however, they adopted both forms, and contemporary landscape architects throughout the Islamic world continue to use them today. (*See also* **Ablution; Bazaar; Mamluk State; Modernism; Mosque; Ottoman Empire.**)

Art

* **theology** study of the nature and qualities of God and the understanding of His will

Islamic art takes root from the basic ideals of Islamic theology*, emphasizing God's role as the creator of all life. Harmonious compositions and regular, repetitive designs suggest the unity of the Islamic community. The absence of human figures on mosques and other religious monuments reflects the idea that to create a human figure is to attempt to rival God. Main features of Islamic art include patterns of curved, interlaced lines, intricately decorated surfaces, and the use of vivid colors.

History

Islamic art developed during the Middle Ages, the period roughly between 500 and 1500. Before 500 Arabs wrote poetry but practiced no other art forms. Mosque and religious architecture became immensely important after the establishment of Islam. The Dome of the Rock, constructed in

Miniature painting, used to illustrate books and manuscripts, emerged as a popular artistic form during the Middle Ages. This Indian miniature from the 1500s features the Mughal emperor Babur passing his crown to his son Humayan.

See color plate 2, vol. 2.

Jerusalem in the late 600s, serves as one of the most revered religious sites in the world. Calligraphy* flourished as well as architecture, and the hand-copying of the Qur'an took on major artistic significance. On pilgrimages to Mecca, Muslims were influenced by people from other societies, mainly the Persians and the Byzantines*.

Early Influences. Until the 1200s, the capitals of the Muslim world were Arab (Baghdad and Damascus), but artisans in various parts of the Muslim world developed their own traditions. From Central Asia to Spain, Islamic crafts took on a distinctive character. In the late 1700s, Western countries

* **calligraphy** artistic, stylized handwriting or lettering

* **Byzantine** refers to the Eastern Christian empire that was based in Constantinople

expanded their empires into Islamic states, and interest in Muslim arts grew. Demand for textiles and other goods, combined with the introduction of Western methods of production, increased artistic output in many Muslim regions.

The influence of other cultures enriched Islamic arts in many ways. From the Chinese, for example, Muslims learned how to make paper, thus enabling calligraphers and painters to adapt their skills for the production of manuscripts and books. A strong tradition of miniature painting, used to illustrate books, also emerged (especially in Persia, under Indian influence). By the end of the Middle Ages, court artists in the Islamic world had access to European painting and had begun to experiment with Western techniques.

See color plate 13, vol. 3.

New Production Methods. Until around the 1800s, artists used traditional methods of production—that is, they crafted objects by hand. In rural areas, most artisans produced items in their homes either for domestic use or for local trade. In urban centers, workshops employed skilled artisans who produced objects for the royal court as well as for the marketplace. Royal commissions for luxurious carpets, jewelry, and other items could sometimes account for all of a workshop's business.

By the 1800s, increased contact with European cultures brought profound changes to the Islamic arts. Western societies had developed an enthusiastic taste for art objects from the Islamic world, and Europe and the United States became huge markets for Islamic goods—particularly carpets. To satisfy the demand, artisans began producing more goods for export, to the extent that domestic production in some areas almost ceased. Artisans also adapted traditional stylistic elements to appeal to Western notions of beauty.

Europeans also introduced modern methods of production, such as the use of mechanized looms and factories. At the same time, they brought inexpensive mass-produced goods from their own countries into Islamic markets. These goods were so much cheaper than traditionally crafted items that it became almost impossible for Islamic artisans to remain profitable. Focus shifted from small-scale production for local consumption to mass production for foreign export. Traditional techniques in some arts, such as carpet weaving, almost disappeared. In recent years, however, many Islamic countries have revived traditional practices, and consumers in the West have shown an interest in buying handmade goods.

Features of Islamic Art

The distinctive visual elements of Islamic art can be classified into two categories: surface decoration and structural form. Surface decoration includes geometric patterning, repetitive design, and calligraphy. Domes, minarets*, arches, and mihrabs* constitute the main structural elements of Islamic architecture.

Surface and Form. The intricate decoration of plain surfaces, such as walls and other parts of buildings, coins, pottery, fabrics, and carpets, is one of the most characteristic features of Islamic art. Artists use geometric motifs—circles, triangles, hexagons, and squares—to create ornate pat-

* **minaret** tall, slender tower of a Muslim mosque from which the faithful are called to prayer

* **mihrab** niche, or recess, in a mosque indicating the direction of Mecca

terns. The graceful curves of the arabesque* and the formal, angular patterns of geometric motifs both express and reinforce the unity of the Islamic world vision.

Unlike Christian art, which often depicts scenes from the Bible and includes images of Christ and even God, early Islamic art does not typically include human or divine representation. Human figures do not appear in mosque decorations, and artists never depict Allah. Such an act would seem an attempt to imitate God's power and a mark of profound disrespect. In nonreligious artwork, artists sometimes represent human beings but in a stylized way to emphasize their decorative purpose. Instead of striving for realistic effects, Islamic artists favor a high level of technical skill and place an emphasis on embellishment.

Mosques contain many of the structural elements associated with Islamic art. Domes are painted or tiled in shades of bright blue or turquoise to represent the heavens. Mihrabs guide the faithful by placing them in the proper position for prayers. The minaret, a tall spire from which the muezzin* calls the faithful to prayer, is usually next to the dome. Together, the dome and minaret symbolize the presence of Islam and serve as a focal point for the Muslim community. Arches also play a significant role in the architecture of Islamic buildings. The rhythmic repetition of rows of arches in mosque architecture provides a sense of community and unity.

Decorative Lettering. The art form most highly revered in the Muslim world is calligraphy—artistic, stylized lettering. More than any other cultures, those in the Islamic world have used the written word to embellish surfaces of buildings and other structures. Quotations from the Qur'an often decorate mosques, serving both to beautify the building and to remind the faithful of God's teachings. The practice of calligraphy originated in the 600s, when scribes began to make hand-copies of the Qur'an. Religious leaders felt compelled to develop a script style worthy of the sacred text. Only the best trained and most pious calligraphers were considered appropriate for the task of copying the Qur'an. According to a saying attributed to the Prophet, a person who makes a beautifully written copy of the *Bismallah*—the phrase meaning "In the name of God, the Merciful the Compassionate"—will enter paradise.

The first Islamic calligraphers copied the Qur'an in a geometric script known as Kufic, named for the Iraqi city of Kufa. This style often appears on wall decorations, with squarish letters complementing the rectangular shape of the glazed tiles. After the Muslims learned how to make paper, calligraphers developed flowing scripts, generally known as *naskh*.

The special qualities of various shapes and surfaces, such as arches and domes, coins, bowls, and metalwork inspired innovations in calligraphy. In Ottoman Turkey in the 1700s and 1800s, different types of mirrored script became popular. To create this type of calligraphy, the artist painted or carved the mirror image of a phrase opposite its original. Calligraphers sometimes created multiple mirror images of a phrase and sometimes twined them together. Another popular trend involved the writing of texts in circular forms, which became widespread as calligraphers imitated the design of Qur'anic texts that adorned the tops of some mosques.

* **arabesque** artistic style that uses foliage, fruit, or figural outlines to produce an intricate pattern of interlaced lines

* **muezzin** person who calls the faithful to prayer

See color plate 2, vol. 2.

Circular calligrams, known as *tughra*, appeared around the name of ruling sultans and bore embellishments corresponding to the artistic perferences of the period. *Tughra* also came to be used on postage stamps, banknotes, and coins, as well as on title pages of books to show the imprint of the publisher. Many calligraphic designs of the 1800s and after display an elaborate and ingenious style. Examples of such works include an Indian prayer scroll with a tiny text written into the letters, a Persian prayer scroll with the words appearing within the figures of imams*, and scrolls with gold lettering on leaf skeletons.

Contemporary artists in the Islamic world continue to find ways to use calligraphy. Even in parts of the world that do not use the Arabic script, such as Bangladesh, Malaysia, and Indonesia, artists have developed an interest in handwriting and letter art. In Turkey, the International Research Center for Islamic Culture and Art (IRCICA) holds competitions in classical calligraphy. Computer-generated calligraphy has developed, and although this method does not conform to the traditional techniques, it shows the possibilities of using Arabic script for decorative purposes.

Islamic Crafts

Muslim artists perfected techniques for making carpets, illuminated manuscripts, pottery and ceramic tiles, metalwork, and jewelry for domestic use and for trade. The only major art form not part of the Islamic tradition is sculpture, possibly because of the religious prohibition against depicting the human form realistically.

Weaving as a Cottage Industry. Carpet weaving is one of the most distinctive and characteristic art forms in the Islamic world. Nomadic tribes who lived in the arid lands of the Muslim empire, from Morocco to northern India and western China, wove carpets from the wool they gathered from their own herds. Most of these carpets were for their family's domestic needs, but some were made for trade. In urban areas, commercial weaving enterprises provided carpets for a growing international market. In Muslim regions, carpets were popular at all levels of society, and members of royalty ordered specially-woven rugs for their palaces.

Carpet weaving gained prominence in Anatolia (western Turkey) in the 1500s. It also flourished in Iran, the Caucasus, and Central Asia. Although rural carpet-making remained stable, urban Anatolian carpet production began to decline in the 1800s because of a shrinking market in Europe. In addition, the introduction of machine looms and artificial dyes affected traditional weaving techniques. By the 1970s, the quality of Turkish carpets had significantly declined. Renewed interest among European collectors, however, stimulated a revival in traditional carpet weaving techniques. Prices rose dramatically, and carpet weavers returned to older methods to improve the quality of their products. By the 1990s, Turkey produced new carpets, using traditional methods, in record quantities.

In the Caucasus, carpet weaving dates back to the 1600s. Local traditions of village weaving lasted through the 1800s, resulting in a limited production of small carpets in traditional designs. While most carpet weavers

* **imam** spiritual-political leader in Shi'i Islam, one who is regarded as directly descended from Muhammad; also, one who leads prayers

See color plate 4, vol. 1.

in the region were Muslim, many of the people who dyed the yarns, as well as those who bought the finished product, were from Christian Armenia. Carpets from the Caucasus became popular in Britain and the United States and were sold by Armenian immigrants at very low prices. After the Soviet Union took control of the Caucasus region in the early twentieth century, however, Western buyers looked elsewhere for carpets. As the Soviets relocated rural communities, the Caucasian carpet weaving industry virtually disappeared.

Iranian carpets are typically large, regularly woven, and intricately designed. The technical skill of the weavers ensures that the carpets lie flat and square when finished. In the late 1800s, Iranian rug weavers manufactured carpets with traditional patterns in sizes that would fit the floorspaces of European and American homes. In fact, some British companies operated their own carpet factories in Iranian cities. Weavers in rural areas contributed to the carpet trade by sending materials and unfinished pieces to the factories. The Iranian Revolution of 1979, however, slowed carpet production and demand from the West ceased. Since then, Iranian leaders have struggled to promote their carpet exports.

Before the 1800s, weavers in Central Asia produced carpets almost entirely for their own use. Because of their relative isolation from other markets, weavers managed to preserve their distinctive traditions even when faced with demand from Western countries. By the late 1800s, when Russian railways into Central Asia opened, rugs from Turkmenistan began to appear in European markets. Although carpet production continued after the Soviet takeover, the traditions of nomadic carpet weaving declined and were replaced by the production of rectangular floor carpets with synthetic dyes.

Tiles and Tableware. Islamic artisans produce many ceramic* products, using a variety of forms, techniques, and decorative styles. Ceramic tiles adorn mosques and other buildings. People drink, cook, serve, store, and carry food using vessels made from clay. In recent years, however, the use of plastic, aluminum, and enamel has increased in Muslim countries and is slowly replacing traditional materials.

In northern Africa, ceramic goods include plates, covered dishes, bowls, oil and butter jars, inkwells, and lamps. Qalliline, a suburb of Tunis, is known for its ceramic panels and tableware decorated in large floral or animal motifs. Ceramists in southern Tunisia typically produce large, unglazed storage jars and popular green and yellow ceramic ware. Although Egypt has a distinguished history of ceramic arts, most pottery produced today serves everyday functions and is of unexceptional quality.

By the 1700s, local traditions of ceramic manufacture were profoundly affected by contact with Europe. In many regions of the Muslim world, traders began to import fine porcelain from the European cities of Meissen, Vienna, and Sevres. A few European firms established factories in Iran and Turkey, where workers used modern methods of production but catered to local tastes. Inspired by European methods, rural potters created new styles of tableware, architectural tiles, and religious objects that they exported mainly to Armenian markets.

* **ceramic** refers to products made from a nonmetallic mineral such as clay and fired at high temperatures

See color plate 4, vol. 2.

Animals from Words

The last Mughal emperor, Bahadur Shah Zafar (died 1862) was not only a fine poet but also a skilled calligrapher. He fashioned holy phrases into drawings of faces, flowers, and trees. Some calligraphers created lion-shaped invocations to the fourth caliph Ali ibn Abi Talib, known as Asad Allah, or God's lion. Many talented artisans used Arabic script to form the shapes of elephants, mosques, and birds. A noted example is a calligram in white of a hawk holding an envelope in its beak—a message for the mystic Abd al-Qadir al-Jilani, known as the "White Hawk." Another artist uses the Arabic inscription that means "There is no god but Allah, Muhammad is the Prophet of Allah," to create the shape of a star and crescent—symbols of Islam.

In Iran, the cities of Kashan, Isfahan, Meybod, Shiraz, and Nain served as centers of ceramic production. Artisans used a variety of decorating styles, including bicolored black and blue patterns, European-influenced multiple color schemes, and luster painting, which involves the use of metallic paint on a white or blue glaze. Production of architectural tiles remains strong, and different types of folk items, such as ceramic beehive covers, are also produced.

Afghan and Central Asian pottery factories were much less affected by Western imports. As a result, ceramics produced there closely resemble those of earlier centuries. Artisans in this region use turquoise glazes with splashes of dark blue and purple and techniques similar to those used in the Chinese T'ang dynasty.

The art of glassmaking flourished in Islamic countries for centuries, dying out in the 1500s when European cities such as Venice became the major centers of export. In Egypt and Syria, glassblowers created cut glass, gilt glass, enameled glass, and lustre glass, which is fired with a thin coating of metal to give it a glistening surface. Craftsmen in Iran, Iraq, and Turkey produced similar items. In a few Islamic cities, such as Cairo and Damascus, studios use recycled materials to create traditional glass items as well as colorful glass beads and bracelets.

Pictorial Art. With a few exceptions, human imagery does not appear in Islamic religious art. Tradition holds that artists who depict human figures are imitating God, who alone can create life. In mosques and other holy sites, painters decorated walls with calligraphy or abstract images. Ornamental chapter and verse headings serve as ornamentations in most religious texts. Books that contain religious subjects, however, sometimes feature human figures. A book about Muhammad, for example, might contain an illustration of a journey he took, although the artist would take care to depict Muhammad and his fellow travelers in a one-dimensional, stylized manner that in no way seemed realistic.

Other Islamic texts, such as histories, the lives of the saints, mystical poetry, folktales, romances, epics, and animal fables were often richly illustrated. Artists typically created such works for wealthy patrons or royalty. A manuscript from the 1200s, now in the Bibliotheque Nationale in Paris, depicts a lively scene in which a pilgrim caravan departs from Mecca. Several camels, one carrying a palanquin (enclosed coach) possibly containing a lady, follow blue-coated men blowing trumpets. The painting, with figures of animals, human beings, banners, and plants, curves to fill the space in a harmonious way. Perspective and shading—painting techniques that create the illusion of three dimensions—are absent. Paintings like this are typical of those used to illustrate books and manuscripts.

By the end of the Middle Ages, Islamic artists—who usually worked in royal courts and thus had the opportunity to meet foreign visitors—had begun to take an interest in European styles of painting. They learned how to use perspective and shading. Landscape painting, an important tradition in Ottoman art, had traditionally focused on presenting precise geographical characteristics. In the 1700s, however, painters began to create more lush, romantic scenes in the European style. At the same time, European painters copied elements of Islamic painting. Important artists, such as Jean-Auguste Ingres and Eugene Delacroix, experimented with an "orientalist" style of painting that included images of Arabic horseman and exotic beauties in the sultan's harem.

Metalwork and Jewelry. In Islamic societies, jewelry often served as part of a woman's dowry*. Women commonly wore such items as bracelets, anklets, and earrings. Men wore jewelry as well, such as turban ornaments, rings, and talismans (charms worn around the neck to protect against harm). Artisans used metals to create pots, pans, perfume bottles and stoppers, water jugs, and other domestic items.

* **dowry** money or property that a bride or groom brings to the marriage

Traditionally, only members of royalty wore gold. Plain or gilded silver served the needs of the wealthy, nobility, and those in the royal court. Islamic leaders sometimes sent gifts of jeweled or metal objects to religious shrines, mosques, and the holy cities. Metalwork and jewelry, particularly turban ornaments, also served as gifts.

Artists created items using techniques such as enameling* or setting jewels in their finished products. In India, works of enamel on gold became decorated in geometric, floral, bird, and animal patterns. Iranian artisans painted portraits and scenes on gold or silver. Both Indian and Iranian artists used images of the sun in their work. In Turkey, metalworkers created floral patterns in painted and cloisonné* enamel. Turkish styles reflected a wide range of influences, including European designs such as rose-filled baskets and vases, ribbons, and pine cone patterns.

* **enameling** process of fusing colored glass to metal to produce a glossy finish

* **cloisonné** style of decoration involving raised enamel

Artisans made vessels and architectural decorations out of bronze, iron, and steel, as well as the preferred brass and copper. Such objects were either plain, or inlaid with gold or silver. Gilded copper was highly valued in Turkey. Artisans in eastern Anatolia and the Caucasus made silver and brass vessels inlaid with jewels and niello, a black metallic alloy of sulfur and copper. In India, artisans used *bidri*, a zinc alloy inlaid with silver or brass. In recent times, however, plastic vessels have come to replace many metallic items.

Jewelers also worked with a wide variety of gemstones. They used emeralds, lapis lazuli, jade, rock crystal, topaz, garnet, turquoise, and beads made from plaster and glass. Gold and precious jewels appeared most commonly in urban areas. In rural regions, people adorned themselves with silver and more modest gems. In Mughal, India, pearls became particularly fashionable and designers embroidered them onto royal garments. In Iran, pearled bandoliers*, armbands, crowns, and clothing were popular until the mid-1800s. Earrings in elongated shapes of domes or half moons were also common in Iran, as were bird pendants.

* **bandolier** belt worn over the shoulder and across the chest

Some Muslim women continue to wear traditional ornaments, but Western styles have influenced fashion in urban areas. In some large cities, women order jewelry from Europe. At the same time, however, Islamic jewelry and jeweled items have gained popularity in the international market.

Artisans also used gems, such as carnelian and agate, to create seals, which people used to authenticate documents and to convey their status. Some people carried their seal in a small pack placed in an inside pocket. Others wore them around their necks or had them set in rings. Jewelers also made talismans from a variety of gems. Talismans came in round, square, rectangular, oval, heart, and teardrop shapes, and people wore them on bracelets or as pendants, or had them sewn into their clothes. (*See also* **Arabic Language and Literature; Architecture; Music; Textiles.**)

Ashari, Abu al-Hasan al-

ca. 873–ca. 935
Founder of Ashari school

* **theologian** person who studies the nature, qualities, and will of God

* **Sunni** refers to the largest branch of the Muslim community; the name derives from sunnah, the exemplary behavior of the Prophet Muhammad

* **Qur'an** book of the holy scriptures of Islam

Abu al-Hasan al-Ashari was the Muslim theologian* who founded the Ashari school of Islamic thought. In doing so, he attempted to bridge the gap between a literal interpretation of the Qur'an and one based on reason. His ideas and those of his followers had a major influence on Sunni* Islam for many centuries.

Born in Basra, a city in southern Iraq, at a time when that region was the center of the Muslim world, al-Ashari received a thorough education. As a young man, he became involved with the Mutazilis, Muslim theologians. Mutazilis taught that the Qur'an* was created by God, meaning that it was not a part of God's eternal essence although it expresses God's eternal will. They also held that people have free will to choose between doing good and doing evil. These beliefs ran counter to views of traditionalist theologians, such as Ahmad ibn Hanbal, who founded one of the four schools of Sunni law (Hanbali). Ibn Hanbal maintained that the Qur'an exists eternally and that God has absolute power over all people and events.

Al-Ashari eventually had a change of heart. He left the Mutazilis and began to attack their views. He insisted that the Qur'an as a revelation is uncreated, but that any physical copy of the scripture is created. In this way, al-Ashari distinguished between essence and existence. In other words, although the Qur'an is uncreated, the words and letters on the pages are themselves created. He also affirmed God's power to create and control all people, objects, and events, including good and evil.

Al-Ashari's break with the Mutazilis is reflected in his book *Kitab al-Luma (Luminous Book)*. His views, however, differed somewhat from those of the traditionalists, and he relied on reason to defend aspects of belief that seemed to defy rationality. In the end, however, al-Ashari and his followers maintained that the ways of God are beyond the ability of ordinary people to understand. They require faith, not explanation, for acceptance.

Ashura

See *Calendar, Islamic.*

Assassins

* **Shi'i** refers to Muslims who believe that Muhammad chose Ali ibn Abi Talib and his descendants as the spiritual-political leaders of the Muslim community

The Assassins were a group whose practices included the murder of political and religious enemies. The term *assassin* is derived from the Arabic word *hashishiyun* or *hashshashin*, which means "smoker of hashish." This name, given to them by their enemies, refers to their supposed use of the drug hashish as part of their violent activities. The Assassins were active from about the 1090s to the mid-1200s.

The Assassins were members of the Nizari Ismaili, a movement within a larger group of Shi'i* Muslims, the Ismaili. The Ismaili had come into being in the 700s. Following the death of the sixth Shi'i imam*, Jafar al-Sadiq, a dispute arose over who was to succeed him. One group, later known as the Ismailis, insisted that Jafar's son Ismail should be the seventh imam.

Over the centuries, the Ismailis experienced a number of divisions over religious and political matters. One of these splits led to the establishment of the Fatimid dynasty* in Egypt. In 1094 Nizar, eldest son and the chosen successor of the Fatimid caliph*, was captured by political enemies and imprisoned. The Ismailis who remained loyal to Nizar became the Nizari Ismailis. A missionary* named Hasan-i Sabbah became leader of the Nizaris Ismailis. Hasan's impressive religious scholarship and strong personality helped him amass a fiercely devoted following, which came to be known as the Assassins.

Hasan's Assassins made their headquarters in a mountain stronghold in Iran called Alamut. From this fortress, the group carried out its murderous campaigns. Targeting enemies among the Fatamids and other groups, their methods included suicide attacks. Murdering their enemies was considered a religious duty.

The Alamut stronghold became legendary through the writings of Marco Polo, the famed traveler from Venice. Polo claimed to have visited Alamut in 1273, and he wrote of the Assassins' use of hashish and of their spectacular gardens. The gardens were designed to resemble the gardens of paradise to which the Assassins would go after completing their missions. Some skepticism exists as to whether Marco Polo ever actually visited Alamut and whether his stories are based on hearsay.

It is known, however, that the Assassins remained active through the 1100s and into the early 1200s. Finally, in 1256, Alamut was captured by the Mongols, an Asian people who conquered vast territories in Europe and Asia. Following the fall of Alamut, the Assassins gave up their violent ways. The Nizari Ismailis eventually established communities in Syria, Iran, Iraq, Central and South Asia, and India. Followers in India became known as the Khojas. Led by an imam known as the Aga Khan, the Khojas continue to thrive. (*See also* **Fatimid Dynasty; Ismaili; Shi'i Islam.**)

* **imam** spiritual-political leader in Shi'i Islam, one who is regarded as directly descended from Muhammad; also, one who leads prayers

* **dynasty** succession of rulers from the same family or group
* **caliph** religious and political head of an Islamic state
* **missionary** person who works to convert nonbelievers to a particular faith

Astronomy

Al-Battani, one of the great Islamic astronomers, declared that astronomy was the most noble of the sciences, second only to the science of religious law. Indeed, astronomy is the only natural science to have escaped the condemnation of the medieval* Muslims opposed to secular* sciences, and it is virtually the only Islamic science that lasted well into the modern age. Islamic scientists practiced the most advanced astronomy of the Middle Ages, studying and improving on the principles developed by the ancient Greeks. Muslims built major observatories, developed the mathematics of trigonometry to measure the angle between the sun and the horizon, and used astronomical observations to support Islamic beliefs.

The origins of Islamic astronomy are varied, deriving from early Indian, Persian, and Greek treatises and observations. Muslim astronomers owed an

* **medieval** refers to the Middle Ages, the period roughly between 500 and 1500
* **secular** separate from religion in human life and society; connected to everyday life

* c.e. Common Era, which refers to the same time period as A.D.

enormous debt to the work of the Greek astronomer Ptolemy (100–170 c.e*), who had written extensively about the motion of the moon and the planets. Muslims translated Ptolemy's works into Arabic during the 800s and 900s and then refined and advanced his ideas. Al-Battani, for example, predicted eclipses of the sun, and Abd al-Rahman al-Sufi produced a fairly accurate chart of the constellations.

Muslim astronomers conducted their studies from observatories, one of which they constructed at Maragha, near present-day Azerbaijan in southwestern Asia. Historians consider it the first observatory, which included 20 astronomers (including one from China), advanced instruments for studying the heavens, and an extensive scientific library. The astronomer Nasir al-din al-Tusi worked there during the 1200s, perhaps influencing the observations and writings of Nicolaus Copernicus, the Polish astronomer who discovered, in the 1400s, that the sun was the center of the solar system.

Astronomy helped Muslims solve various problems related to worship—determining the times for daily prayers and the time of sunrise and sunset in relation to fasting, and observing the phases of the moon to determine the beginning of the lunar month. Scientists used their astronomical observations to determine celestial longitude and latitude. These calculations were especially important in the architecture of mosques throughout the Muslim world. Each mosque had to have a *qibla*, a wall into which the mihrab (niche) is set, indicating the direction of Mecca. The positioning of the wall in each building was different, depending on the mosque's location. Astronomical handbooks usually contained chapters describing methods for accurately finding this direction.

Before the invention of clocks, Muslim astronomers calculated the altitude of the sun to determine the time of day. This was important because Muslims were expected to pray five times daily at specific hours. To facilitate time keeping, Muslim scientists made improvements to the astrolabe—a device that measures the altitude of the sun and other heavenly bodies. (*See also* **Architecture; Mathematics; Mosque; Science.**)

Atatürk, Mustafa Kemal

1881–1938
Turkish political leader

* **autocratic** characterized by unlimited authority

* **liberal** supporting change, especially in existing political and social institutions

* **abdicate** to give up a throne or other high office

Mustafa Kemal Atatürk is regarded as the founder of the modern Turkish state. He was a successful military commander during World War I, a political leader, and the creator of a parliamentary government in Turkey during the 1920s.

Mustafa Kemal (later called Atatürk, meaning "Father of the Turks") was born in Thessalonika, which is now part of Greece. As a boy, he went to military schools and eventually graduated as a captain in the infantry in 1905. At that time, the Turkish-based Ottoman Empire was in decline. Known as the "sick man of Europe," the weakened empire, ruled by an autocratic* sultan, Abdul Hamid II, had lost control of territories in the Balkans (a region in southeastern Europe) and in North Africa.

Meanwhile, a group of political leaders, known as the Young Turks, wanted to reform the government and restore Turkish prestige. Members of the Turkish army, including Mustafa Kemal, joined them. In 1908 the Young Turks forced the sultan to accept a more liberal* constitution and a year later forced him to abdicate*. By this time, however, Mustafa Kemal had broken with the

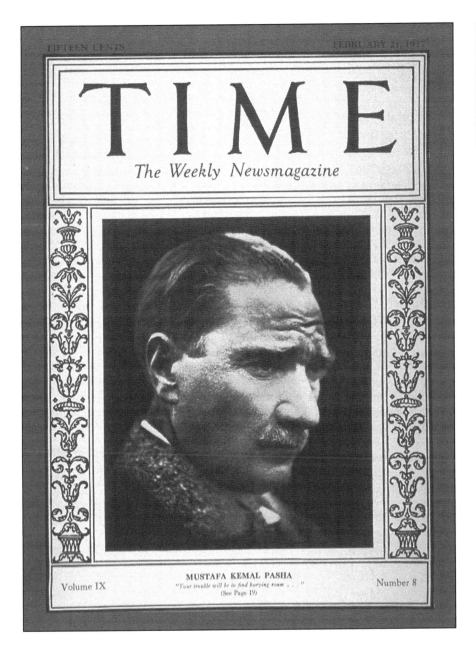

TIME

The Weekly Newsmagazine

FIFTEEN CENTS   FEBRUARY 21, 1927

MUSTAFA KEMAL PASHA
"Your trouble will be to find burying room . . ."
(See Page 19)

Volume IX   Number 8

The father of modern Turkey, Mustafa Kemal Atatürk ruled as a virtual dictator with goals of modernizing and strengthening the country. Although he never completely realized his dreams, Atatürk instituted many important reforms that helped guide the country towards becoming an independent state with a strong national identity.

See map in Ottoman Empire (vol. 2).

leadership of the Young Turks. He feared that they would undermine the power of the military by creating political divisions within the empire. Instead, he spent time writing and suppressing revolts that erupted in the region.

When World War I broke out in 1914, Ottoman Turkey allied itself with Germany and Austria-Hungary. Mustafa Kemal led Turkish troops in successfully defending Gallipoli, a peninsula off the east coast of Turkey that extends into the Aegean Sea, against the British and their allies. Promoted to brigadier-general, he was widely admired throughout Turkey because of his victory at Gallipoli. Nevertheless, the Allies eventually defeated the Turks, who then faced the problem of preserving their existence against attempts to dismember what remained of the empire.

Mustafa Kemal formed the Turkish Nationalist Party and established a new capital at Ankara, replacing the one at Istanbul. He strengthened the armed forces, which subsequently defeated Greek and French troops during the early 1920s. In 1923 the major powers recognized Turkish independence and Mustafa Kemal's presidency.

Over the next ten years, Mustafa Kemal instituted radical changes in the government and society. A new constitution called for a parliament and a president to be elected by all male citizens. Mustafa Kemal won the election three times and served as president until his death in 1938.

Although he appeared to consider the views of the parliament, Mustafa Kemal ruled the country as a virtual dictator. He feared that disunity might undermine Turkey's future, especially during the period when he was attempting to effect significant change in the country. Believing that the Western powers had succeeded because of a strong sense of nationalism*, Mustafa Kemal sought to replace loyalty to the Ottoman sultan with allegiance to the Turkish state. He favored education as a means for people to control their own lives. He sought to free the economy from foreign dominance and to separate religion from politics. Mustafa Kemal considered Muslim tradition too conservative* and a hindrance to his plan for Turkey's modernization. Indeed, he believed that Turkey, like other Muslim countries, had been weakened by strict adherence to Islamic teachings that encouraged blind acceptance of its precepts.

Mustafa Kemal's reforms represented a political revolution—a significant change from a multinational empire to the establishment of a modern state with a strong national identity. He instituted important social reforms, such as granting women the right to vote and the freedom to participate in other areas of society. Mustafa Kemal's principles of government have come to be known as Kemalism, which consists of several important elements. Kemalism includes a republican* form of government that is responsible for and to the people, a secular (nonreligious) government, and a strong Turkish identity. (*See also* **Ottoman Empire.**)

* **nationalism** feelings of loyalty and devotion to one's country and a commitment to its independence

* **conservative** generally opposed to change, especially in existing political and social institutions

* **republican** refers to a type of government in which the citizens elect officials to represent them in a legislative assembly

Averroes

See *Ibn Rushd.*

Avicenna

See *Ibn Sina.*

Ayatollah

See *Religious Scholars.*

Azhar, al-

* **c.e.** Common Era, which refers to the same time period as A.D.

* **caliph** religious and political leader of an Islamic state

Established in about 970 c.e.*, al-Azhar is the greatest mosque-university in the world. After Jawhar al-Siqilli conquered Egypt for the Fatimid caliph* in 969, Cairo became the new capital and construction began on al-Azhar, which was intended to serve as the city's official mosque. Al-Azhar was probably named for Fatimah "al-Zahra" (meaning "the brilliant"), daughter of the Prophet Muhammad and ancestor of the Fatimid dynasty.

When Egypt was restored to Sunni* Islam in 1171, al-Azhar lost some of its prestige and became one of many Islamic learning centers in Cairo. Even when the Ottoman conquest of the region in 1517 transferred world power to Istanbul, Cairo remained a major cultural center—and al-Azhar regained some of its importance as the center of Arabic-Islamic learning. It also became a vital link between the Arabic-speaking population and the Turkish-speaking military elite.

Similar to other Islamic schools at the time, al-Azhar had no formal admissions procedures, academic departments, required courses, written exams, or even classrooms. Professors lectured from a favorite pillar in the mosque, with students gathered at their feet. Lectures included the Qur'an and law in the morning; grammar, rhetoric*, and science after noon prayer; and various "nonessential" subjects after sunset.

The influence of al-Azhar spread throughout Egypt and beyond, attracting students from Iran, Iraq, Syria, Chad, Somalia, Afghanistan, India, and other countries in the region. Students entering the school from outside Cairo joined learning groups called *riwaqs*. Some of these groups were supported by religious endowments that paid for food, and sometimes for libraries and living quarters.

From the early years, students from poor, rural families with little previous education mingled with students from wealthy urban backgrounds. But in the late 1800s, privileged families began to send their sons to private and state-run schools, where the training they received prepared them for more prestigious careers.

Efforts to modernize al-Azhar met with resistance from conservatives* in the university. State reformers bypassed Azhari shaykhs* who headed the school and founded specialty institutions, such as the School of Law (called Administration and Languages), the Dar al-Ulum teacher's college, and the state-run Egyptian University. Students at these schools successfully competed for jobs with the unspecialized graduates of al-Azhar. In 1902 new subjects and required examinations were introduced, but they were subsequently cancelled after protests from students and faculty.

A law passed in 1961 greatly changed al-Azhar by establishing new departments and programs. Among these were the Islamic Research Academy, the Department of Cultural and Islamic Mission, and the College of Islamic Women. The new curriculum included engineering, commerce, agriculture, medicine, science, and education. The location of the new colleges in the suburbs of Cairo further separated the conservative and progressive* factions.

Al-Azhar has always attracted students from outside Egypt. In 1903 more than 630 students were enrolled. By 1990 foreign student enrollment at al-Azhar campuses had reached about 6,000 students from 75 countries. That number continues to grow. Outside Egypt, al-Azhar remains the foundation of learning of Sunni Islam and the Arabic language, although study of a Western language is now a requirement. Graduates and professors from al-Azhar are in demand throughout the Islamic world to help establish and improve local Islamic institutions. Meanwhile al-Azhar remains true to its conservative origins. School officials have regarded Islamic activists with disfavor in the past, and battles to change their ways will likely continue. (*See also* **Education, Egypt, Universities.**)

* **Sunni** refers to the largest branch of the Muslim community; the name derives from sunnah, the exemplary behavior of the Prophet Muhammad

* **rhetoric** art of speaking and writing effectively

* **conservative** person generally opposed to change, especially in existing political and social institutions

* **shaykh** tribal elder; also, title of honor given to those who are considered especially learned and pious

* **progressive** inclined to support social and political change through government action

Babism

A revivalist* Shi'i movement of the 1840s, Babism was founded by an Iranian merchant named Sayyid Ali Muhammad Shirazi. In 1844 at the age of 25, Shirazi claimed leadership of a Shi'i school of thought known as Shaykhiyah, which had followers in Iran and Iraq. Although he lacked formal religious training, Shirazi declared himself Bab (gateway to knowledge), a traditional term for an individual acting on behalf of an imam*. Babism emphasized innate (or inborn) knowledge over clerical* training, strict observance of Islamic law, and the imminent return of the Hidden Imam, or messiah*. The movement gained wide support among merchants, government officials, and other social groups that were traditionally secular, or nonreligious.

Traditionalist Shi'i clerics opposed Babi teachings and had Shirazi placed under house arrest. In 1848 he announced that he was the Hidden Imam and that he had begun a new religious era. A series of bloody clashes with Iranian troops nearly wiped out the Babi leadership. Executed in 1850, Shirazi left behind a body of writings that his followers regarded as divine.

Persecution of the Babis in Iran intensified after a failed attempt to assassinate the shah* in 1852. A group of survivors fled to Baghdad, where two brothers founded separate strands of what came to be known as Middle Babism. Mirza Yahya, the designated successor of the Bab, based his teachings on Babi doctrines. Mirza Husayn Ali Nuri, however, gained a wider following among those inside and outside the sect with a new and simpler revelation—one more easily understood by laypersons. This movement gradually evolved into the Baha'i faith.

Babism was the last of a series of movements that began in the Middle Ages calling for a revival of radical Shi'i values. It was the only one, however, whose teachings evolved into a religious system, Baha'i, that extended beyond Islam. Many Muslim historians consider it a failed attempt at social and religious reform and a modern heresy*.

Baha'i

The word *baha'i* derives from the Arabic word *baha*, which means "glory" or "splendor." It now refers to the Baha'i faith, which was established during the 1800s by Baha Allah (1817–1892).

History of Baha'i. In 1844 Sayyid Ali Muhammad Shirazi declared himself the leader, or Bab (gateway to knowledge), of a Shi'i sect in Iran. He was eventually executed in 1850 as a result of his clashes with Iranian troops and Shi'i clerics who opposed his claim to leadership. His followers, the Babis, fled to Baghdad after a failed attempt in 1852 to assassinate the shah* led to intensified persecution of the sect. Two half-brothers, Mirza Husayn Ali Nuri and Mirza Yahya, continued to lead the Babis in Baghdad.

Before his death, Shirazi had designated Mirza Yahya as the head of the Babi sect. The more charismatic brother, Mirza Husayn Ali Nuri, who had taken the title Baha Allah (glory of God) in 1848, also had a significant following within the Babi sect. A split between the two men had resulted from differing interpretations of the Bab's prophecy of the coming of a messenger who would have the authority to change the Bab's laws. In 1866 Baha Allah (Nuri) publicly announced that he was the divine messenger the Bab had predicted would appear on earth. He also stated that the Baha'i faith would replace Babism.

In 1868 Ottoman authorities exiled the two brothers and their followers. Baha Allah was sent to Acre, a seaport city in present-day Israel. There, he entrusted most of the affairs of the community and religion to his eldest son Abbas, known as Abd al-Baha (servant of Baha). Following Baha Allah's death in 1892, the leadership of the faith passed to Abd al-Baha, who already commanded enormous respect within the Baha'i community.

Some members of the Baha'i faith emigrated to the United States where they established a religious community in Chicago in 1894. Abd al-Baha's correspondence with the community and his 18-month visit there around 1912 led to a strengthening of the Baha'i faith in the West. Today the faith has over seven million followers worldwide, with the largest community in India.

Basic Religious Beliefs. The followers of the Baha'i faith believe in the idea of progressive revelation—that God continually makes his will known through prophets and messengers. Among these men was Muhammad, the founder of Islam, as well as Baha Allah, who called himself a divine manifestation. Muslims believe that Muhammad was the last prophet. Members of the Baha'i faith, however, maintain that religious beliefs are constantly evolving and that God continuously reveals His word through new divine manifestations.

The Baha'i faith supports the concept of a single god, the importance of spiritual values as the foundation of society, equality of men and women, and education for everyone. Believers accept the unity and harmony of all peoples. Baha Allah was reported to have said in 1890:

> That all nations should become one in faith and all men as brothers; that the bonds of affection and unity between the sons of men should be strengthened; that diversity of religion should cease, and differences of race be annulled—what harm is there in this?

The Universal House of Justice, located in Haifa, Israel, is the seat of government for the Baha'i faith. This body is considered infallible in matters of religious doctrine because the faithful believe its rulings are inspired directly by God. At the local level, the Baha'i faith has established Local Spiritual Assemblies to carry out the rulings of the Universal House of Justice.

Baha'i followers use a solar calendar that consists of 19 months, each with 19 days. On the first day of each month, the faithful come together to pray and read or to listen to the teachings of their religion. In addition, Baha'is over the age of 15 observe a month of fasting each year, during which, like Muslims during Ramadan, they do not eat or drink between dawn and sunset. (*See also* **Babism; Islam: Overview; Muhammad.**)

See *Albania; Bosnia; Kosovo.*

Balkan States

Bangladesh

Bangladesh, "the land of Bengal," is a country in South Asia that is bounded by India to the west, north, and northeast. Bangladesh is one of the most densely populated nations in the world, with an average of almost 2,000 people per square mile. It is also one of the poorest.

Bangladesh sits on a flood plain crisscrossed by numerous rivers and streams. These waterways make the land fertile for farming, the nation's most important industry. But the region is vulnerable to floods, cyclones, and other natural disasters, which take a toll on crops and citizens alike. In 1998, for example, extensive flooding left almost two-thirds of the country underwater for two months. More than 1,000 people died and over 30 million people lost their homes. Such natural disasters drain the nation's resources and destabilize the economy. As a result, the leaders of Bangladesh face endless challenges, and opposition to the government runs high. Bangladesh has been plagued by intense political unrest since its formation in 1971.

Today about 83 percent of the Bangladeshi population is Muslim. Most of the remaining people are Hindu*. Although Bangladesh is not officially an Islamic state, much of its history is closely linked to its religious identity.

Early Bangladesh. Prior to the 1200s, Bengal—a large portion of which is now called Bangladesh—was ruled by a series of Buddhist and Hindu dynasties*. In 1200 Turkish Muslims conquered what is now northern India, bringing Islam to the region. Bengal remained under independent Muslim rule until 1576 when it became a province of the Mughal Empire, which had gained control of most of Afghanistan, India, and the land that would become Pakistan. Muslim culture flourished under Mughal rule, and many Hindu Bengalis converted to Islam during this time. The Mughal Empire began to disintegrate in the early 1700s, and for about 50 years Bengal was an independent state. As such, it drew large numbers of Muslims from both western India (which was dominated by Hindus) and the Middle East. However, when the British brought a formal end to the Mughal Empire in 1857, Bengal became a province of British-controlled India.

During the late 1700s and 1800s, the people of western Bengal, many of whom were still Hindu, profited from industrial and educational reforms implemented by the British. The Muslims of eastern Bengal, however, did not. They continued to farm and remained poor and largely uneducated. Tensions between the two regions ran high until the end of British rule in 1947.

Bangladesh From 1947 to 1971. When Britain granted India its independence in 1947, it also established the new nation of Pakistan. Pakistan had two parts: West Pakistan, to the northwest of India, and East Pakistan, which had previously been eastern Bengal. Western Bengal, which was primarily Hindu, was absorbed into India as a state.

Although East Pakistanis and West Pakistanis shared a common religion—Islam—they spoke different languages and had very different cultures. East Pakistan had the larger population, but West Pakistan controlled the government and the economy. Over time, East Pakistanis became increasingly dissatisfied with the lopsided distribution of wealth between the two

* **Hindu** refers to the beliefs and practices of Hinduism, an ancient religion that originated in India

* **dynasty** succession of rulers from the same family or group

See map in India (vol. 2).

parts of the nation. In 1971 East Pakistan declared itself independent and adopted a new name—Bangladesh. A bloody civil war followed, and East Pakistan, with help from India, ultimately prevailed.

Bangladesh After 1971. Reacting against the oppression they had experienced under the Muslim rule of West Pakistan, the leaders of the new nation set up a secular* government. The new government, controlled by a group known as the Awami League, banned religious-based political parties. In addition, ordinary Muslims who observed traditional rituals were often shunned or mocked by supporters of the Awami League.

As a result, many Bangladeshi Muslims grew highly uncomfortable with the nation's secularism. Taking advantage of this discontent, an Islamic group based in India became active in Bangladesh. Known as Tablighi Jama'at, this group aimed to strengthen Islamic faith and practice among believers. It attracted large numbers of followers in Bangladesh and moved toward an Islamic revival.

In 1975 the Awami League government, which had grown increasingly dictatorial, was overthrown by the Bangladesh military. The new government under President Zia (Ziaur Rahman) began to strengthen ties with the broader Islamic world. Although Zia was assassinated in 1981, the government that followed continued to develop the nation's Muslim identity, and in 1988 Islam was declared the state religion of the country. Nevertheless, the *shari'ah,* or Muslim sacred law, was not instituted as state law. Strictly speaking, therefore, Bangladesh remained a non-Islamic state.

In 1991 the Bangladesh Nationalist Party (BNP) regained control of the government in the nation's first free elections, and Zia's wife, Khaleda Zia, became the nation's first female prime minister. Although the BNP lost the 1996 elections to its rival, the Awami League, it prevailed once again in the 2001 elections and restored Khaleda Zia to the office of prime minister. Opposition to the BNP remains high, however, and the political climate continues to be volatile and unstable. (*See also* **India; Mughal Empire; Pakistan; Sufism.**)

Sufi Warrior-Saints

Many historians wonder how the population of Bangladesh came to be so overwhelmingly Muslim. The answer may lie in the era of the Mughals. During that time, land-hungry peasants without firm religious beliefs cleared much of the forest from Bengal's delta—a triangle of land between the region's two main rivers. Seeing a population ripe for conversion, Sufi missionaries moved into the region. These pioneer leaders, known as *ghazi-pirs* or "warrior-saints," organized the peasants, established communities, and protected farmers from the dangers of the forest. Over time the devoted followers of these Sufi pioneers came to view them as saviors, and the Sufis' religion, Islam, took hold in the delta.

* **secular** separate from religion in human life and society; connected to everyday life

Banks and Banking

In the non-Muslim world, banks operate according to standardized procedures. Individuals and businesses deposit money in banks, and those deposits earn interest. Banks also make loans and charge a fee for the privilege of borrowing money. These institutions are important for the movement of money through an economy. Banks in many Islamic countries, by contrast, operate according to the requirements for business practices set forth in the Qur'an*. In recent years, this alternative form of banking has gained widespread acceptance.

The Origins of Banking. Historically, trade has played a fundamental role in Muslim economies. Moneychangers, people who exchanged one type of currency for another, carried out business in many cities including the Arabian cities of Mecca and Medina. Nevertheless, because the Qur'an pro-

* **Qur'an** book of the holy scriptures of Islam

hibits lenders from charging interest (*riba*) to borrowers, Muslims were reluctant to become involved in the lending and collection of money. Consequently, traders developed another means of conducting business with people who did not have the money to make a purchase. Instead of lending money and then charging interest, traders extended credit based on the value of property owned by the borrower or his family, often charging a set fee.

Starting in the mid-1800s, commercial banks began to appear in Muslim countries. These early banks, however, were all owned by Europeans. They existed mainly to serve the governments and businesses of European empires, such as Great Britain and France. They did not serve the local Muslim business community.

Muslim-Owned Banks. In the 1920s, Muslims realized that traditional business practices were inadequate in the modern world and decided to establish their own banks. Thus, the Bank Misr of Egypt, the Arab Bank (a Palestinian institution), the Habib Bank in British India, and other similar institutions were created. There was, however, some resistance to the founding of Western-style banks. King Abdul Aziz of Saudi Arabia refused to allow the Bank Misr to open a branch in his country. Eventually, the king granted local money changers a license to open the National Commercial Bank on the condition that it operate under strict Qur'anic rules. The bank charged fees for its services but did not pay interest on deposits or collect interest on loans.

Nationalization. In the 1950s, anticolonial revolutions in Egypt, Syria, and Iraq brought independence to Muslim nations. The new governments assumed ownership of both colonial banks and private Muslim banks and placed them under state control, a practice called nationalization. Banks in Pakistan were nationalized a decade later. Such measures reflected a new approach to economic development that included the introduction of state-run industries.

Government-owned banks were generally unsuccessful. They failed to attract new depositors, in part because they offered a limited range of financial services. Following nationalization, bank deposits were worth less in Syria and Iraq than they were in Jordan, a country that did not have nationalized banks.

In Malaysia, Indonesia, and the countries that border the Persian Gulf, governments have favored privately owned banks. The majority of owners, however, are local Muslims. Branches of the British Bank of the Middle East, for example, were sold to local investors following the independence of Kuwait in 1961. In Saudi Arabia, 60 percent of Citibank's operation was made available to the public in the mid-1970s. Thus, the Saudi American Bank was created.

The Spread of Islamic Banking. Significant growth in Islamic banking came in the 1970s, largely as a result of a boom in the oil industry. Additional growth occurred in the 1980s, when Iran and Pakistan declared the paying and charging of interest illegal. In most other Muslim countries, Islamic banks have had to compete with Western-style banks. The Islamic institutions have succeeded in attracting deposits.

A Financial Alternative. Some Muslims, including Islamic scholars and members of the general public, have expressed dissatisfaction with commercial banking practices in Islamic countries. Despite the Qur'an's ban on *riba*, in some areas banks openly charge interest to borrowers. In Turkey, for example, a small interest charge on a loan—to account for rising prices— is acceptable. Nine out of ten banks in Egypt offer customers a fixed rate of interest.

Pious Muslims believe that banks receive an "unearned gain" by charging interest. They also impose an "unfair obligation" on the borrower, who must repay the loan plus charges. With regard to a depositor receiving interest, fundamentalists argue that people should not be rewarded for merely saving money. Earning a share of a bank's profit in return for sharing in the bank's risk is acceptable, however. For this reason, banking based on profit sharing, or *mudarabah*, has emerged as an Islamic banking alternative.

Islamic banks offer two types of accounts that operate according to the principle of profit sharing. Savings accounts pay depositors a sum periodically, depending on the bank's profits. Depositors can withdraw money from this type of account at any time. Investment accounts also enable depositors to share in a bank's profits, but account holders may withdraw money only after a predetermined period of time has passed.

Current accounts are similar to checking accounts in conventional banks. Depositors can access funds by writing checks or by using a debit card at an automatic teller machine. These accounts earn neither interest nor a share of the profits.

Islamic banks may help their clients finance large, expensive purchases. This type of assistance comes in a variety of forms. The bank may purchase an item on behalf of a client and later resell it to the client, marking up the price. Leasing is another practice of Islamic banks. The bank buys a piece of equipment or machinery, and the customer makes monthly payments to the bank for the use of the equipment. Finally, banks may help clients by becoming a partner in a business venture. (*See also* **Capitalism and Islam; Economics; Nationalism.**)

A Different Way of Doing Business

In the mid-1970s, the Muslim nation of Bangladesh was in the midst of a severe famine. University of Chittagong professor Muhammad Yunus decided to apply the economic theories taught in his classroom to the dire situation in his country. He founded Grameen Bank, an institution that caters to the needs of the poorest segment of the population in Bangladesh. The bank operates on the idea that in order to break the cycle of poverty, landless peasants need access to credit. It offers very small loans—typically about $100— without any collateral. The large majority of the bank's 2.4 million borrowers are women. Grameen Bank grants loans for a variety of purposes, including the purchase of farm animals and agricultural equipment as well as the construction of housing and sanitation facilities.

Barakah

Barakah refers to the "blessing" of humans by God. *Barakah* is believed to be granted by God to holy persons such as mystics or saints. In the Maghrib (coastal region of North Africa), and elsewhere from the 1400s onward, *barakah* was believed to be a hereditary trait passed along certain family lines, usually those descended from the Prophet Muhammad. In Morocco, for example, the sultans* of the Alawid dynasty* were believed to be endowed with *barakah*, which gave them unprecedented political wisdom.

Barakah was also believed to survive death so that the tombs of saints became shrines where people could pray for favors. Thus, saints came to be regarded by many as intermediaries of God. The person having *barakah*, living or dead, had to be able to transmit it to ordinary people, giving them good health, material gain, or spiritual rewards. This confirmed a blessed person's special relationship with God. The most visible proof of *barakah* was the ability to perform miracles.

* **sultan** political and military ruler of a Muslim dynasty or state

* **dynasty** succession of rulers from the same family or group

Some Muslim saints are known for their specialized *barakah*. A female holy person might be sought out to help women to become fertile or settle domestic problems. In Islamic folk traditions, *barakah* is also associated with certain foods, animals, plants, and even words and gestures. Folk medicine and healing are also associated with *barakah*. The qualities of barakah often existed in charms and amulets used to ward off evil spirits. (*See also* **Health Care; Saints and Sainthood.**)

Bazaar

See color plate 8, vol. 1.

The term *bazaar*, Persian for "market" or "shop," has several different meanings in Islamic society. It may refer to the actual marketplace—the shops or stalls where people buy, sell, or trade goods and services. The term also applies to the sector of the economy operating outside government control where individuals exchange goods and services. The bazaar is also a place of personal jihad (or ethical struggle) where services are performed for the communal good. In other words, Muslims must resist the temptation to profit at the expense of the community.

From ancient times to the present, the bazaar has taken on a variety of forms in the Islamic world. Fictional accounts provide insight into the social and economic structure of the bazaar. Such accounts include R. K. Narayan's novel *The Financial Expert* and the traditional folktales of *The Thousand and One Nights*. Although most ancient bazaars have been modernized over the centuries, this entry focuses on the traditional Persian bazaar.

The Bazaar as Marketplace. The structure of the traditional Persian bazaar depended on the setting in which it operated. Large facilities with roofs or awnings were common in urban centers, while open-air markets dotted the countryside. In small towns, shops or stalls lined neighborhood streets and alleys.

* **patronage** support or financial sponsorship

Many of the covered bazaars were built under the patronage* of kings or governors. As the masses gathered in a central location to buy and sell, the authorities could collect taxes easily. Some smaller covered bazaars were constructed by groups of merchants. Generally, the rents that shopkeepers paid to conduct business in the bazaar went to support local mosques*. This created a strong link between the marketplace and the religious establishment.

* **mosque** Muslim place of worship

* **guild** association of craftspeople and tradespeople that set standards for and represented the interests of its members

Sometimes a group of merchants in the same industry would organize a guild*. These associations regulated bazaar activities, including the production and pricing of goods. Guilds also enabled their members to regulate competition. The baker's guild, for example, determined where new shops could be located. Bread shops and a few other businesses, such as butchers and grocers, had to be distributed within a city's central bazaar as well as throughout a city to ensure the availability of food for all the people. Some businesses, including cloth merchants and blacksmiths, clustered together in their own specialized bazaars. At the center of most traditional Persian bazaars were moneychangers and credit suppliers. Their shops typically had heavy doors that could be shut at night in order to provide extra security.

This bazaar in Tehran, Iran, offers a typical assortment of goods for sale, such as clothing, rugs, food, and other items.

* **artisan** skilled craftsperson

The Bazaar as Economic Sector. Bazaars were central to the economy in many Islamic nations. At a basic level, they provided an outlet for agricultural products and traditional crafts. People working in bazaars represented a wide range of occupations, including peddler, wholesaler, broker, moneychanger, artisan*, and shop assistant.

Among the key participants in this system were large merchants and small shopkeepers. Large merchants frequently guaranteed business loans for small shopkeepers. In this way, large merchants exercised control over small shopkeepers. Failing to repay a loan was considered the ultimate sin, and it led to exclusion from the entire bazaar economy. Small shopkeepers funded mosques and religious meetings within the bazaar and supported religious leaders who opposed state policies that negatively affected the marketplace.

Governments occasionally tried to control the bazaar economy, but their attempts to influence the guilds or regulate prices were usually unsuccessful. In the 1970s, the government of Iran tried to promote alternative sources of credit through state banks. The banks, however, required too much collateral and were unable to provide loans as flexibly as the bazaar. The Iranian people greatly resented the government's attempt to control the bazaar economy. Hostility toward the state intensified and may even have contributed to the revolution that occurred in Iran in 1979.

A Delight for the Senses

Walking through the crowded alleys and streets of the traditional Persian bazaar is an experience for the senses. The sounds of potters, cabinetmakers, and metalworkers transforming raw materials into finished products fills the air. Merchants hawk everything from bread to luxury items. The sweet smells of spices, incense, perfumes, candies, and pastries are accompanied by other, more pungent, odors, including leather, paint, and sweat. The sights are also mesmerizing. There are shimmering skylights in domes and thousands of flickering candles and oil lamps, and the lights are scattered by glazed arches and ceilings.

* **Qur'an** book of the holy scriptures of Islam

The Bazaar as Moral Battleground. The bazaar has been described as an arena of jihad, an internal struggle to maintain one's morality when there is temptation to take unfair advantage. People participate in the activities of the bazaar to make money, yet it is also supposed to be a place where goods and services are provided for the welfare of the community. Muslims consider a merchant to be a servant of the community, not someone who seeks personal gain. Although the temptation to profit is inherent in commercial transactions, people accept the risk, because ultimately merchants perform a job that enables the community to function.

Traditionally, the bazaar has operated according to Islamic codes of conduct. The main Shi'i commercial code is more than 100 years old, and there have been few attempts to update it. The code establishes the rules for exchange. For example, it states that children may not buy or sell in the bazaar, except on behalf of competent adults. It also indicates that a buyer may return goods if he or she discovers that the price paid was more than the fair price. There are even rules for what must be said for a transaction to be considered a final sale. Judges and experts in religious law have been called on to enforce the commercial code on many occasions.

Credit practices in bazaars have also generated debates among Muslims. People who seek loans must pay interest, which is usually high. However, the Qur'an* prohibits the receiving or charging of *riba* (interest). As a result, interest is often disguised instead of eliminated. For example, interest loans are referred to as "loans of kindness" or "contracts." (*See also* **Banks and Banking; Economics; Trade.**)

Bin/Ibn

The prefixes *bin* or *ibn* mean "son of" in Arabic. Names with these prefixes can be found under *B*, as in *Bin Laden, Osama;* or under *I*, as in *Ibn Sina*.

Bin Laden, Osama

1957–
Islamic militant

To many people, Osama bin Laden is best known as the alleged mastermind of the terrorist attacks in the United States on September 11, 2001. On that day terrorists hijacked four airplanes and crashed two into the World Trade Center towers in New York City, one into the Pentagon outside Washington, D.C., and one into a field in western Pennsylvania. High-ranking officials in the U.S. government accused bin Laden and his followers of committing these deadly acts. September 11, they claimed, marked the latest in a series of attempts to harm the United States and its interests. Bin Laden's actions appeared to be part of his declared war against what he saw as the enemies of Islam.

Osama bin Muhammad bin Awad bin Laden was born in Riyadh, the capital of Saudi Arabia, in 1957. The son of a highly successful businessman, bin Laden inherited a large fortune, which he has used to finance his many activities.

In 1979, the year bin Laden graduated from university, the Soviet Union invaded the largely Muslim nation of Afghanistan. Bin Laden, like many other

Muslims, went to Afghanistan to aid in the resistance against the Soviets. Throughout the ten-year struggle, bin Laden helped recruit Afghan soldiers and financed their training. According to some sources, he also served as a commander of the Afghan opposition forces, known as the mujahidin*. With American support and assistance, the mujahidin eventually defeated the Soviets in 1989.

Bin Laden returned to his home in Saudi Arabia. In August 1990, neighboring Iraq invaded and occupied Kuwait, an independent state on the Persian Gulf coast. Iraq ignored a call from the United Nations Security Council to withdraw from the small, oil-rich country. The United States led a coalition of 32 nations, including Saudi Arabia, to liberate Kuwait. Bin Laden denounced the Saudi government for allowing the United States to use Saudi soil as a military base from which to operate. He considered the Americans infidels* whose presence in the land of Mecca and Medina—Islam's most holy places—was unacceptable. Bin Laden's opposition so angered the Saudi government that they accused him of subversion*, and revoked his citizenship. He fled the country in 1991.

Bin Laden then committed himself to the destruction of the United States and its allies. From his new location in Khartoum, the capital of Sudan, he worked to expand an organization called al-Qaeda (Arabic for "the base"). Appealing to Muslims throughout the world, al-Qaeda's broad goal was to overthrow all moderate or "corrupt" Muslim governments, eliminate Western influence, erase state boundaries, and establish a single fundamentalist* Muslim state. To support this effort, al-Qaeda used terrorism* against its enemies. Throughout the 1990s, al-Qaeda built training camps and allegedly took part in a number of terrorist attacks. Bin Laden was suspected of involvement in two terrorist incidents in 1993— the bombing of the World Trade Center that killed 6 people and injured more than 1,000 others, and the battle in Mogadishu, Somalia, in which 18 U.S. soldiers died.

Under pressure from the United States and Saudi Arabia, Sudan expelled bin Laden in 1996. He moved his operation to Afghanistan, set up at least two terrorist training camps, and issued statements encouraging Muslims to strike at American interests and citizens. He was believed to be responsible for the 1998 bombings at United States embassies in Tanzania and Kenya that killed over 200 people and injured more than 4,500. In response to these attacks, the United States bombed suspected terrorist training camps in Afghanistan and a pharmaceutical plant in Sudan that was believed to be producing chemical weapons for bin Laden. The plant was later shown to be producing products for civilian purposes.

The attacks of September 11, 2001, were by far the deadliest ever experienced by the United States. Some 3,000 people were killed in the plane crashes and the resulting collapse of the World Trade Center buildings. Suspicion for the attacks immediately fell on Osama bin Laden, and the United States demanded that the Islamic fundamentalist rulers of Afghanistan, known as the Taliban, cooperate with efforts to bring bin Laden to justice. When the Taliban refused to hand over bin Laden, the United States and 20 allied nations, among them the United Kingdom, Australia, Canada, and Germany, launched a military campaign in Afghanistan in late 2001.

* **mujahidin** literally "warriors of God"; refers to Muslim fighters in proclaimed jihads, such as the war against the Soviet invasion of Afghanistan

* **infidel** unbeliever; person who does not accept a particular faith

* **subversion** attempt to overthrow or weaken a government

* **fundamentalist** generally refers to the movement that promotes a literal interpretation of scripture; in Islam, a movement that promotes politicization of religion to create an alternative public order

* **terrorism** use of violence against people, property, or states as a means of intimidation for political purposes

Osama bin Laden is the presumed mastermind behind several terrorist attacks against the United States. The most deadly of those assaults occurred in the United States on September 11, 2001, when he allegedly arranged and financed the hijacking of four airliners to be flown into several American buildings.

The American-led military action succeeded in removing the Taliban from power, but bin Laden escaped. In November 2002, threatening and inflammatory audiotapes believed to have been made by bin Laden were released to the media, but his whereabouts were still unknown. Groups associated with bin Laden continue to train thousands of potential terrorists, who remain at large throughout the world. (*See also* **Afghanistan; Iraq; Jihad; Saudi Arabia; September 11, 2001; Somalia; Sudan; Taliban; Terrorism.**)

Black Muslims

See *Nation of Islam*.

Body Decoration

* **Qur'an** book of the holy scriptures of Islam

* **hadith** reports of the words and deeds of Muhammad (not in the Qur'an, but accepted as guides for Muslim behavior)

* ***shari'ah*** Islamic law as established in the Qur'an and sunnah, the exemplary behavior of the Prophet Muhammad

* **surah** chapter of the Qur'an

* ***hijab*** refers to the traditional head, face, or body covering worn by Muslim women

* ***abaya*** cloak worn by women that covers the head and body

* **chador** veil worn by Muslim women that covers the whole body except the face, hands, and feet

* **henna** reddish dye that comes from the leaves of the henna plant

Islam provides Muslims not only with spiritual and theological guidance, but also with directives on many aspects of daily life, such as contact between men and women, dress, and body decoration. The display of the self in public and private is a matter of considerable concern to Muslims. Instructions on the care, treatment, and presentation of the human body are drawn from the Qu'ran* and the hadith* and are codified in the *shari'ah**.

Gender Boundaries. Islam draws a clear distinction between public and private domains. It views the family as central to the survival of society and sets boundaries that separate the realms of domestic and public life and define the roles of men and women. Islamic tradition clearly states that a woman must not display her personal adornments or physical charms to anyone but her husband (surah* 24:31).

The effects of these boundaries can be seen in dress and body decoration. The *hijab** worn by many Muslim women ensures that women keep an appropriate distance from men and promotes respect and moral behavior among men and women in public spaces. In private, women do not veil themselves, and in public, women may wear attractive clothing and elaborate jewelry under their *abayas** or chadors*.

Media images of veiled women in Islamic countries have led many non-Muslims to assume that Muslim women avoid all displays of beauty and any form of body decoration. In fact, Islam places high value on the relationship between husbands and wives, and many traditions encourage women to make themselves attractive to their husbands. Some of the most elaborate practices of bodily ornamentation center on the rituals of preparing a bride for her new life and her role as a wife.

Henna* figures prominently in the body decoration of brides and married women throughout the Islamic Middle East. Elaborate, women-only parties prior to weddings involve the removal of all the bride's bodily hair, including her pubic hair. Then friends and family members use wooden or silver sticks to apply henna to the bride's hands and sometimes her feet, creating artistic and regionally distinctive designs. The designs resemble tattoos, but they are temporary. Islam does not approve of permanent tattooing, though many women in tribal areas of North Africa and the Arabian Peninsula have pre-Islamic* designs and symbols tattooed on their chins, hands, and chests.

Cosmetics, Charms, and Fragrances. Cosmetics also have an important role in many parts of the Islamic world. Indeed, in some settings, a thick layer of makeup is viewed as a protective mask for women. Traditionally, cosmetics consisted of heavy creams made from crushed flowers, herbs, powdered precious stones, and spices. In the Middle East, kohl* is the most popular and ancient cosmetic. Muslims value it for the beauty it lends to the eye no less than for its health-giving properties and its ability to protect them from the sun's rays. In many communities, men and children as well as women use kohl on the inner rim of their eyelids.

In the Islamic world, the eye is considered a very powerful part of the body. It is seen as the window to the soul and profoundly erotic and expressive. Even the veils and headscarves worn by observant Muslim women in public accentuate the eyes or the curve of the face in a manner that emphasizes, though modestly, a woman's best features. Scarves and veils are often embroidered and edged with lace designs for added effect within the bounds of Islamic propriety.

The eye also has symbolic value as a force of evil. Malicious people are believed to be able to harm others with the "evil eye," a malevolent glance. To protect themselves against hostility, many women and children throughout the Middle East wear blue beads in necklaces, bracelets, or amulets pinned to their clothing, in the belief that the properties of the color blue can counter evil intentions. Although not mentioned in Islamic teachings, beliefs concerning the evil eye are widespread in the Islamic world and also throughout much of Catholic southern Europe.

Last but not least, the use of fragrances in the Islamic Middle East is an important part of bodily adornment and ornamentation. Strong fragrances, such as musk, amber, sandalwood, and rose, have been popular since ancient times. Islamic teachings do not prohibit women or men from using such fragrances. In fact, any practice that ensures bodily health and hygiene is valued and encouraged, including the use of henna leaves for underarm deodorant and the use of henna dye as a fingernail polish. Many Islamic scholars prefer henna dye to polishes made of artificial ingredients that create a barrier to water, violating requirements for proper ritual cleansing. (*See also* **Clothing; Hair and Beards; Hijab; Magic and Sorcery; Women.**)

* **pre-Islamic** refers to the Arabian Peninsula or to the Arabic language before the founding of Islam in the early 600s

* **kohl** black powder applied to the membrane between the eyelashes and the edge of the eyelids

See color plate 12, vol. 3.

Bosnia

Bosnia, officially known as the Republic of Bosnia and Herzegovina, lies on the Balkan Peninsula in southeastern Europe. The country's population includes Muslims and ethnic* Serbs and Croats. The largest population group, about 45 percent, is Muslim. Traditionally, Croats are Roman Catholic and Serbs are Eastern Orthodox Christian. Bosnia is a country with a rich past. Its capital, Sarajevo, is one of the cultural centers of the region. Its history has been marked by both warfare and communal coexistence. Recent years have added a new chapter to the region's troubled history.

* **ethnic** relating to groups of people who share a common racial, national, tribal, religious, linguistic, or cultural background

At the center of a fierce civil war in the 1990s, Bosnia's capital of Sarajevo endured considerable damage and the loss of thousands of lives. This photo from that period shows barricades marking off an area of the city called "Sniper's Alley," named for daily shootings by Serbian forces.

* **duchy** territory ruled by a duke or duchess

A Brief History. The land of Bosnia has, over the centuries, been a battleground for foreign powers. The Romans conquered the territory over 2,000 years ago and were driven out by the Goths, who were themselves replaced by the Byzantine Empire in the 500s. Soon afterward, Slavic peoples began to settle the area—including Serbs and Croats, two groups who would have a deep impact in the centuries ahead. Bosnia also enjoyed some periods of independence from the 1100s to 1300s. In the 1300s, Bosnia joined with Herzegovina, a duchy* to its south, to form Bosnia-Herzegovina.

Ottomans and the Arrival of Islam. The Ottomans—Muslims who came from Turkey—invaded Bosnia in the late 1300s. Completing the conquest in 1463, Bosnia became part of the vast Ottoman Empire. A major effect of the Ottoman conquest was the conversion of much of Bosnia's population to Islam. Conversions happened gradually and mostly in large cities, such as Sarajevo and Mostar. The Ottoman era was marked by costly and exhausting wars, during which Bosnia was often called on to supply soldiers for the empire. Some battles occurred on Bosnian soil, and the Ottomans levied heavy taxes on the people to pay the costs of the fighting. Despite these burdens, however, the city of Sarajevo flourished.

By the 1800s, the power of the Ottoman Empire was fading, and the Bosnians had become restless under Ottoman rule. In 1875 peasants staged a revolt against Ottoman tax collectors. The revolt spread, eventually touching off a war in which several European powers took part. By 1878 the Ottoman Empire had lost control of Bosnia. A new power, Austria-Hungary, took over the country.

Bosnia Under Austria-Hungary. In the years following Austria-Hungary's occupation, Muslims, Serbs, and Croats in Bosnia continued to develop a strong sense of their religious and national identities. As part of their growing desire for independence, these groups wanted Austria-Hungary out of Bosnia. In 1914 a Serbian nationalist* murdered Archduke Francis Ferdinand, the heir to the Austria-Hungarian throne, and his wife while they were visiting Sarajevo. The murder set in motion a series of events that led to the outbreak of World War I. The war broke Austria-Hungary's grip on Bosnia. In its aftermath, Bosnian Serb, Croat, and Muslim leaders joined other peoples in the region to create a new state of Yugoslavia. Bosnia ceased to exist as an independent political unit.

Bosnia in World War II and After. In 1939 World War II erupted in Europe. Germany and its allies invaded Yugoslavia in 1941 and quickly subdued the nation. The Germans established a puppet* Croatian state that included Bosnia. A period of terrible brutality followed. Serbs were massacred by the new regime*. In response, Serbs organized a movement which often targeted Muslims. Some Muslims, in turn, cooperated with Germany in attacks against Serbian populations. In all, some 300,000 Yugoslavs perished. When the fighting ended, a communist* force led by Josip Broz Tito won control of Yugoslavia. Tito formed a new communist state—the Federal People's Republic of Yugoslavia, which included Bosnia. The new government discouraged the practice of all religions, including Islam. Muslim schools, mosques, and other institutions were closed. In the 1960s, however, Tito softened his position somewhat and allowed Muslims to identify themselves as Muslims. This was viewed, however, as an ethnic rather than a religious identity.

The End of Communism. By the late 1980s, the communist system practiced in Yugoslavia and many other Eastern European nations had produced wide public dissatisfaction. By 1990 communism in Yugoslavia had collapsed. The separate republics of the Yugoslavian federation began to establish themselves as independent countries. The Serbs in the new Bosnia were not happy. They declared the creation of their own Serbian republic within Bosnia. Supported by the government and troops of the former Yugoslavia, which by then was basically a Serbian state, they went to war against the Bosnian Muslims, using terror tactics to drive them away. Serbs also targeted mosques and other symbols of the Muslim presence in Bosnia. In 1992 Serbs besieged* Sarajevo. By 1994 they controlled 70 percent of Bosnia. Some 200,000 people were dead and two million had been forced from their homes.

The crisis abated somewhat in 1994, when forces sent by the North Atlantic Treaty Organization (NATO) struck Serb targets. Bosnia's Muslims and Croats joined forces to force Serbian withdrawal. In 1995 the United States helped to bring about a peace agreement in which Bosnia was divided into two parts—the Bosnian Serb Republic and the Republic of Bosnia and Herzegovina. Although the agreement ended the bloodiest fighting, Bosnia still faces many challenges as a result of the war. These include the relocation

Spotlight on Sarajevo

Sarajevo, the capital of Bosnia, is also the home of many of the country's leading Muslim institutions, including over 100 mosques.

In addition to being the heart and soul of Bosnia, Sarajevo has been in the spotlight on the world stage several times. In 1984 the city hosted the Winter Olympics, attracting visitors and athletes from around the world. It was a moment of great pride for Sarajevans. That would soon be followed by a horrible civil war. Although the fighting destroyed the city and its people, it also helped draw world attention to the situation in Bosnia.

* **nationalist** one who advocates loyalty and devotion to his or her country and its independence

* **puppet** refers to a government that is controlled by an outside power

* **regime** government in power

* **communist** follower of communism, a political and economic system based on the concept of shared ownership of all property

* **besiege** to surround with armed troops for the purpose of cutting off supplies and forcing a surrender

of people forced from their homes by Serb forces. Another effect of the war has been the growing Muslim identity among the Bosnian Muslims. This has in part resulted from the response of Muslims worldwide to the suffering of the Bosnian Muslims. (*See also* **Ottoman Empire.**)

Brunei

* **sultanate** government of a sultan, the political and military ruler of a Muslim dynasty or state

* **sultan** political and military ruler of a Muslim dynasty or state

* **protectorate** country under the protection and control of a stronger nation

* **hajj** pilgrimage to Mecca that Muslims are required to make once in their lifetime

* **socialist** refers to socialism, the economic system in which the government owns and operates the means of production and the distribution of goods

Brunei is a tiny, oil-rich sultanate* located in Southeast Asia on the north-west coast of the island of Borneo. The country is bound on the north by the South China Sea and on all other sides by the Malaysian state of Sarawak, which also divides the country into two parts.

Brunei probably adopted Islam during the 1400s, or possibly as early as the 1300s. During this time, the first leader of Brunei to rule as a sultan* was installed by the sultan of the Malaysian state of Johore. Islam provided a unifying base for religion and politics. Brunei supported itself by trading jungle produce and attained the status of empire during the 1500s. By the 1800s, however, because of internal disagreements, European colonial expansion, and piracy, Brunei was near disintegration. In 1888 Brunei became a British protectorate*, a move that may have saved the country. Britain supported the government while Brunei's sultan maintained responsibility for the country's customs, traditions, and religious affairs. They enjoyed a friendly relationship for nearly a century.

Substantial oil deposits were discovered in Brunei in 1929. Production was expanded to offshore oil and gas fields in the early 1960s. During the course of the twentieth century, Brunei became wealthier and more self-sufficient. Sultan Omar Ali Saifuddin addressed the concerns of Brunei's poor with the creation of a social welfare system. To promote Islam, he built one of Asia's largest mosques and subsidized the hajj* for many Muslims.

In 1959 a new constitution returned much of the governing power to the sultan. Britain still maintained a presence and even tried to install a democratic government. Meanwhile, tensions mounted between the common people and the ruling elite. The socialist* Brunei People's Party (BPP) formed and staged an unsuccessful rebellion in 1962. The ruling elite reversed its stand on adopting democracy. Although invited to join the newly created Malaysian Federation during this period, Brunei declined, and instead became self-governing in 1971. Full independence from Great Britain came on January 1, 1984.

Today two–thirds of Brunei's population of 350,000 are Muslim. Many Chinese immigrants, who make up about 15 percent of the population, and people from small indigenous tribal groups have converted to Islam. Other religions include Buddhism and Christianity. Brunei is still ruled by a sultan, who encourages Islamic codes of behavior. The same family has ruled Brunei for over six centuries. The country's main exports continue to be oil, natural gas, and petroleum products.

Brunei's leaders are concerned that increasing integration into the world economy may undermine the country's internal social order. Today there is a rift between those who want an Islamic state and those who are more open to Western values. The role of Islam in Brunei government will continue to be examined and contested. (*See also* **Great Britain; Sultan.**)

Calendar, Islamic

In 622 the Prophet Muhammad and his followers moved from the city of Mecca to Medina, where they established the first Islamic community. This famous journey, known as the Hijrah*, marks the beginning of Year One of the Islamic calendar.

Lunar Calendar. The traditional Islamic (or Hijrah) calendar consists of twelve months and coincides with the phases of the moon. Each month lasts from the first sighting of the crescent moon to the next sighting, which is 29 or 30 days. One year comprises 354 days. The names of the calendar months are Muharram, Safar, Rabi' al-Awnal, Rabi' al-Thani, Jumada al-Ula, Jumada al-Akhirah, Rajab, Sha'ban, Ramadan, Shawwal, Dhu al-Qa'dah, and Dhu al-Hijjah.

Because the sightings of the moon depend on weather conditions and the location of the observer, the Islamic calendar may vary from place to place. The calendar also differs from the Gregorian, or universal solar calendar, which is based on 365 days. To offset these differences, Muslims use solar calendars for nonreligious purposes.

Like the Gregorian calendar, the Islamic calendar observes a seven-day week. As in the Jewish calendar, the days run from sunset to sunset. Some days have special rituals attached to them. Friday is the day of congregational prayer, with many businesses closing to allow Muslims to attend midday prayers at a mosque. Thursday is a day of fasting for some Muslims.

Sacred Days and Months. Some dates in the Islamic religious calendar commemorate events that occurred during the early period of Islamic history. The calendar also designates as sacred certain days and months that have no connection to particular historical events. They simply provide opportunities for religious observances and festivals.

Muslims celebrate numerous days in Islamic history, including the birth and death anniversaries of important individuals such as the Prophet, his daughter Fatimah, and the twelve imams*. Among these historical events, the most significant one (especially for Shi'i* Muslims) is the martyrdom* of the Prophet's grandson, Imam Husayn ibn Ali, on the tenth of Muharram in 642. During the first days of Muharram, Muslims remember and honor the sacrifice of Husayn by participating in daily ceremonies of mourning. On the tenth day of Muharram, huge public assemblies and processions occur. Shi'is, who view allegiance to the Prophet and his successors as a necessary part of obedience to God, wear dark clothing and carry replicas of coffins and tombs through their neighborhoods.

The Islamic calendar also includes major public religious observances. Ramadan, the ninth month, is a period of daily fasting. From sunrise to sunset, Muslims do not eat or drink, and they abstain from smoking and sexual relations. The fast is broken with a small meal at sunset before the evening prayer. During Ramadan, Muslims might gather to hear discussions on religious topics. Over the course of the month, some might recite the entire Qur'an, which is broken down into 30 equal sections for this purpose. The fast of Ramadan ends with the celebration of Eid al-Fitr on the first day of the next month (Shawwal).

* **Hijrah** celebrated emigration of Muhammad from Mecca in 622, which marks the first year of the Islamic calendar

Remembering the Martyr

The tenth day of the month of Muharram is known as Ashura. On this day, Shi'i Muslims mourn the martyrdom of Husayn, Muhammad's grandson and the third imam. In 680 Husayn, along with his family and several followers, was traveling to Kufa to claim his rightful position as caliph. Yazid, Husayn's Sunni rival, attacked the party. A battle ensued in which some people were killed and others were captured and imprisoned. Husayn has become a symbol of resistance and revolution and has inspired political and religious movements in Iran and Lebanon. Shi'i Muslims consider pilgrimages to Husayn's tomb in Karbala second in importance only to the hajj.

* **imam** spiritual leader in Shi'i Islam, one who is regarded as directly descended from Muhammad; also, one who leads prayers

* **Shi'i** refers to Muslims who believe that Muhammad chose Ali ibn Abi Talib and his descendants as the spiritual-political leaders of the Muslim community

* **martyrdom** act of dying for one's religious beliefs

Ramadan, the ninth month of the Islamic calendar, is a period of daily fasting and nightly prayer for Muslims. In this photo, Palestinian women gather around the Dome of the Rock Mosque to worship during the final Friday of Ramadan.

* **hajj** pilgrimage to Mecca that Muslims are required to make once in their lifetime

During the month of Dhu al-Hijjah (the 12th month), millions of Muslims make their hajj*. On the tenth day, pilgrims celebrate Eid al-Qurban, or Eid al-Adha, a commemoration of Abraham's willingness to offer his son Ismail as a sacrifice to God and God's substitution of a lamb for Ismail. Muslims ritually slaughter an animal—a sheep, goat, or cow—and give portions of the meat to the poor. They share the rest with family and friends.

Mawlids are popular holidays throughout the Islamic world. *Mawlid,* which means "birth," technically refers to the birth of the Prophet. It also refers to the celebration of the birth of a holy person who has died. The commemoration of a *mawlid* can take place at the holy person's tomb or at a historic site. Muslims throughout the world make pilgrimages to these sacred places to pay tribute. Rituals may include circling the tomb seven times, sacrificing an animal, donating money, and touching the tomb to receive a blessing.

In parts of the Muslim world with Persian heritage, a major festival is Nawruz, which marks the beginning of spring. It marks the beginning of Iran's solar calendar and is celebrated with a week of festivities. The people of Kyrgyzstan celebrate with traditional games, music, drama, and street art. Afghans prepare special foods—wheat for the women and veal for the men. (*See also* **Abraham; Hajj; Muhammad, Birthday of; Ramadan.**)

Caliph

Caliph is the title held by those who succeeded Muhammad as rulers of the Islamic world between 632 and 1924. As Muslim heads of state, early caliphs held powers similar to those of other rulers. These powers included enforcing the law, defending and expanding the realm of Islam, and distributing funds. In later years, however, the office of caliph lost much of its power, and the title became little more than ceremonial.

Muslim leaders elected the first caliph, Abu Bakr, after the Prophet Muhammad died in 632. The three caliphs who succeeded him—Umar, Uthman, and Ali ibn Abi Talib—were also elected. Sunni Muslims call these four caliphs the Rashidun, or "rightly guided." Their reign ended with the death of Ali in 661. Some Muslim writers have argued that the true caliphate (office of the caliph) ended here, and that the caliphs who succeeded Ali were merely kings or sultans, rulers with political power but not religious authority. They had inherited the title and often abused their position.

Not all Muslims believed that the Rashidun caliphs were the rightful heirs of Muhammad. This controversy led to the division of the Islamic world into two major sects. Muslims who accepted the authority of the Rashidun became known as Sunni Muslims. Those who rejected the authority of the early caliphs became known as Shi'i Muslims.

Between 661 and 750, caliphs of the Umayyad dynasty* ruled the Islamic world. The Abbasid caliphs followed the Umayyads, retaining power until the Mongol conquest in 1258. After the Mongol conquest, Egyptian rulers maintained figurehead* caliphs in the region until 1517, but these positions were not recognized elsewhere. Occasionally, Muslim rulers used the term *caliph* as an honorific* title, but most rulers were identified as sultans rather then caliphs. In the later centuries of the Ottoman Empire, sultans also took the title of caliph. In 1924 after the fall of the Ottoman Empire, the new Turkish government abolished the caliphate altogether. (*See also* **Mongols; Ottoman Empire; Shi'i Islam; Sultan; Sunni Islam; Titles, Honorific.**)

> See color plate 2, vol. 1.

* **dynasty** succession of rulers from the same family or group

* **figurehead** in name only; without real authority or responsibility

* **honorific** giving honor or showing respect

Caliphate

The caliphate was the ruling institution of the Islamic state, which included Muslims and the lands they conquered. The caliphate began with the death of Muhammad in 632 and continued in some form until 1924, when the Turks formally abolished it.

The caliphate, which comprised a large staff of officials, scribes*, servants, and other workers, was ruled by a caliph (Arabic for "successor"). The caliph provided political and military leadership, and to some degree, religious leadership. Caliphs were chosen and claimed their authority based on their link with Muhammad. Throughout much of its history, disputes over succession of the caliphs plagued the caliphate.

The "Rightly Guided" Caliphs. When Muhammad died in 632, the Muslim community needed leadership. Community elders selected Abu Bakr,

* **scribe** person who keeps records and copies manuscripts by hand to preserve them

Umar's Influence

Umar I, whose full name was Umar ibn al-Khattab, was a close friend and adviser of Muhammad. It was Umar who first urged Muhammad to put his teachings into writing and make them public. According to tradition, Umar was responsible for preserving the pages recording the revelations that were collected in the text of the Qur'an. Umar also decided to begin the Islamic calendar with the Hijrah, Muhammad's flight from Mecca to Medina, which took place in the year 622 C.E.

* **Sunni** refers to the largest branch of the Muslim community; the name derives from sunnah, the exemplary behavior of the Prophet Muhammad

Muhammad's father-in-law, as the first caliph. This choice was based on Abu Bakr's close personal relationship with Muhammad and his devotion to the highest standards of behavior.

Abu Bakr died in 634 and was succeeded by Umar I (634–644), Uthman I (644–656), and then Muhammad's son-in-law, Ali ibn Abi Talib (656–661). These men had been companions of the Prophet and ruled by virtue of their personal connections to him. These first four caliphs are remembered by many Muslims as the Rashidun or "rightly guided" caliphs. Muslims believe their rule reflected the ideals and goals of Muhammad. Their rule also marked a time of great expansion of the Islamic empire. Muslim victories in Syria, Jordan, Palestine, Egypt, Iran, and Iraq, among others, brought enormous wealth and power to the caliphate.

Not everyone, however, was satisfied with the rightly guided caliphs. Umar's policies, for example, angered some groups in the cities of Medina and Mecca and led to his assassination. Uthman sought to expand the authority of the caliph into a range of social, economic, and religious matters. His measures created such anger that he, too, was assassinated. Uthman's successor, Ali ibn Abi Talib, could not escape from the bitterness that lingered over Uthman's murder. Uthman's cousin Mu'awiyah challenged Ali's leadership. Ali was assassinated, and Mu'awiyah declared himself the next caliph.

The Muslim Community Splits. The Muslim community split over who had the legitimate right to occupy the caliphate. One group, the Sunnis*, believed that the Prophet had not designated a successor. They accepted the leadership of Abu Bakr and the caliphs who followed him. Sunni Muslims believed that because the first four caliphs had been selected on a nonhereditary basis, their successors should be chosen in the same way. Another group, the Shi'is, rejected the authority of the Rashidun and followed the tradition that Muhammad had designated Ali, his son-in-law, to be his heir, and that only Ali's descendants should succeed as caliphs. Over time, these groups developed their own communities, each with its own set of political ideas. Although their religious practices are virtually the same, they remain distinct Muslim communities to this day.

In spite of these divisions, Mu'awiyah continued as caliph. His rule marks the beginning of the Umayyad caliphate, in which leadership was passed on within the Umayyad family. This was a period marked by growing divisions in the Muslim world, including a civil war among disgruntled groups that raged for 20 years. Military success also characterized the Umayyad years. The caliphate expanded into new territory, including North Africa and Spain, and absorbed more groups into the Islamic empire. The growth produced great strain in the Muslim world.

The Rise of the Abbasids. Following the death of the Umayyad caliph Hisham in 743, the empire again fell into civil war. The armed forces of the caliphate were worn out from years of battle on behalf of the empire. Groups of discontented subjects rose up against Umayyad authority. They were led by the Abbasids, who were descendants of an uncle of Muhammad. Among their supporters were the Shi'i Muslims, who believed the Abbasids supported their cause of installing a descendant of Ali as caliph.

The Umayyad caliphate ended in 750 with the battle of Great Zab. The victorious Abbasids named their own caliph, contrary to the hopes of the

Shi'is. This marked the beginning of the Abbasid caliphate, which, like the Umayyad caliphate, was dynastic in nature.

A key development of the Abbasid era was the establishment of Baghdad as the new capital of the caliphate. This city grew in population and became a center of trade and industry. Baghdad, however, was remote from much of the territory under the caliphate. While the Abbasid caliphs tried to hold the empire together, they actually had little control over many diverse groups and communities within the realm. Rebellions occurred regularly, and the caliphate had trouble collecting taxes in many areas. In both Africa and Spain, opponents of the Abbasids proclaimed new caliphates—one called the Fatimid caliphate and another proclaimed by a descendant of the Umayyads. Clearly, the empire was coming apart.

The End of the Caliphate. The Abbasids managed to hold power and even reclaim some of their influence in remote areas of the caliphate. But they were unable to resist the power of the Mongols. In 1258 these Asian people, who were in the process of conquering vast territories in Europe and Asia, captured Baghdad. The Abbasid caliph escaped to Egypt, but as a political and military force, the caliphate had been greatly weakened. The title of caliph was subsequently adopted by various rulers for ceremonial purposes. The Ottomans later merged the titles of caliph and sultan. The Turks formally dissolved the caliphate in 1924, shortly after the fall of the Ottoman Empire. (*See also* **Abbasid Caliphate; Caliph; Shi'i Islam; Sunni Islam; Umayyad Caliphate.**)

See *Art.*

Calligraphy

Canada

Canada's Muslim population has grown rapidly in recent years. The 1991 government census reported about 253,000 followers of Islam. It is estimated that there are as many as 500,000 to 650,000 Muslims in the country today. Despite the significant growth of this community, Christianity is still the dominant religion in Canada. This environment poses many challenges to Canadian Muslims.

Immigration to Canada. Muslim immigration to Canada began in the latter part of the 1800s. Most of the new arrivals came from Turkey and the territory known as Greater Syria during Turkish Ottoman rule. Some Muslims came from South Asia. Census figures show that there were 300 to 400 Muslims in Canada in 1901 and 1,500 in 1911. Over the next few decades, changes in government policies caused the size of the Muslim community to decrease markedly. In 1907 Canada placed restrictions on the admission of immigrants from Asia. During World War I (1914–1918), the government classified many Turkish immigrants as enemy aliens and deported them. Tight controls on immigration remained in place through World War II, which ended in 1945. Thus, by 1951, there were only 2,000 to 3,000 Muslims in Canada, which was largely a result of the number of births exceeding the number of deaths.

During the 1960s, the Canadian government amended its immigration policy, eliminating discrimination based on race, religion, and national origin. Muslim immigration increased rapidly. By 1971 the Canadian Muslim population was over 33,000. During the 1980s and 1990s, the number of new arrivals continued to multiply.

Ethnic Diversity. The Canadian Muslim population is changing rapidly as it grows. Historically, immigrants have comprised the majority of Canada's Muslims. Today approximately half of the Muslim population is native born. These two groups tend to differ in their approach to Islam. Generally, immigrants hold more conservative* views on religious practices and observances than Canadian-born Muslims.

Most Muslims in Canada are Sunni. In addition, the community consists of various Shi'i groups, including Ismailis and Twelvers. The Muslim population of Canada is ethnically diverse. The large majority of Muslims are of Asian and North African descent, including Indo-Pakistanis, West Asian and North African Arabs, Iranians, and Turks. Most Muslims have settled in the large urban areas of Ontario, Quebec, Alberta, and British Columbia.

Common Concerns. The Muslim community in Canada faces several important issues. Among these challenges is the difficulty of practicing Islam in a largely Christian environment. For example, praying five times a day and following strict dietary rules can be complicated in a society that does not support these practices. Muslims must also strike a balance between preserving their Islamic heritage and integrating into the mainstream culture. Immigrant parents are especially concerned about the marriage of their children to non-Muslims—a practice that often results in children who are not Muslim.

At a broader societal level, Muslim immigrants encounter prejudice because they represent a region of the world that often is the focal point of international crises. During the Persian Gulf War in 1991, members of the Canadian Muslim community faced public expressions of concern about "internal terrorism." Some people were harassed and intimidated. After the terrorist attacks on the United States on September 11, 2001, the National Anti-Racism Council of Canada reported an increase in mosque burnings and hate mail to Arabs.

As negative images and stereotypes of Islam proliferate in the media, many Canadian Muslims remain concerned for their safety. Another area of interest is education and the content of textbooks, which some feel lack unbiased information about Islam.

At an internal level, Canada's Muslims confront the challenge of building a united community. Although Islam connects immigrants from different countries and backgrounds, apart from religious activities, contact between different ethnic groups is limited. Many recent arrivals bring cultural traditions that create controversy within the Canadian Muslim community and in the larger society. Such practices include traditional dress, specifically the *hijab* (veil), and female circumcision, a custom of some African Muslims. (*See also* **Clothing; Dietary Rules; Hijab; Prayer.**)

* **conservative** generally opposed to change, especially in existing political and social institutions

Muslim Pioneers

During the Great Depression of the 1930s, a small group of Muslims in Edmonton (in western Canada) met frequently to support one another and to maintain their religious traditions. Despite the tough economic climate, they raised money to build a mosque near the center of town. Through the efforts of Muslim families in the provinces of Alberta and Saskatchewan and contributions from some non-Muslims, the Al-Rashid Mosque opened in 1938. Al-Rashid was the first mosque in Canada. The original structure is now preserved in a historical park honoring early Canadian pioneers.

Capitalism and Islam

The relationship between capitalism* and Islam is the subject of much debate. Some Muslims argue that the basic doctrines of Islam oppose the aims of capitalism, a system geared toward maximizing profits. The majority of Muslims, however, believe that the Qur'an* does not prohibit capitalism, private ownership, or free enterprise, although it does impose restrictions on the profit motive. In recent years, some Muslim thinkers have developed an alternative economic model to traditional capitalism, which they believe reflects Islamic values without interfering with free enterprise.

Muhammad and Merchants. Historically, Islam supported a form of capitalism. Muhammad was a wealthy merchant in the Arabian city of Mecca, and some of his early followers also earned their living in commerce. The Qur'an endorses private property, honesty in commercial transactions, and competition balanced by a concern for the poor and needy.

For many centuries, Muslim merchants carried their goods and culture across a vast trade network that linked the major cities of Asia and Africa. The traders often acted as missionaries*, urging potential customers not only to purchase their wares but also to be thrifty, modest, and hard-working—in other words, to be good Muslims. Furthermore, traditional Muslim bazaars—where people bought, sold, or traded goods and services—were essentially capitalistic ventures.

Scholars note that the flourishing of Muslim commerce might have led to the rise of industry throughout the Islamic world. Beginning in the 1300s, however, western Europe experienced an intellectual and scientific revival that led to the colonization of parts of Asia and Africa. These political developments along with western technological advances of the 1700s and 1800s caused many aspects of Muslim commerce to change. Cheap, mass produced goods from the West displaced native crafts and manufacturing. Ultimately, the trade network of Islamic civilization could not survive the forces of Western industry and imperialism*.

The Islamic Alternative. As capitalism became more firmly linked to Western control, it became less attractive to Muslims. After achieving independence from colonial rule in the 1950s and 1960s, Muslim business leaders developed their own economic model. In many aspects, the Islamic economic system resembles capitalism. It stresses the importance of private property and free enterprise and emphasizes cooperation between the private sector and the state.

The distinguishing feature of contemporary Islamic economies is a powerful banking system. Several dozen large, state-sponsored banks centralize investment and power. These institutions respect the Islamic ban on interest (*riba*) by offering depositors a share in the bank's profits in return for sharing in the bank's risk.

Islamic banks unite the Muslim world by forging relationships with government agencies, political parties, ruling families, and social groups. These institutions also handle an array of transactions that cut across national borders. For example, they might use profits from oil-producing countries in the Persian Gulf to help unemployed Egyptians purchase farmland. Rooted in fi-

* **capitalism** economic system in which businesses are privately owned and operated and where competition exists in a free market environment

* **Qur'an** book of the holy scriptures of Islam

* **missionary** person who works to convert nonbelievers to a particular faith

* **imperialism** extension of power and influence over another country or region

nance rather than in trade, the new Islamic capitalism uses political ties to make up for its weakness in industry.

Despite Islam's growing economic power, many Muslims are wary of any form of capitalism and the trend toward global markets. They fear that a free market economy will focus solely on profit rather than on shrinking the gap between rich and poor. They also worry that the increased international exchange of goods, services, and technology will lead to greater Western control of Muslim countries. Moreover, they view Western culture as a threat to Islam's religious ideals. (*See also* **Banks and Banking; Economics; Trade.**)

See color plate 6, vol. 1.

Capital Punishment

Capital punishment refers to a government's use of the death penalty on individuals convicted of particular crimes. Islamic law requires this form of punishment for certain offenses, and several countries in the Muslim world have incorporated the death penalty into their criminal and penal* laws. Nonetheless, the practice of capital punishment varies greatly among Muslim nations. According to Amnesty International, a human rights organization, the Islamic government of Iran conducted over 7,000 executions between 1980 and 1990. By contrast, in Tunisia, capital punishment is rare.

The practice of capital punishment in the Muslim world has led to international criticism. Opponents argue that the crimes for which Islamic law prescribes the death penalty do not deserve such severe punishment. They also object to some methods of execution, such as stoning. In addition, they claim that governments in Muslim countries often apply the death penalty unjustly for political objectives.

Muslims who defend the practice of capital punishment maintain that it effectively deters people from acting in ways that violate God's divine law. As a result, its use promotes Islamic values in Muslim societies. Furthermore, they assert that the practice of capital punishment should not be judged based on the standards of Western or secular* societies. Instead, it should be considered as a part of the distinct Islamic order.

Paying the Price. Islamic law either requires or permits three types of punishment for crimes: *hudud*, *qisas*, and *tazir*. The acts for which an individual incurs the mandatory penalties known as *hudud* are specifically defined in the Qur'an* and the sunnah*. Generally, Muslims believe that classifying such acts as crimes is necessary to uphold the public interest and God's moral order.

The Qur'an prohibits sex outside of marriage and identifies it as a sin comparable to murder or stealing. Those convicted of this crime receive harsh punishment, either flogging or stoning. For a married person suspected of committing adultery, Islamic law requires four male eyewitnesses or the voluntary confession of the individual before the state can enforce the death penalty. However, more controversially, some legal scholars consider the pregnancy of a married woman whose husband is absent as sufficient evidence of the crime. Islam also condemns same-sex relationships. Most schools

* **penal** refers to punishment

* **secular** separate from religion in human life and society; connected to everyday life

* **Qur'an** book of the holy scriptures of Islam

* **sunnah** literally "the trodden path"; Islamic customs based on the exemplary behavior of Muhammad of Islamic law require punishments for homosexual activities. In Iran, Iraq, Saudi Arabia, and Sudan the penalty is execution.

Converting to another religion, worshipping idols, or rejecting the principles of Islam are considered acts of apostasy (abandonment of faith) and are punishable by death. Individuals who commit such crimes have the opportunity to reconsider their position, and if they do so, the death penalty cannot be applied. International critics maintain that punishment for apostasy is a violation of the human right to freedom of religion. Other crimes that require capital punishment include an armed robbery in which the victim dies and an act of rebellion, defined as rising up against the leadership of the Islamic community through force, and according to some jurists, without justification.

Crimes that involve murder are subject to punishment known as *qisas*. The rationale behind the penalties for such crimes is "an eye for an eye," cited in both the Bible and the Qur'an. Therefore, a person convicted of murder can be executed, unless the victim's family chooses to pardon that person or agrees to accept financial compensation instead.

The crimes that fall into the *tazir* category are generally not defined by Islamic sources of law. As a result, the leaders and judges in an Islamic community have the authority to establish rules, within the spirit of the Qur'an, to punish such acts. In modern times, the death penalty has been instituted for *tazir* crimes such as drug trafficking (in Iran) and blasphemy* (in Pakistan).

* **blasphemy** lack of respect toward God, a religion, or something considered sacred

The Debate. Both domestic and foreign developments have led to increased debate among Muslims regarding the morality, appropriateness, and effectiveness of capital punishment and capital punishment methods prescribed under Islamic law. Some maintain that various safeguards found in Islamic law—such as the requirement of witnesses and severe punishment for false accusations of adultery or the emphasis on pardoning in the case of murder—are designed to limit the practice of capital punishment in Muslim societies significantly. Others claim that severe punishments such as the death penalty are appropriate only when complete Islamic justice exists and poverty and other social ills that lead to criminal behavior are eliminated. A growing number of Muslims believe that interpretations of Islamic law must evolve with the changing needs and conditions of society. A punishment that may have been appropriate at the time of the Prophet may not be desirable today. Many Muslims in the United States oppose its application of the death penalty on the grounds that it affects poor people and minorities more than other groups.

International human rights law states that governments must restrict their use of capital punishment to the most serious crimes. Today many human rights advocates argue that capital punishment is by nature "cruel and inhumane punishment" and should be abolished completely. In early 2003, in response to pressure from reformist members of its parliament* as well as the European Union, the Iranian government agreed to cease the practice of stoning for adultery. The change came about only after religious scholars declared that it would be possible to establish an alternative punishment for the crime. In Nigeria a heated legal and political debate over the punishment of stoning for adultery persists. As the debate continues to unfold, the ques-

* **parliament** representative national body having supreme legislative power within the state

tion of capital punishment is certain to remain central to legal, policy, and human rights discussions throughout the Muslim world. (*See also* **Human Rights; Law; Sexuality; Sin.**)

Caribbean

The Caribbean region, also referred to as the West Indies, includes the islands in the Caribbean Sea from the tip of the Florida peninsula to the northern coast of South America. Cuba, the Virgin Islands, Jamaica, Barbados, and 19 other islands comprise the West Indies. Muslims are part of many of the societies in the Caribbean region as small minority communities and as part of larger cultural groups.

Although Islam provides a clear religious identity for individuals, Caribbean Muslims frequently define themselves by ethnic* origin rather than by faith. Islamic peoples have lived in the Caribbean region since at least the beginning of the 1500s, when individual Muslims participated in various western European expeditions. Today most Caribbean Muslims are immigrants or descendants of immigrants who came to the region in the 1800s and 1900s. Muslims in the West Indies make up three distinct ethnic groups—South Asian, Arab/Syrian, and African.

The majority of the Muslims in the Caribbean region have their origins in South Asia. They are descendants of thousands of indentured servants* who came to the West Indies from British India after the abolition of the slave trade. The ending of slavery in the Caribbean, especially after the Act of Abolition in 1833, created a labor shortage when former slaves refused to continue working on the plantations. Plantation owners found an alternative source of cheap labor in India and established a system of indentured servitude. Between 1845 and 1917, more than 400,000 workers from India came to Trinidad and British Guiana (now Guyana), and smaller but significant numbers of workers arrived in Jamaica and other British colonies. Landowners in Dutch and French colonies also brought large numbers of laborers from South and Southeast Asia to work on their plantations in the Caribbean.

The majority of the South Asian workers were Hindu, and they established large Hindu communities, especially in Surinam, Guyana, and Trinidad and Tobago. However, a significant percentage of the immigrants were Muslim. In some cases, as in Trinidad, as many as one out of every five were Muslim. Muslims currently represent a significant minority group within every South Asian community in the Caribbean. By the end of the twentieth century, over 400,000 Muslims (including South Asians) lived in the West Indies, with the largest communities in Trinidad, Surinam, and Guyana. More than 100,000 live in smaller communities on at least a dozen islands, including Barbados, Puerto Rico, and Jamaica.

The second major grouping of Caribbean Muslims is historically identified as Syrian or Arab. This group descended from immigrants who came from eastern Mediterranean countries in the late 1800s. They came as individuals or with families and were entrepreneurs, typically working as ped-

* **ethnic** relating to groups of people who share a common racial, national, tribal, religious, linguistic, or cultural background

* **indentured servant** one who agrees to work for another for a certain number of years, usually in return for travel expenses, room, and board

dlers, local storeowners, and merchants. Although they arrived in small numbers, they became an important part of the commercial elite in many societies. They played, and continue to play, an important role in the economic life of such countries as Trinidad and Tobago, St. Kitts, and Haiti. The majority of Syrian/Arab immigrants, however, were not Muslim. Most were Christian, either Orthodox or Catholic. Those who were Muslim established small mosque communities in many places.

The third and smallest group of Muslims in the Caribbean region descended from African slaves. Although many of the enslaved Africans working on plantations were Muslims, the conditions of slave labor made it virtually impossible for them to maintain a clear Islamic identity. While reminders of their Islamic origins are still apparent in some aspects of Afro-Caribbean popular culture, few slaves remained visibly Muslim within the Caribbean societies of the 1700s and 1800s. An awareness of Muslim heritage, however, inspired many Afro-Caribbean people to convert to Islam in the 1900s. The development of Afro-Caribbean Muslim communities during the last century has been aided by interactions with African-American Muslim groups in the United States. Organizations in the West, such as Nation of Islam and the World Community of Islam, have worked to support the growth and expansion of Muslim communities in the Caribbean region.

Although Caribbean Muslims view themselves as belonging to a global religious community, they define themselves primarily in terms of their ethnic and cultural heritage. In politics, for example, Indian Muslims are more likely to work with other Indians than with Muslims who come from outside the South Asian community. Similarly, Arab Muslims in the West Indies are more likely to emphasize their identity as Arabs and to participate in the local Arab/Syrian community.

Ethnic differences sometimes create tensions between different Muslim groups, as happened in 1990 in Trinidad and Tobago, when a group called the Jamaat al-Muslimeen attempted to take over the government in an unsuccessful coup*. The group consisted of Afro-Trinidadian Muslims and received no support from Indian or Syrian Muslims. Instead, the Jamat al-Muslimeen accused the Indian and Syrian Muslims of belonging to the economic elite that exploited people of African heritage.

In the last decades of the twentieth century, a number of regional Muslim organizations emerged in the Caribbean region to unite Muslim communities and to dissolve ethnic and community boundaries. Muslims formed the Federation of Islamic Organizations of the Caribbean in 1977 and the Association of Islamic Communities of the Caribbean and Latin America in 1982. Some communities established Muslim schools and attracted students from several countries. Although these efforts reflect a growing sense of the importance of regional connections for Muslims, the essence of Caribbean Muslim life today continues to be the religious associations linked to the various immigrant and ethnic heritages. (*See also* **Latin America**.)

* **coup** sudden, and often violent, overthrow of a ruler or government

See Art; Prayer.

Carpets

Caucasus

* **ethnic** relating to groups of people who share a common racial, national, tribal, religious, linguistic, or cultural background

* **aristocracy** upper class made up of hereditary nobility

* **mosque** Muslim place of worship

* **Sufi** follower of Sufism, which seeks to develop spirituality through discipline of the mind and body

* **missionary** person who works to convert people to a particular faith

The Caucasus, also known as Caucasia, refers to a mountainous region that lies between the Caspian and Black Seas. The Caucasus Mountains are traditionally considered to be a boundary between Europe and Asia. Islam was first introduced to this area in the 600s and spread throughout the region, despite repeated efforts to suppress it. Today Islam is the major religion of the Caucasus.

The Land and Its People. The main range of the Caucasus Mountains divides the region in half. The northern section is called the North Caucasus and the southern part is referred to as Transcaucasia, or the South Caucasia. The entire area consists of forested mountains, high grassy plateaus, fertile river valleys, and low-lying coastal plains along the Caspian and Black Seas. The climate ranges from semitropical along the coasts to temperate at higher elevations. The area is rich in minerals, especially oil. Constant invasions and migrations have made the Caucasus one of the most complex linguistic and ethnic* regions in the world, with over 50 distinct peoples speaking dozens of languages. Modern-day Caucasian countries include Georgia, Azerbaijan, Armenia, and the southwestern portion of Russia.

Early History. Since ancient times, the Caucasus has served as a vital link between Europe and Asia. Arabs conquered the eastern part of Transcaucasia in the mid-600s, bringing Islam to the region. Within a hundred years, the majority of people in the area had become Muslim. Over the next few centuries, Islam penetrated further into Transcaucasia, spread by Muslim merchants along fur and silk trade routes.

During the 1200s, Mongols from the East invaded the Caucasus. Many Mongol leaders were Buddhists or Christians, and their rule was strongly anti-Islamic. Islam survived in Transcaucasia during this period largely through the efforts of Muslim groups that spread Islam widely among the people. Eventually, Mongol leaders became Muslims themselves. In the 1400s, Mongols introduced Islam into the North Caucasus for the first time. Ottoman Turks and other invaders also helped spread Islam into the North Caucasus.

Russian Expansion. Around the same time, Russia was expanding its empire and attempting to counter the spread of Islam. Ivan the Terrible, who ruled in the mid-1500s, treated Muslims in the Caucasus as Russian subjects and denied them the rights given to Christians. Ivan took over the Muslim aristocracy* and encouraged conversion to Christianity. He expelled Muslim religious leaders and destroyed mosques*.

Despite these efforts to repress Islam in the Caucasus, the religion remained strong. It grew even stronger during the reign of Catherine the Great in the mid-1700s. She believed Islam had a more civilizing influence on Asia than Christianity, so she supported it. She guaranteed religious freedom to Muslims, sponsored the construction of mosques, and created Islamic institutions with broad authority over the Muslim population throughout her empire. She also encouraged Sufi* missionaries* to work in the North Caucasus.

Chechnya, a land-locked region of the North Caucasus close to Russia, was one of the last areas of the North Caucasus to undergo conversion to

Kabardiner Bogenschütze. *Fürst der kleinen Kabarde*

Islam. The Russians began to invade Chechnya in the early 1700s, taking over the region around 1800. At that time there were some local mullahs* in Chechnya, but they still had little influence.

Resistance and Conquest. Russian efforts to control the Caucasus continued throughout the 1800s, but they were often met with Muslim resistance. In the early 1800s, for example, a succession of imams* led rebellions of peasant landowners and aristocrats against the Russians. Although the rebels were defeated, they paved the way for later Sufi resistance leaders. The most famous of these men, a Sufi named Shamil, tried to create an Islamic state in the Caucasus in the mid-1800s. Although Shamil failed, Islam became stronger.

By 1900 Russia had completed its conquest of the Caucasus, instituting a strongly anti-Islamic policy. This policy gained greater strength after the Bolshevik Revolution of 1917 and the beginning of Soviet rule. Over the next several decades, Soviet policy toward Muslims alternated between repression and tolerance. In the 1930s, for example, Soviet authorities closed or

Despite Russia's attempts to expand its empire into Caucasus, the Muslims of the region fought hard to keep their lands and their religion. Those Muslims, such as the warriors shown here, helped pave the way for later resistance leaders.

* **mullah** Muslim religious scholar

* **imam** spiritual-political leader in Shi'i Islam, one who is regarded as directly descended from Muhammad; also, one who leads prayers

destroyed thousands of mosques and shot or imprisoned Muslim clergy. During World War II, the authorities relaxed the anti-Islam policy, hoping to gain the support of Muslims in the war against Germany. The change of policy proved ineffective, however, and thousands of Muslims defected to the German side to fight against Russia.

In the 1950s, the Soviets launched a new anti-Islamic campaign and closed the majority of mosques in the country. Russian leaders later relaxed this policy, viewing Islam as a useful tool for helping the Soviet Union gain acceptance in the larger Islamic world. To that end, Soviet leaders created a variety of official Islamic institutions in Soviet regions with primarily Muslim populations, including territories in the Caucasus. This policy continued throughout the 1970s. Then, in the 1980s, the Soviet Union went even further by launching a policy of religious freedom.

Islam in the Caucasus Today. After the Soviet Union collapsed in 1991 the newly independent states of Azerbaijan, Armenia, and Georgia were created in the Caucasus, along with the official establishment of autonomous (self-governing) regions in Chechnya and Daghistan that remained part of Russia. The majority of peoples in Azerbaijan and the autonomous regions are now openly Muslim and have re-established ties with the larger Islamic world.

In 1991, Chechnya declared its independence and became involved in a brutal war with Russia. Although a peace accord brought a pause in the fighting, the conflict resumed in 1999. The future political status of Chechnya remains uncertain. (*See also* **Communism and Islam; Mongols; Sufism.**)

Caucasian: Place or Race?

The term *Caucasian* means "of or belonging to the region of the Caucasus." It is used much more commonly, however, to refer to a light-skinned race of people, regardless of their geographic origins. The term was first used as a racial label by German anthropologist Johann Blumenbach in the late 1770s. He was obsessed with the beauty of the people of the Caucasus and believed that humans first arose in that region. Like most other scientists of his time, Blumenbach also assumed that the first humans had light-colored skin. The word *Caucasian*, therefore, soon became synonymous for light-skinned people everywhere. Modern anthropologists have rejected Blumenbach's ideas and his use of the term *Caucasian*.

Central Africa

The region of Africa that lies along the equator, drained by the vast Congo River system, is known as Central Africa. The region includes the Democratic Republic of Congo, the Republic of Congo, the Central African Republic, Gabon, and the island republic of Sao Tome and Principe that lies off the coast of Gabon. Angola, Rwanda, and Burundi are also sometimes considered part of Central Africa.

Profile of Central Africa. There are numerous ethnic* groups in Central Africa. Pygmies live in forests throughout the area. Groups in Congo and Gabon include the Fang, the Teke, the Kongo, the Chokwe, and the Lunda. The Baya and the Banda occupy Central African Republic, and the Hutus and the Tutsis live in Burundi and Rwanda. The island republic of Sao Tome and Principe has a mixed population due to its history of slavery and ties to Angola and West Africa. Most languages spoken in Central Africa belong to the Bantu group.

Although the population in Central Africa expanded greatly during the second half of the 1900s, most people live in rural areas clustered around kinship groups dominated by the head of the family. Polygyny, or the practice of having more than one wife, is common. Families live in houses built from plants and mud.

Most rural groups worship ancestors and believe in a creator—a god associated with nature and natural occurrences. The influence of missionaries*

* **ethnic** relating to groups of people who share a common racial, national, tribal, religious, linguistic, or cultural background

* **missionary** person who works to convert nonbelievers to a particular faith

caused some Central Africans to turn to Christianity, although Christians make up less than 30 percent of the population in this region. Most Christians in Central Africa are Roman Catholic, with a smaller percentage practicing various Protestant faiths. Muslims are a small minority in the Central African states. For example, Muslims account for 15 percent of the population in the Central African Republic, 10 percent in the Democratic Republic of Congo and Burundi, and only 2 percent in the Republic of Congo. In Gabon, Muslims comprise less than 1 percent of the population.

Many Central Africans, however, practice more than one faith. They may adhere to the beliefs of either Christianity or Islam, as well as to the beliefs of their tribal religion. Although Muslim and Christian groups have clashed on occasion, the tolerant aspects of most tribal religions ensure that interactions between groups generally remain peaceful.

Islam in Central Africa. Islam first arrived in Central Africa in the 1800s, when Arab and East African traders introduced it to the region. Muslim slave hunters journeyed to Central African lands as they searched for captives for the Ottoman Empire*. Traveling imams*, healers, and teachers served as missionaries, spreading Islam throughout the continent.

In 1908 Islam gained more followers in Central Africa when Muslims migrated in from Tanzania, Kenya, Uganda, and Sudan to escape European rule in those countries. In postcolonial* Africa, Islam gained converts as people sought refuge from harsh conditions, such as famine or drought. The hardships experienced by many Africans resulted in a resurgence of faith and spirituality. Some embraced Islam as a way of resisting Western values spread by the growth of capitalism* in the region.

In the 1990s, the Muslim population in Rwanda underwent an especially rapid growth spurt. After the 1994 Rwandan genocide* in which Hutu extremists slaughtered around 800,000 minority Tutsis, large numbers of Rwandans began to convert to Islam. By 2002, Muslims comprised 14 percent of Rwanda's population—nearly double its pre-genocide numbers. Converts explained that they felt betrayed by Protestant and Catholic leaders, some of whom had supported the killing of the Tutsis. Although some Christians made efforts to protect the Tutsis, the betrayal by others drove the Tutsis to seek solace in another faith.

Rwandan Muslims had traditionally lived apart from the rest of Rwandan society and had never taken part in the longstanding ethnic rivalry between the Hutu and Tutsi groups. The Muslim community in the capital city of Kigali was segregated in the Biryogo neighborhood, and people needed special permits to leave that area. Knowing that the Hutus would not invade their area, Muslims helped to hide and save families regardless of ethnicity or religion. They protected both neighbors and strangers. In the aftermath of the conflict both Tutsis and Hutus converted to Islam. Tutsis converted for protection and to honor the religion of their rescuers. Some Hutus also embraced Islam. For them, Islam offered symbolic purification for the crimes Hutus had committed.

Both Hutu and Tutsi Muslims appreciate the lack of ethnic rivalry in the mosque and the concept that God considers all groups equal. The struggle to heal the differences between Hutus and Tutsis has been referred to as the new jihad, or spiritual struggle, of the Rwandan Muslim community. (*See also* **East Africa; North Africa; Slavery; Southern Africa; West Africa.**)

* **Ottoman Empire** large Turkish state existing from the late 1200s to the early 1900s

* **imam** spiritual-political leader in Shi'i Islam, one who is regarded as directly descended from Muhammad; also, one who leads prayers

* **postcolonial** refers to the condition of a state after the departure of conquering powers

* **capitalism** economic system in which businesses are privately owned and operated and where competition exists in a free market environment

* **genocide** deliberate destruction of a racial, political, or cultural group

Central Asia

* **atheistic** denying the existence of God

Islam has existed in Central Asia for more than 1,000 years. Despite threats from the Mongols, Russian conquests, and the atheistic* policies of Soviet rule, Islam has survived as a political, cultural, and religious force.

The Land and Its People. Central Asia, which includes the present-day countries of Kazakhstan, Kyrgyzstan, Tajikistan, Turkmenistan, and Uzbekistan, covers more than 1.5 million square miles. This vast area shares its borders with the nations of Russia, China, Afghanistan, and Iran. The region's varied geography consists of mountains, grassy plains, and deserts, which comprise 60 percent of its total area.

Centuries of intermarriage in Central Asia have blurred ethnic distinctions in the region. Most groups here can trace their language to Turkic origins. The Tajiks—the only exception—speak an Indo-Iranian language. Religion provides a unifying force among Central Asia's diverse population. The majority of the estimated 58 million people who live in the region practice Sunni* Islam and follow the Hanafi school of law.

* **Sunni** refers to the largest branch of the Muslim community; the name derives from sunnah, the exemplary behavior of the prophet Muhammad

Early History. Beginning in the 900s, Islam spread among the Turkish peoples of Central Asia. They learned about this new religion through their contact with Muslim merchants who traveled the silk and fur trade routes that crisscrossed the region. Missionaries* and Sufi* brotherhoods were also influential in the conversion of the Turks to Islam.

* **missionary** person who works to convert nonbelievers to a particular faith

* **Sufi** refers to Sufism, which seeks to develop spirituality through discipline of the mind and body

During the 1200s, the Mongols invaded and conquered much of Central Asia. Mongol rulers, most of whom were Buddhists and Nestorian Christians, strongly opposed Islam. Sufi brotherhoods helped preserve the religion's hold on the region by preaching extensively among the masses. Eventually, several important Mongol rulers converted to Islam, ensuring its survival.

By the mid-1300s, the Russians began to seize power from the Golden Horde, a branch of the Mongol ruling family that had its capital at Saray on the lower Volga River. Over the following centuries the Russians expanded their control across Central Asia and incorporated Muslim territories and people into their empire. As the Russians occupied the region, they drove Muslims from major cities and valuable lands. In some areas, they destroyed mosques* and forced Muslims to convert to Christianity. Catherine the Great reversed such policies when she became the ruler of Russia in the late 1700s. Catherine allowed Muslims to worship freely, supported the building of mosques, and created Islamic institutions to oversee the Muslim population of the Russian empire.

* **mosque** Muslim place of worship

Islam in the Soviet Union. By 1900 Russia ruled all of Central Asia. In 1917 Vladimir Lenin led a revolt against the Russian government and established the world's first communist* state—the Union of Soviet Socialist Republics (USSR). Lenin and most of the members of his Bolshevik party were hostile to all religions, including Islam. Their need for political and military allies, however, led them to alternately tolerate and oppress the Muslims living within the Soviet sphere of influence.

* **communist** refers to communism, a political and economic system based on the concept of shared ownership of all property

The Soviets launched a campaign to secularize* the lands under their control. They believed that if they could destroy the religious identity of the

* **secularize** to separate religion from other aspects of human life and society

Until 1991 the Central Asian republic of Uzbekistan was under the control of the Soviet Union and before that, the Russian empire. At various times, both powers took steps to suppress Islam in the region, destroying or closing down mosques. These ruins of a mosque in Uzbekistan serve as a reminder of the country's long Islamic history.

people and replace it with a national identity, they would be better able to promote the principles of communism. Between 1925 and 1936, the government established the republics of Uzebekistan, Turkmenistan, Tajikistan, Kazakhstan, and Kyrgyzstan. The Soviets imposed the use of new standardized languages in these territories.

The structure of Islamic societies in Central Asia also came under attack. The communists considered the patriarchal, or male-dominated, Muslim family to be a potential challenge to the state. Consequently, they banned polygyny*, and they passed a law that gave Muslim women equal rights to obtain a divorce and to own property. Furthermore, the government arrested and killed opposition Muslim religious leaders and closed mosques and Islamic schools. During World War II (1939–1945), the Soviets adopted a more relaxed approach to Islam in an effort to win the support of Muslims in the fight against Germany. Nonetheless, thousands of Muslims joined the opposition.

Tolerance of Islam continued in the Soviet Union until the late 1950s. Under the leadership of Nikita Khrushchev, however, anti-religious sentiment resurfaced. Soviet authorities closed more than 1,000 mosques within ten years. After Khrushchev was removed from power in 1964, the communists revised their strategy to curb religious activity. Instead of relying on forcible measures, they created an anti-religious propaganda campaign. Publications, films, radio broadcasts, and research reports emphasized the in-

* **polygyny** practice of having more than one wife at the same time

Islam in Uzbekistan

Following independence in Uzbekistan, President Islam Karimov created a dictatorial regime. Fearing the threat of Islamic fundamentalist movements, he began a campaign to crack down on Muslims not affiliated with government-approved Islamic institutions. Popular independent religious leaders disappeared, and the media labeled observant Muslims as fanatics and terrorists. The government banned the public call to prayer, and police and security officers arrested thousands of Muslim men on fabricated charges. Observers worried that Karimov's tactics would fuel the growth of Islamic militancy. In fact, the Islamic Movement of Uzbekistan did engage in terrorist activities and guerrilla tactics in an effort to remove Karimov from power.

See color plate 5, vol. 2.

feriority of religion in general, and Islam in particular, as compared with communism.

The period following World War II was characterized by a nonmilitary rivalry between the United States and the Soviet Union, known as the Cold War. Soviet leaders believed that their official support of Islam could help them win favor in the Muslim world. To this end, they created Islamic organizations within the Soviet Union to forge diplomatic ties with Arab countries and to spread anti-American feelings in the Middle East and Africa. This policy lost much of its appeal after Soviet forces invaded Afghanistan in 1979.

When Mikhail Gorbachev became president of the Soviet Union in 1985, he introduced a policy of glasnost, or openness. Greater freedom of religious expression was permitted. Muslim groups in the Soviet republics staged antigovernment protests and began to compete for political power. When the government of the Soviet Union collapsed in 1991, most of the former Soviet republics joined to form the Commonwealth of Independent States. Islam reemerged, and by 1993 thousands of mosques and hundreds of Islamic schools had opened in the Muslim states of Central Asia.

Present Concerns. Although the former Soviet republics gained their independence, serious problems plague the Central Asian states. The political situation in these states is very unstable. Authoritarian regimes, led by former communist party members, run the government. Security forces ensure the power of the state, and freedoms of assembly, speech, and the press are restricted. The status of Muslims and Islamic political parties varies among the countries of Central Asia. In Uzbekistan, for example, Islamic political and social movements are subject to strict controls. Shortly after achieving independence, Tajikistan became the site of a civil war between the ex-communists who ruled the country and opposition forces calling for the formation of an Islamic state.

Another important issue for Muslims in Central Asia is reconnecting with the Islamic world. The antireligious policies of the Soviet state and isolation from historic centers of Islamic learning had caused Muslims to lose much of their religious identity. Since the collapse of the Soviet Union, Central Asian states have established diplomatic ties with neighboring Islamic countries, such as Saudi Arabia, Turkey, and Iran.

Central Asia also faces economic challenges. Under Soviet rule, the region's economy depended on cotton production, mining, and light industry. The Soviet system of central economic planning guaranteed a market for these goods. Today the Central Asian states must export their products to other countries, making them vulnerable to changes in demand. Although the region has abundant supplies of oil and gas, especially in Kazakhstan and Turkmenistan, regional and international political disputes over pipeline routes have limited their potential to generate income.

Central Asians must additionally deal with environmental and health issues. The extensive use of pesticides and fertilizers has caused water and air pollution. Infant mortality rates are high in Central Asia, particularly in rural areas. Near the Aral Sea, for example, about one in ten babies die in infancy. Moreover, Central Asians have a lower life expectancy than those living in the more economically developed regions of the world. (*See also* **Communism and Islam; Mongols; South Asia; Sufism.**)

Charity

Since the days of Muhammad, followers of Islam have supported many educational, religious, and social welfare causes. Governments and individuals regularly contribute to charitable activities. In the Islamic world, giving serves both social and spiritual purposes.

Setting Aside for Giving. The Arabic word *waqf* refers to the practice of reserving property and the income it generates for a charitable donation. This custom dates back to ancient times, when the Egyptians, Greeks, and Romans dedicated properties for educational and religious purposes. Today variations of *waqf* and charitable giving exist throughout the world and in all cultures.

Three different types of *waqf* exist in the Islamic world. Religious *waqf* includes mosques* and real estate that provides funds for their operation. The first religious *waqf* was the Kaaba in Mecca. Philanthropic *waqf* promotes the interests of the poor as well as the general public by providing funding for libraries, schools, and health services. It may also be used for loans to small businesses and the construction of roads and bridges. Muhammad initiated philanthropic *waqf* when he donated seven orchards to assist the poor and needy. The third type, a posterity or family *waqf*, benefits the family and descendents of its founder.

*mosque Muslim place of worship

Several rules govern the creation of a *waqf*. The property must be something of real or enduring value, such as land, buildings, herds, jewelry, tools, or books. The donation must be an act of charity that is made on a permanent basis. At the time of donation, the founder must be legally fit and able to make the donation. The founder specifies the conditions for *waqf* and decides who will manage it. These conditions must be followed as long as they are in accordance with Islamic law. All revenues generated by *waqf* must be used for the original purpose set forth by its founder.

By the early 1800s, corruption had become common in the management of *waqf* properties. Muslim governments established agencies to regulate the practice. During the colonial period of the 1800s and 1900s, and after independence, many government leaders seized possession of *waqf* properties. Today however, a growing number of Muslim countries seek to revive the custom of privately-run *waqf* foundations.

Helping the Poor. *Zakat*, setting aside a portion of one's wealth for the poor, is one of the Five Pillars of Islam. Both the Qur'an* and sunnah* require this form of personal giving. All Muslims who are able must give 2.5 percent of their net worth annually. Wealth counted for *zakat* includes gold, silver, livestock, crops, currency, and items that can be quickly converted to cash, such as stocks and bonds. Early caliphs* decreed that failing to pay *zakat* violated the law.

*Qur'an book of the holy scriptures of Islam

*sunnah literally "the trodden path"; Islamic customs and beliefs based on the exemplary behavior of Muhammad

*caliph religious and political leader of an Islamic state

Zakat serves both a functional and a religious role in Islamic societies. It helps redistribute some wealth to the poor in order to reduce tension among the classes and promote a greater sense of community. *Zakat* also stimulates the economy. It encourages wealthy Muslims to invest in physical assets, such as equipment, factories, and tools, because such assets are not included when calculating a person's net worth. This type of giving also increases the purchasing power of the lower classes. On a religious level, paying *zakat* provides a sense of completion for satisfying a pillar requirement. In addition, giving enables Muslims to overcome greed and materialism in favor of spiritual advancement.

The secular, or nonreligious, governments set up by colonial powers in the 1800s and 1900s eroded *zakat* practices. Secular tax systems replaced mandated religious giving. Recently, however, several Muslim states have restored *zakat*. Since the 1980s, Sudan and Pakistan have established agencies to collect and distribute *zakat* funds.

Sadaqah is a voluntary offering, above and beyond what is required, that may serve a variety of purposes besides charity. According to the Qur'an, *sadaqah* can be a way of atoning for offenses. Some Muslims use *sadaqah* to compensate for failing to perform certain rituals. (*See also* **Muslim Brotherhood; Pillars of Islam.**)

China

With 1.2 billion people, China is the most populous country in the world. Its civilization and culture are thousands of years old. Over the millennia, China has drawn people of many different backgrounds to settle within its borders. In 1978 China recognized 55 minority nationalities, groups who view themselves as non-Chinese and who speak the same language, live in a particular area, and share common values. Chinese Muslims represent ten ethnic groups and number about 20 million. The Hui comprise more than one-half of the Muslims in China.

The Golden Age of Islam. According to ancient records of the T'ang dynasty, in 650 a Muslim emissary* traveled from Arabia to China to pay tribute to Emperor Yung-Wei. Although the emperor did not embrace Islam, he honored the religion by building China's first mosque at Ch'ang-an. Muslims consider this event the beginning of Islam in China. Fourteen centuries later, this mosque still stands.

* **emissary** official agents of a ruler sent on a special mission

Following the emissary's visit, Muslims traveled to China for trade. Many settled there and formed small, independent communities. By the time of the Sung dynasty* (960–1279), Muslims had gained firm control over the import/export business in China. Because of the prosperity they brought to the country, they enjoyed a friendly relationship with the government and the people.

* **dynasty** succession of rulers from the same family or group

At the start of the Ming dynasty (1368–1644), Muslims were fully integrated into Chinese society. Many had intermarried with the Chinese, discarded their Muslim last names and blended their customs with those of the Chinese. Nevertheless, they maintained their dress code and dietary restrictions.

Conflicts Arise. During the Ch'ing dynasty (1644–1911), life became increasingly difficult for Muslims. The Ch'ing emperors spread anti-Muslim sentiment throughout the country. In 1911 the Republic of China replaced the ruling Ch'ing dynasty. Sun Yat Sen, the leader of the republic, declared that the country belonged equally to the Chinese, the Muslims, the Mongols, and the Tibetans. Relations between these groups and the government improved over the next several decades, but any progress that had been made quickly disappeared during the communist revolution in 1949. Chinese leader Mao Zedong established the People's Republic of China. During Mao's many years as head of the Chinese communist government, Muslims suffered terrible persecution. The violence peaked during what is known as the Cultural Revolution (1966–1976), when the communists sought to eliminate all traces of religion, including Islam, in China. The government closed Muslim schools and mosques and tortured and executed hundreds of thousands of Muslims.

Muslims in China Today. After the death of Mao in 1978, the Chinese government changed its policies toward Islam. New laws gave Muslims and other minority groups the right to practice their religion and to observe their traditional customs. Religious freedom has its limits in China, however. Muslims must worship in government-approved mosques, and imams* are not allowed to criticize the government's communist policies. (*See also* **Communism and Islam; Trade.**)

* **imam** spiritual-political leader in Shi'i Islam, one who is regarded as directly descended from Muhammad; also, one who leads prayers in Sunni Islam

Chishtiyah

Of all the Sufi brotherhoods, or orders, in South Asia, Chishtiyah is one of the most important. The order takes its name from the village of Chisht in western Afghanistan. The supposed founder of the brotherhood in India was Mu'inuddin Chishti (died 1236), a shadowy figure shrouded in legend.

Like all Sufis, the Chishtis are mystics* who engage in practices that they believe will gain them direct knowledge of God. One of the Chishtis' central practices is referred to as ecstatic listening. By immersing themselves in mystical music and poetry, the Chishtis believe they enter into a spiritual union with God.

The golden age of Chishtiyah began with the founding of the order in the early 1200s and extended into the mid-1300s. The great Chishti leaders of this period were neither religious scholars nor intellectuals. Instead, their mysticism was both practical and emotional, focusing primarily on the relationship between a spiritual guide and his disciple. These early leaders left no written records. During the 1300s, however, conversations of followers were recorded and gathered together. These writings are valued today for the insights they provide into early Chishti practices.

During the 1400s and 1500s, Chishti writers worked to clarify the order's central beliefs. They also defended some of the brotherhood's more controversial practices. Muhammad Gisu Daraz (died 1422), for example, linked Chishtiyah to traditional Sufism, but he also defended the Chishti practice of prostration* before one's spiritual guide. Chishti writer Abd al-Quddus (died 1537) incorporated some Hindu practices into Chishti tradition. He also strongly defended the practice of worshipping upside down while hanging by a rope tied around the ankles.

After a period of decline, the order enjoyed an era of popularity in the late 1600s and early 1700s. Throughout the next two centuries, many Chishtis were supported by the donations of pilgrims who visited the shrines of the

* **mystic** one who seeks to experience spiritual enlightenment and truth through various physical and spiritual disciplines

* **prostration** act of lying facedown in respect, submission, or worship

early leaders of the brotherhood. In exchange for donations, the Chishtis gave advice and charms. Today Chishti shrines are the sites of music and poetry performances that draw from both Muslim and Hindu cultures.

Chishti groups exist throughout India, Pakistan, and Bangladesh. In recent years, the Chishti order has lost its place as the most popular Sufi order to its rival, the Qadiriyah. Nevertheless, Chishtiyah remains an important reflection of Islamic and Indian culture. (*See also* **Sufism.**)

Christianity and Islam

Before the rise of Islam in the early 600s, the Byzantine Empire (the eastern half of the Roman Empire) and the Persian Empire controlled most of the Middle East. The Persians soon fell to Muslim invaders, but the Byzantine civilization, which was largely Christian, endured for almost 1,000 years. Throughout history, relations between Christians and Muslims have been characterized by cooperation and conflict. Their followers have fought in wars for political dominance. At the same time, Muslims and Christians have benefited from cultural and economic exchanges. Today interaction between the world's two largest communities of faith continues to be marked by ambivalence.

Conquest and Collaboration. At the time of Muhammad, Jewish and Christian tribes lived in Arabia. Muhammad reached out to these groups, hoping that they would accept his message of social and religious reform and become his allies. Debate and dialogue between Christians and Muslims soon developed. Muhammad, for example, discussed theological* issues with Christians from Najran and eventually allowed them to pray in his mosque.

* **theological** refers to the study of the nature, qualities, and will of God

In the years following the Prophet's death, Muslim armies extended the boundaries of the Islamic world from the Arabian Peninsula to Spain, Central Asia, and the Indian subcontinent. During that time, Muslims captured Egypt and Syria, which had been controlled by the Byzantines. Although many welcomed the Muslims as liberators from Roman rule, some Byzantine Christians viewed them as agents of Satan sent to destroy their religion. In 829 the Coptic Christian community in Egypt even rose up against the Muslim government.

Despite occasional religious battles, relations between Christians and Muslims living in the Islamic empire were generally good. In accordance with Islamic law, Muslim leaders extended legal protections to Christians living under their rule. Muslims considered Christians and Jews to be People of the Book, meaning that these groups were guided by scripture—sacred writings that contained revelations from God. Furthermore, the caliphs* permitted greater religious freedom and imposed lower taxes than had the Byzantine rulers. Many Christians held government positions in the Islamic empire. In Andalusia, for example, they served as translators, engineers, physicians, and architects.

* **caliph** religious and political leader of an Islamic state

Cultural exchanges between the Muslim and Christian worlds were also common during this time. Scholarship provided a way for the different traditions to communicate. The caliph al-Ma'mun founded an academy to translate works of science, philosophy, and medicine from Greek into Arabic. The

Bible was one of the few religious works translated into Arabic. Christians studied at Islamic universities in Córdoba and Cairo. Such institutions became the models for universities in western Europe. The exchange of knowledge between Muslims and Christians eventually helped Europe to emerge from its intellectual "dark age."

Rise and Fall of Empires. By the 1000s, the Holy Roman Empire, a European power composed of several states, controlled northern and central Europe. The Christians within the empire considered Islam to be an enemy and a threat to their religion. At that time, the Holy Land* was under Muslim control, and European Christians believed they would be in danger if they attempted to make pilgrimages to Jerusalem. In addition, Alexius I, the ruler of the Byzantine Empire, believed that his capital city of Constantinople was vulnerable to attack. In 1095 Pope Urban II called for a Christian army to free the Holy Land from Muslim rule. Four years later, the Christian forces captured Jerusalem and massacred Muslims and Jews living there, including women and children. This event was the first in a lengthy series of bloody military expeditions that came to be known as the Crusades. Muslims still regard the Crusades as a clear example of the aggression and imperialism* of the Christian West.

Muslim forces recaptured Jerusalem in 1187. Subsequent Crusades failed to dislodge the Islamic armies, except for brief periods. Muslim victories eventually gave rise to a powerful Ottoman Empire in the 1300s. The vast

From the 1000s to the 1300s, Muslims and Christians fought over possession of the Holy Land in a series of bloody battles known as the Crusades. This decorated tile from the 1200s commemorates the Third Crusade, during which Richard I of England and Muslim leader Saladin signed a three-year truce. It provided for Jerusalem to remain in Muslim hands, while allowing Christian pilgrims access to shrines in the city.

* **Holy Land** refers to Palestine, site of religious shrines for Muslims, Jews, and Christians

* **imperialism** extension of power and influence over another country or region

Own Worst Enemy

Over the centuries, the battle lines between Christians and Muslims were often blurred, and Christians were sometimes their own worst enemies. In 1204 for example, Roman Catholic Crusaders sacked the Byzantine capital of Constantinople, which was controlled by Eastern Orthodox Christians. This assault weakened the Byzantines in their struggle against Muslim forces. In 1453, Mehmed II, the leader of the Ottoman Empire, attacked Constantinople. To overcome the city's strong walls, he used a cannon built and operated by Christians from Transylvania. After knocking down the walls, Mehmed's forces captured the city. The Byzantine Empire crumbled, and Muslim rulers established a powerful state in the region.

* **Vatican** government, office, or authority of the pope

Muslim state ultimately encompassed southeastern Europe, most of the Middle East, and the Mediterranean coast of North Africa. Christians living in the conquered territories served in the Ottoman government and military, and Islamic law protected their churches.

The hold of the Ottomans gradually weakened, however. Inept leaders and corruption plagued the empire. Beginning in the mid-1700s, Europe experienced the Industrial Revolution, which generated military and technological advances, further shifting the balance of power in its favor. In the 1800s, European nations established colonies in Algeria, Tunisia, Egypt, and other Muslim lands and helped Greece, Serbia, and Romania gain independence from Muslim rule. After World War I, the victorious European powers completed the destruction of the Ottoman Empire. Colonization brought Western government and education and Christian missionaries to the Islamic world.

Most Muslims considered Western imperialism to be a serious challenge to their way of life. They viewed colonization as an attack on their society, education, religion, and culture. In response, some Muslims joined militant resistance groups. Anticolonial movements gained strength after World War II. By the early 1960s, most Islamic regions had achieved independence from colonial rule and had established Muslim nation-states.

In 1948 the United Nations divided the Arab territory of Palestine into two parts, creating the state of Israel. Muslims regarded Israel as a Western colony in Arab land. Arab nationalists and Islamic activists have fought to regain possession of this land.

Renewed Interest in Islam. East-West geographic divisions are no longer a defining factor in Muslim-Christian relations. Followers of both religions are now spread throughout the world. Centers of Christianity and Islam exist in Asia, Africa, Europe, and the Americas. Approximately six million Muslims live in the United States alone. Nonetheless, the relationship between Christianity and Islam still retains a dual nature. Though cooperation has reached new levels, suspicion and violence still separate the two faiths.

By the 1950s, Christian scholars renewed their interest in the study of Islam. Dialogue between Christians and Muslims grew as the World Council of Churches and the Vatican* organized meetings for representatives of various faiths. In 1965 the Vatican officially recognized the legitimacy of Islam and called for greater understanding between Catholics and Muslims. In the late 1990s, the Methodist Church, the second largest Protestant denomination in the United States, called for increased tolerance of Muslims. In 2002 Christian and Muslim leaders met in London to improve relations and to promote mutual understanding.

Muslims and Christians have also worked together to solve many world problems including poverty, hunger, and trade barriers. During the 1990s, the administration of President Bill Clinton helped Muslim groups take a more active role in public life in the United States.

Despite recent progress, conflict remains a major factor in Muslim-Christian relations. The 1970s marked the beginning of an Islamic revival. Some experts attribute this trend to increased revenue from oil in the Middle East and the corresponding rise in economic and political power of Muslim governments. Others point to the defeat of Egypt, Syria, and Jordan in the 1967 war against Israel and the continued statelessness of many Palestinians as a reason for renewed distrust of Christians among Muslims. Radical* Muslims became committed to victory over Christian culture and Western political systems. In 1979 Islamic fundamentalists* overthrew the Western-supported government in Iran. Islamic militancy grew in nations around the world, aggravating tensions between Muslims and Christians. Since the 1980s, Muslim and Christian mobs in northern Nigeria have battled in the streets. Sudan has been embroiled in a 20-year civil war between Arab Muslims in the north and Christians in the south. Since 1999 an estimated 10,000 people have died in Muslim-Christian violence on the Indonesian island of Ambon.

Most radical Muslims see the United States as their chief Christian enemy. They oppose its military and economic support of Israel and what they consider to be oppressive anti-Islamic regimes. Beginning in the 1990s, Islamic militant Osama bin Laden's al-Qaeda network launched a series of terrorist attacks against American targets around the world. Bin Laden seeks to unite Muslims in a global jihad* against Christians and Jews. Al-Qaeda's devastating attacks on the World Trade Center and the Pentagon on September 11, 2001, demonstrated the intensity and potential for tragedy in this ongoing conflict. (*See also* **Bin Laden, Osama; Colonialism; Crusades; Israel; Ottoman Empire; Qaeda, al-.**)

* **radical** favoring extreme change or reform, especially in existing political and social institutions
* **fundamentalist** person who believes in a literal interpretation of scripture; Muslim who accepts Islam as a comprehensive belief system that can be applied to modern times
* **jihad** literally "striving"; war in defense of Islam

Cinema

Economic, political, and cultural factors have shaped cinema in Islamic countries since the first film productions in the early 1900s. Initially, European and American influence on the film industry was strong. Later, movies became a vehicle for Muslim filmmakers to comment on the social and political issues in their countries.

Foreign Influences on Film. By the late 1800s, people had discovered how to make pictures move and how to project them. Using a combination camera, printer, and projector, French inventors Louis and Auguste Lumière began public showings of films in Paris in 1895. At that time, many Muslim countries were European colonies with large immigrant populations. Foreign residents introduced cinema to the Muslim world. They arranged film showings in cities with high concentrations of immigrants, such as Cairo and Algiers. At first, screenings catered to the upper classes—foreign residents and westernized Muslims. Eventually, movie operators targeted popular Muslim audiences. A two-tier system of film distribution remains common in many parts of the Islamic world. Imported films play in luxurious, air-conditioned movie theaters for elite audiences. Low-budget films play in simple, unadorned spaces for the masses.

Europeans produced most of the early films in Muslim lands, and they based their work on foreign models. Most Turkish films of the 1920s, for example, were adaptations of European stage plays. Although film production in Islamic countries remained low during the silent film era of the 1920s,

A crowd gathered outside a theater in Cairo, Egypt, in 2002 to watch the Egyptian film *Maali el-Wazir* (His Highness the Minister). The subject of the film was the corruption of Egyptian officials.

some Islamic lands were desirable as film locations. North Africa, for example, was the site of more than 60 European feature films.

The influence of foreigners on the industry remained strong during the 1930s. The advent of sound increased technical demands and production costs, forcing Muslim filmmakers to hire foreign directors. Furthermore, local producers could not match the budgets of their Western rivals. Instead of offering financial support, the government imposed high taxes on the industry. As a result, Muslim film production remained limited.

The Industry Expands. Following World War II, which ended in 1945, the film industry experienced a boom in the Muslim world with Egypt dominating the field. Production levels in national studios rose to more than 50 films per year. As a result, Egyptian movies became the most popular Arabic films. Prior to the early 1950s, most of these movies were adventure tales, dramas, or musicals that featured a love story in an exotic setting. Directors soon began creating serious films that offered realistic views of Egyptian life.

In 1961 the government created a state film organization to provide funding for Egyptian cinema. The experiment was a financial disaster, and many Egyptian filmmakers moved to Lebanon to produce movies. Although the government officially ended its financial support of cinema in 1971, the state's

High Cinema Institute remained in operation. The institute, located in Cairo, makes Egypt the only Arab nation that provides training for its filmmakers.

Film production increased dramatically in several Islamic nations in the 1960s and 1970s. Annual output in both Turkey and Iran peaked in 1972 after reaching 298 and 90 films, respectively. Indonesia produced 124 movies in 1977. By the 1980s, however, changing economic and political conditions in many Muslim countries had caused production levels to drop significantly.

Obstacles to Overcome. Cinema has faced numerous obstacles in the Islamic world. Soon after the first film screenings in the early 1900s, religious groups protested the new form of entertainment, calling it immoral. Other Muslims rejected movies for promoting foreign values. These critics believed films had a corrupting influence on culture and religion. Islamic governments also became wary of the film industry. Muslim leaders worried that movies might incite opposition to their regimes. Unlike books, motion pictures reached the mostly illiterate masses.

Egypt provides an example of film censorship in a Muslim country. Generally, rules regarding unacceptable material have been closely tied to the type of government in power at the time. In 1914 British and Egyptian officials established a censorship bureau. It forbade criticism of the government, religion, and foreigners. Films could not portray the lifestyle of workers or farmers. Furthermore, the bureau banned plots that supported nationalism or socialism. In 1936 a new Egyptian regime barred films from expressing positive views of the upper class. Egyptian officials later prevented filmmakers from portraying poverty and from questioning traditional customs. Today Egyptian filmmakers still face considerable censorship. Government representatives review scripts before filming begins and remain on the set during filming.

Iran offers another example of film censorship. For most of the industry's history in that country, film production and distribution have been subject to government control. In the 1950s, Iranian officials banned criticism of the government and portrayals of poverty. After 1979 Ayatollah Khomeini's regime established more stringent rules. Religious extremists destroyed many theaters, and officials outlawed around 2,000 films.

Today the Iranian government must approve all scripts. Filmmakers cannot depict social conditions in Iran if the material makes a political statement. Films may not show physical contact between men and women, and actresses have to follow strict Islamic dress codes. In 2001 the Iranian government arrested filmmaker Tahmineh Milani for portraying the political struggles that followed the 1979 Islamic revolution.

Winning Awards. After almost 100 years of filmmaking, true Islamic cinema does not exist. Instead, movies in the Muslim world are either low-budget films for local audiences or artistic works for foreign film festivals.

Iran has emerged as a leader in the latter category. In the 1980s, Iranian officials sought to revive cinema and encouraged the production of artistic films that could bring their country international prestige. The strategy worked. Iranian films have won hundreds of awards, and critics praise Iran's national cinema as one of the world's best.

In the 1990s, Abbas Kiarostami and Mohsen Makhmalbaf emerged as two of Iran's leading filmmakers. Despite censorship and financial con-

Coming to a Theater Near You

Virtually unknown to Americans prior to the 1990s, Iranian films are now attracting attention in the United States. In 1996 major museums showed Jafar Panahi's comedy-drama *The White Balloon*. Mohsen Makhmalbaf's *Gabbeh*, a tale based on the lives of Iranian carpet weavers, toured the American museum circuit the following year. In 1998 Abbas Kiarostami's *Taste of Cherry*, a film that addresses the subject of suicide, opened in New York and Los Angeles to critical acclaim. Iranian movies have also begun to appear in American video stores.

straints, they have produced complex works that realistically portray the hardships of ordinary people. Using subtlety and symbolism, these filmmakers have highlighted many contradictions in Iranian society. (*See also* **Radio and Television.**)

Circumcision

See *Rites and Rituals.*

Citizenship

For most of the history of Islam, the concept of citizenship referred to a person's duties as a member of the Muslim community rather than to the individual's rights as a participant in a political process. During the 1900s, nation-states emerged among Muslim populations, and citizenship became less closely linked to religion.

The concept of citizenship first arose in the city-states of ancient Greece. It was not until the modern era, when Europe established countries, that the term *citizen* became associated with active membership in a society as well as with certain rights and responsibilities. Today in modern Western democracies, citizens can affect public decisions by voting for representatives to the government. Citizens must pay taxes and many serve in the military. The citizens of a state or country exercise authority over its affairs in accordance with the law. An individual's place of birth determines his or her citizenship, although people from other countries may acquire citizenship by fulfilling certain requirements.

In Islam, as in Christianity, God has absolute authority over all matters. In the ancient Western world, and throughout Islamic history, there was no distinction between religion and the state. The caliph* or sultan* ruled over the community in accordance with the teachings of the Qur'an* and the sunnah*. Muslims did not have political rights, and they did not think in terms of geographical boundaries. Rather, they were members of a universal Islamic community. In principle, all Muslims were equal regardless of race or ethnic background.

During the late 1800s, Muslims came close to establishing a modern concept of citizenship. In 1869, for example, the Ottoman government issued the law of nationality and naturalization. This law recognized the right of individuals born in the territories of the Ottoman Empire to claim Ottoman nationality. These and other political developments in the Muslim world were interrupted by colonization. European countries, mainly Great Britain and France, took control of most of the Muslim world. Political, economic, and social development in the Muslim world stopped until the end of European control. By the early 1960s, most other Islamic regions had achieved independence from colonial rule.

As new governments formed, they defined the rights and duties of their citizens. Citizenship specifically referred to national boundaries, not general membership within the Islamic community. The criteria for citizenship varied according to the politics, historical experience, and social customs of each

* **caliph** religious and political leader of an Islamic state

* **sultan** political and military ruler of a Muslim dynasty or state

* **Qur'an** book of the holy scriptures of Islam

* **sunnah** literally "the trodden path"; Islamic customs based on the exemplary behavior of Muhammad

country. Turkey, for example, established a democracy and granted full political rights and duties to the entire population. In some states, such as Egypt and Indonesia, both Muslims and non-Muslims are involved in public affairs. Other governments, including those of Kuwait and Saudi Arabia, limit the privileges of citizenship. Individuals who arrived in Kuwait after 1945 are not considered for citizenship, and women—even with Kuwaiti citizenship—do not have the right to vote. Under repressive regimes and dictatorships, the exercise of political rights does not truly exist for anyone. (*See also* **Democracy; Ottoman Empire; Saudi Arabia; Turkey.**)

Civil Society

Civil society refers to the group of social institutions organized freely by civilians—and independent of the government—for the advancement of specific goals and interests. The phrase also refers to associations based on equality, autonomy*, freedom of movement, and the recognition of the rights and duties of their members. Political parties, nongovernmental organizations, and trade unions are just a few of the components of civil society.

* **autonomy** self-government

In modern times, many Muslim states are governed by authoritarian regimes—led by kings, military officers, or former military officers. These governments have systematically hindered the development of civil society. Without effective social institutions of their own, citizens lack the means to challenge the authority of an autocratic* government. Consequently, many scholars consider the existence of civil society to be a reliable indicator of the level of democracy in a country.

* **autocratic** characterized by unlimited authority

Determining Compatibility. The Western political experience has demonstrated that civil society is critical to the advancement of democracy. In recent decades, Muslims have engaged in heated debate about the usefulness of importing the concept of civil society. The debate has included both religious and secular* scholars associated with seminaries and universities, respectively. Traditional Muslim leaders regard the idea of a civil society as an imposition from the West. They consider individual freedom in civil and social matters to be a threat to traditional values, which are based on the integration of spiritual and material life. In contrast, the secular nationalist* leaders who support the institutions of civil society want to replicate the form as well as substance of Western modern society in the Muslim world. Nevertheless, they also acknowledge that Muslims may subject democratic institutions to traditional religious values, resulting in institutions that differ significantly from those existing in the West.

* **secular** separate from religion in human life and society; connected to everyday life

* **nationalist** one who advocates loyalty and devotion to his or her country and its independence

Another issue that currently impedes the formation of democratic institutions in the Muslim world is the domain of civil society. In most countries, it is restricted to a relatively small portion of citizens. Some Muslim thinkers believe that these nations can further democracy by involving and educating the population at large. This requires assuring the public that Islam encourages such associations and that they are not simply a product of the modern West.

Inclusive or Exclusive? The subject of a civil society also raises the question of whether Islam teaches anything about the separation of church and state. Any free association has to include all citizens. The traditional Islamic model divides the people into believers and nonbelievers. By contrast, a modern nation-state functions as the protector of the interests of all of its citizens, regardless of their religious or ethnic* affiliations, while trying to separate religion from politics.

Religious and secular scholars agree that civil society in the Muslim world will have to be inclusive. This prospect poses a challenge to some Muslims: to accept all people as equal or to insist on their uniqueness and claim to special privilege in the state. Muslim extremists rule out any option that requires the equality of all citizens. They want to exclude non-Muslims from participating in, and benefiting from, these institutions. Muslim modernists, by contrast, have produced much evidence in Islamic heritage to support the concept of civil society. Islamic sources demonstrate the necessity of building social-civil institutions on the basis of freedom of conscience and human dignity and promoting the good of all people living within the borders of a Muslim country without any discrimination. Nevertheless, the progressive opinions of modernists are still far from being accepted by either the secular authoritarian or the explicitly Islamic regimes in many Muslim states. (*See also* **Government; Iran; Iraq; Modernism.**)

Clothing

In Muslim countries, a person's clothing may reflect practical, religious, social, cultural, and political considerations. For centuries, Muslims typically wore long, flowing garments. Today some Muslims prefer Western-style clothing to traditional attire, and others opt for modern variations of customary dress.

Practical Functions. Practicality has been a significant factor in the clothing choices of Muslims. Long, loose-fitting garments have many advantages in the hot, dry climates of the Middle East. Covering the body provides protection from sun exposure and allows perspiration to remain on the skin, which keeps the body moist. In addition, traditional Arab head coverings, such as those worn in Saudi Arabia, shield the head and neck from wind and sand. Of course, clothing varies according to geographic region. Muslims in mountainous areas wear woolen garments for warmth.

Traditional styles have other functional advantages. Long, flowing garments enable wearers to sit and stoop without compromising modesty. Loose fitting clothes do not impede work. Women often tie back the sleeves of their garments in order to accomplish their household chores.

The availability of tools and equipment has also influenced Muslim clothing styles. Traditional looms produced large rectangular pieces of fabric for robes and outer wraps. The introduction of the sewing machine enabled the clothing industry to modify dress styles.

Religious, Social, and Cultural Functions. Islamic clothing serves a variety of religious functions. The Qur'an* stresses modesty for both men

Daily Life

PLATE 1

Prayer is an integral part of the daily life of Muslims. Here hundreds of thousands of pilgrims assemble for evening prayer in the holy city of Mecca. Every Muslim who is physically and financially able is required to make at least one pilgrimage to Mecca.

PLATE 2
The Qur'an plays a very important role in the lives of Muslims. The oldest and most sacred text of Islam, it is the foundation of Islamic belief and practice and an important source of Islamic law.

PLATE 3
The Qur'an functions as a basic source of Muslim religious education. In areas of the world where the people do not speak Arabic, young Muslim children usually learn the Arabic alphabet in order to read the Qur'an in its original language. Here a young girl in Nigeria learns to read the Qur'an.

PLATE 4
In Iran, a woman skilled in embroidery adds ornate decoration to a fabric. The woman wears a traditional hijab over her head and shoulders.

PLATE 5
In March 2003, soon after American and British forces attacked Iraq, a group of Iraqi Shi'ites gathered in Qom, Iran. The occasion was a mourning session to commemorate the martyrdom of Husayn ibn Ali, the grandson of the Prophet.

PLATE 6

Tradition and technology intersect on a busy street corner in Riyadh, Saudi Arabia. This man has set up shop—a rug, typewriter, and mobile phone—to write letters and other documents for customers who want their papers properly prepared.

PLATE 7

A tailor in the city of Zaria in northern Nigeria works at his sewing machine. Zaria was part of the Sokoto Caliphate, an Islamic state founded in the early 1800s by Usuman Dan Fodio.

PLATE 8
The lively market of Djenné, Mali, takes place weekly in front of the impressive Great Mosque. Shoppers can buy food and clothing, catch up on gossip, and discuss community affairs.

PLATE 9
Young girls attend a religion class at school in the Southeast Asian sultanate of Brunei. More than 80 percent of the women in this tiny, oil-rich country can read.

PLATE 10
Soccer is a popular sport in the Middle East and Africa. Nigeria's soccer team won the gold medal in the 1996 Summer Olympics. Here fans in Iraq cheer their team in a championship match.

PLATE 11
Traditionally, Bedouins have lived as nomads in desert areas of North Africa and the Middle East, herding camel, sheep, goats, or cattle. This camel-riding Bedouin keeps in touch with a mobile phone.

PLATE 12
A Chinese Muslim relies on a donkey to draw his cart.

PLATE 13
Muslim women in a modern classroom in Amman, Jordan, use earphones in their language studies.

PLATE 14

Founded more than 2,500 years ago, Tunis is a modern city with a very long history.
It is also the capital of Tunisia. Shaded arcades surround the city's Government Square,
where the prime minister and many other government officials work.

PLATE 15

Muslims make up less than 2 percent of China's 1.284 billion people. In the northwestern province of
Xinjiang, a group of Muslim women work together to produce handicrafts.

Some Muslims prefer Western-style clothing to the traditional dress of their religion. This street in Jordan shows the mixture of styles that Muslim men and women have adopted.

and women, and Muslims generally regard the covering of the body as a way to conform to this teaching. Traditionally, the degree of covering increases if an individual is in public or with members of the opposite sex. Specific areas of the body are regarded as sexual in nature, and as such, must be hidden. Men cover their bodies from their waists to their knees, cover their heads, and don outerwear in public. Women traditionally conceal their hair and neck and cover themselves from the neck to ankles. Arm coverings extend to the wrists. Muslims believe that a woman demonstrates virtue by wearing such dress. In some parts of the Muslim world, women also wear an outer layer that covers the face or a *burqa* (face mask).

Another religious function of Muslim clothing relates to the hajj*. During the ceremonies, men wear two seamless lengths of white cloth and a waistband. This garment signifies that all believers are equal. Men do not cover their heads while praying during the hajj, but they cut their hair or shave their heads on completing this Pillar of Islam. Muslims from India and Pakistan often wear a green cloth to cover their heads after the hajj.

Dress may signify status. In some Muslim societies, a woman traditionally wore certain colors to reflect her marital status. Red or orange embroidery on a garment indicated that a woman was married, and blue stitching showed that she was single. Veiling—the wearing of loose-fitting clothing and/or a headscarf—has been a custom of Muslim women for centuries. It

* **hajj** pilgrimage to Mecca that Muslims are required to make once in their lifetime

Changing Hats

The fez *(tarbush)* is a brimless hat made from red felt. It was popular among Turkish men during the late Ottoman Empire. Men wore the fez to show their status as gentlemen or professional workers, thereby separating themselves from the lower classes. After the collapse of the Ottoman Empire, Mustafa Kemal Atatürk founded the Republic of Turkey (1923). He wanted to emphasize a modern European outlook for the country. As president, Atatürk forced Turkish men to abandon the fez in favor of a European-style hat. Although these brimmed hats interfered with prayer, the fez had virtually disappeared by the mid-1900s.

* **secular** separate from religion in human life and society; connected to everyday life

* **fundamentalist** generally refers to the movement that promotes a literal interpretation of scripture; in Islam, a movement that promotes politicization of religion to create an alternative public order

originally meant distinction and honor. Upper-class women wore the veil to separate themselves from the lower classes.

Some Muslims wear non-traditional garments, reflecting the economic and cultural impact of the West. In urban areas, women may dress in contemporary fashions based on styles originating in Europe or elsewhere. Shoes and stockings take the place of sandals or slippers. For some Muslims, traditional dress is associated with an older, conservative, rural status. Men, for example, may refuse to wear the *jallabiyah* (robe) because of its lower class connotations.

Muslims have various perspectives regarding Western dress for women. Some men view modern clothing styles, such as sleeveless garments or miniskirts on women, as a threat to their virtue. Men often harass women who wear modern attire in public. Some women prefer Western-style clothing because they believe that it enables them to express their individuality and freedom. By contrast, others argue that veiling protects them from being treated as sexual objects. They see the *hijab* (veil), not as a sign of oppression, but as a symbol of devotion, discipline, and respect. These Muslim women believe they are more liberated than their Western counterparts who wear uncomfortable clothes to meet their culture's expectations of beauty.

Clothing styles in the Islamic world also include unique ethnic variations. Some notable historic examples are the Moroccan bridal headdress, the Palestinian embroidered jacket, and the Lebanese *tantur*, a tall silver cylinder with a flowing veil worn on the head by Druze women. In Malaysia, Islamic dress distinguishes Malays from Indian and Chinese Malaysians.

Political Functions. Islamic dress may also reflect a political agenda. Some Muslims don traditional clothing as a way of applying religious principles to society, and others use this type of dress to demonstrate their commitment to replace a secular* political system with an Islamic one. During the 1970s, for example, Muslim women in Iran wore traditional clothing to show their opposition to the government of the shah. After Islamic revolutionaries seized control of the country, the new religious government made traditional dress a requirement.

Over the past century, Muslims have often worn various articles of clothing to display political loyalty. Certain colors and specific garments have been worn to reflect a variety of causes. For example, in Palestine and Jordan, men who wear the *kaffiyah* (head cloth) show support for Palestinian nationalism. Wearing the colors of the Palestinian flag also has political symbolism. Dress may indicate membership in an association or party. Members of the Taliban— the Islamic fundamentalists* who ruled Afghanistan in the late 1990s—often wear turbans. (*See also* **Body Decoration; Hair and Beards; Hijab; Modesty.**)

Coffee and Coffeehouses

Coffee has had a significant impact on the Islamic world for several centuries. Many scholars believe that the beverage originated in Ethiopia during medieval times, when it was discovered that a delicious and energizing beverage could be made when beans of the coffee plant were boiled or

Coffee has held an economic and social importance for Islamic countries for hundreds of years. This painting from the 1500s shows a coffeehouse, where men come to talk, drink coffee, and enjoy the music.

roasted. By the 1400s, coffee had become a popular drink in Yemen on the Arabian Peninsula. A century later, people in Egypt, Syria, Turkey, and Persia were enjoying the rich, flavorful beverage. By the end of the 1500s, coffee had reached all parts of the Islamic world.

Coffee's popularity helped boost the economy of the Islamic world. Muslim merchants lost much of their income when, beginning in the early 1500s, European ships began to sail around the tip of Africa to do business at Asian ports. The coffee trade helped them replace their losses.

Muslims made great profits selling mass quantities of coffee to Europe in the 1600s and 1700s. In the 1700s, however, Western nations started growing coffee in their own colonies in the Americas and Asia, cutting into the Muslim share of the world coffee trade.

In addition to its economic importance, coffee also had a major social impact. People enjoyed the drink at home as well as in public. In the 1600s, coffeehouses appeared across the Middle East. Although usually not elaborate structures, they became important social gathering places. Muslim men of all ages and social classes came to talk and tell stories. Sons joined in the discussions with their fathers. The coffeehouse became home to a variety of activities, including chess, backgammon, book readings, Qur'an* recitations, and puppet theater performances. Some coffeehouses catered to special groups and professions, such as the military.

* **Qur'an** book of the holy scriptures of Islam

Coffeehouses also served as important information centers. When illiteracy rates were high, men gathered to hear the newspaper read. In the 1900s, Muslims met to listen to the radio or to watch television. Coffeehouses were often the first place in a town to have such devices. Men sometimes pooled their money to buy a television for their favorite coffeehouse, because they could not afford one of their own. Coffeehouses were such important information centers that they became known as "schools of the wise."

* **imam** spiritual-political leader in Shi'i Islam, one who is regarded as directly descended from Muhammad; also, one who leads prayers

* **mosque** Muslim place of worship

Not long after its introduction, coffee attracted the attention of Muslim religious officials. In the 1500s, many imams* sought to ban coffee, complaining that people went to coffeehouses more often than to mosques*. Religious leaders did not like that coffeehouses were beyond their authority. In some areas, they succeeded in having the government ban coffee. Few Muslims obeyed the ban, however, and Islamic officials soon lifted the prohibition. Religious opposition to coffee ended in the 1600s, especially after many coffeehouse owners began to donate money to help support the local mosque. Today coffee remains a significant part of Muslim society. Coffeehouses still attract men from all walks of life. Even those with televisions at home gather at coffeehouses for the social interaction. These men enjoy the stability of being a part of a group. For many centuries Muslims have lived according to the old Turkish proverb: "One cup of coffee is worth 40 years of friendship." (*See also* **Radio and Television.**)

Colonialism

Colonialism—the process by which a powerful country takes possession of a weaker one for economic or military gain—had a profound effect on the Islamic world. In some instances, permanent settlers were sent to colonies along with colonial administrators. Such territories were considered to be an integral part of the mother country and might eventually be given some local self-government. Territories that were directly controlled by the colonial power were considered by the colonial powers as formal parts of their respective empires. Thus, the term *colonialism* may be used interchangeably, in many cases, with the word *imperialism*. While the term *imperialism* may have

Members of the All India Muslim League marched in London in 1946 to show support for the partition of British India. The partition created Pakistan, where India's Muslims could live free from European control.

been—or might still be—regarded by some with a degree of respectability for its introduction of European institutions (such as parliamentary government), the term *colonialism* generally has been viewed from the vantage point of those territories and peoples who have been colonized or exploited.

Establishing Colonial Rule. By the 1700s, several European nations had emerged as world powers. Technological advances had greatly increased their military strength, and the Industrial Revolution had given them the ability to manufacture goods more cheaply and efficiently than ever before. With industry growing, Europeans needed raw materials, such as cotton, that they could not produce in their own countries. They also sought new markets for their products. With the decline of the Ottoman Empire*, Europeans had little difficulty invading nations that could provide necessary materials. They weakened native industries, forcing workers to produce goods for Western factories and creating a need for European imports.

In 1798 the French invaded Egypt, and other European powers rushed to the region to take their share. Britain took over India, Palestine, Iraq, and part of the Sudan and took Egypt from the French. The French then colonized Algeria, Morocco, and Tunisia. Russia took over Muslim lands in Cen-

* **Ottoman Empire** large Turkish state existing from the early 1300s to the early 1900s

This chart lists European powers and the Muslim countries that were under their colonial rule. Independent, non-colonial Muslim states with major Muslim populations include Afghanistan, Iran, Saudi Arabia, Turkey, and Yemen.

Colonial Power

Great Britain

Bahrain	Gambia	Malaysia	Sierra Leone
Bangladesh	India	Maldives	South Yemen
Brunei	Iraq	Nigeria	Sudan
Cyprus	Jordan	Pakistan	Tanzania
Egypt	Kuwait	Qatar	United Arab Emirates

France

Algeria	Comoros	Lebanon	Niger
Burkina-Faso	Djibouti	Mali	Senegal
Central African Republic	Guinea	Mauritania	Syria
	Ivory Coast	Morocco	Tunisia
Chad			

Netherlands [Dutch]
Indonesia

Italy

Libya	Ethiopia	Somalia

Portugal
Guinea-Bisseau

Spain
Western Sahara

USSR

Albania	Kazakhstan	Tajikistan	Uzbekistan
Azerbaijan	Kyrgyzstan	Turkmenistan	

tral Asia. The Dutch moved into Indonesia, and Italy seized Libya, Ethiopia, and parts of Somalia. The colonizers of Islamic lands tended to view their subjects as either inferior or as "noble savages" who possessed a purity and innocence that the Europeans lacked.

Effects of Colonization. To maintain order and advance their interests, Europeans imposed harsh laws and crushed any threats to their rule. They also ridiculed Islamic traditions and practices. For example, the British applied the term *caliph*, one of the most important titles in Islamic society, to refer to Muslims who held low positions, such as barbers. They used the term *mullah* (cleric) to refer to common workers. Colonization also led to an influx of missionaries who denounced Islam as a false religion and encouraged Muslims to convert to Christianity.

European rule had some benefits. In Egypt, for example, the British built railroads, increased the amount of arable* land, and improved tax collection processes. European powers, however, structured colonial economies for their

* **arable** fit for growing crops

own benefit, showing little concern for the consequences their actions might have on the population. British reforms in Egypt slowed the growth of industry and left the economy almost completely dependent on cotton exports.

European powers eliminated Islamic studies from school curricula, and in India, the British made English the official language. Colonial governments used the local education system to instill Western values into the population and to train low-level employees to serve the colonial bureaucracy*.

Muslims Respond to Colonial Rule. Muslims responded to imperialism in a variety of ways. Many fell into poverty and opposed colonial rule. Some believed that a return to Islamic roots would build strength and unity in the Muslim world. Others viewed modern reform as the key to restoring their power. By the mid-1900s, nationalism* emerged as the primary response to colonization. Muslims increasingly sought to establish and govern their own nation-states.

Colonial powers began to falter after World War I (1914–1919) when the losing countries (Italy and Germany) had to relinquish their colonies to the winners (France and Great Britain). The League of Nations, the predecessor of the United Nations, designated these colonies administrative units called mandates with the understanding that the mandatory powers (the victors) would help prepare them for eventual independence. In effect, it represented a continuation of colonialism under the guise of liberalism*.

The Western grip on its colonies was further weakened after World War II (1939–1945), when Europe lay in ruins. No longer able to maintain their empires, the European powers allowed the colonies to establish their own governments. By the 1960s, most had succeeded. The countries of Central Asia—Kazakhstan, Turkmenistan, Kyrgyzstan, Tajikistan, and Uzbekistan—were the last to gain their independence, which occurred in 1991 with the collapse of the Soviet Union.

The effects of European imperialism continue to plague Islamic nations in the early twenty-first century. Because colonial governments neglected the education of their Muslim subjects, many areas still suffer from intense poverty. Islamic governments struggle to build their economies and compete in the global marketplace. The growth of the oil industry has helped some Islamic nations to become prosperous. Scores of Muslims, however, retain deep resentments against Europe and the United States for their imperialist actions. This bitterness remains a barrier to the establishment of closer ties between Islamic and Western nations. (*See also* **Christianity and Islam; Education; Modernism; Nationalism.**)

* **bureaucracy** agencies and officials that comprise a government

* **nationalism** feelings of loyalty and devotion to one's country and a commitment to its independence

* **liberalism** political philosophy based on a belief in the ability of individuals to decide how they should be governed

Communism and Islam

Communism, a system of economic and political organization, dominated many parts of the world during the 1900s. Muslims who lived in areas under communist rule experienced periods of religious freedom as well as repression. More often marked by conflict than consensus, the relationship between communism and Islam came to an end with the collapse of the Soviet Union in the early 1990s.

Communism and Islam

Differences in Theory. Communism began with the work of German political thinker Karl Marx in the mid-1800s. Russian revolutionary leader Vladimir Lenin extended Marx's ideas in the early 1900s. Marxist-Leninist theory argues that societies progress through historical stages, with each transition involving the replacement of the existing social and economic system with one that is more effective and efficient. The final stage of this process would produce a society in which the community, not individuals, owns all property and means of production, including machinery and factories. The community would share wealth and distribute it among the citizens according to their need. To achieve this ideal, the government might have to control the economy for a period.

Marx considered religion a human creation designed to help people cope with the depression, anger, and other negative aspects of life. He claimed that these problems would not exist in a communist society, making religion—and therefore God—unnecessary.

The Islamic view of human society differs from that of communism on several levels. Fundamentally, Islam is based on the belief in the existence of one God. Furthermore, the Qur'an* provides guidelines regarding property and the distribution of wealth in Muslim society. Owning property is a right sanctioned by the Qur'an. With the exception of *zakat*, the requirement that Muslims give 2.5 percent of their net worth annually, sharing wealth is voluntary. Finally, Islam does not predict the historical progression of secular* society. Instead, the Qur'an describes the end of the world and a day of judgment for all people.

Competing Societies. The initial interactions between communism and Islam occurred in Central Asia. By 1900 Russia had conquered much of this largely Muslim region. In 1917 Vladimir Lenin led a revolt against the Russian government and established the world's first communist state—the Union of Soviet Socialist Republics (USSR). Lenin and most of the members of his Bolshevik party were hostile to all religions, including Islam. Their need for political and military allies, however, led them to alternately tolerate and oppress Muslims.

Generally, the new Soviet government sought to secularize Central Asia, by closing or destroying thousands of mosques. The authorities also killed many Muslim clerics. Communist party leaders eliminated Islamic social and economic practices that posed a challenge to their goals. They changed the status of women and seized traditional public institutions, such as *waqf* (endowments for the public good). During the 1920s and 1930s, the communists divided Central Asia into separate territories, such as Uzbekistan and Turkmenistan, and imposed the use of new standardized languages. As a result of these policies and isolation from historic centers of Islamic learning, Muslim identity in Central Asia lost much of it religious aspect. Being Muslim meant little more than an ethnic identity and observance of a few traditions, such as avoidance of pork and alcohol.

The communist takeover of Russia fueled a global movement. After World War II ended in 1945, Yugoslavia, Albania, and China came under the control of communist regimes*. In each country, communist leaders sought to eliminate the religious identity of the Muslim population. In south-

* **Qur'an** book of the holy scriptures of Islam

* **secular** separate from religion in human life and society; connected to everyday life

* **regime** government in power

eastern Europe, Islamic institutions were less of a threat to the ruling communist parties. Muslims there were better able to preserve their religion.

During the postwar era, communists and Islamic activists discovered a common enemy in Western colonialism. Communist parties rose to prominence in countries where they were perceived to be involved in the anticolonial movement. Important communist parties existed in Sudan, Iraq, and Syria. After these countries gained independence and established their own governments, however, most of these parties were effectively eliminated. During the 1950s, communism also lost support in some parts of North Africa. Muslims resented the French communist party because it did not firmly oppose the French colonial governments of Algeria and Tunisia. In fact, in 1956, the communists voted to give the French government emergency powers to suppress a nationalist revolt in Algeria.

The period following World War II was characterized by a nonmilitary struggle, known as the Cold War, between the United States and the Soviet Union. The leaders of America's democratic government were determined to limit the influence of communism worldwide, while the Soviets intended to expand their authority. Each nation wanted a strong presence in the Arab countries of the oil-rich Middle East. As a result, communist nations often provided aid to Muslim governments. For example, although Egyptian president Gamal Abdel Nasser dissolved his country's communist party in 1957, he bought arms from the Soviets. Nasser also embraced several Marxist principles and incorporated them into the 1962 constitution. After Egypt's defeat in the 1967 Arab-Israeli War, however, Nasser moved away from Marxist ideas and sought to restore Islamic values.

Communists and Muslims battled for power in some parts of the world in the 1960s and 1970s. Political unrest led to the massacre of hundreds of thousands of communists by Muslims in Indonesia in 1965. During the 1970s, a powerful communist party tried to win control of the government of Iran. By 1984, however, the revolutionary Islamic government had destroyed its Marxist rivals.

Perhaps the most significant Muslim victory came in Afghanistan. A communist regime had seized power in 1978. Muslim factions organized an armed resistance movement, causing the Soviet Union to send military forces to the region in 1979. The invasion only served to further strengthen the Islamist groups. After suffering heavy losses, the Soviets pulled out of Afghanistan in 1989, and the communist government there collapsed.

Demise of Communism. When Mikhail Gorbachev came to power in the Soviet Union in 1985, he introduced a policy of glasnost, or openness. Greater freedom of religious expression in the USSR was permitted. Communism in East Europe crumbled in 1989, and the government of the Soviet Union collapsed two years later. With the breakup of the USSR, most of the former Soviet republics joined to form the Commonwealth of Independent States. Islam reemerged, and by 1993 thousands of mosques and hundreds of Islamic schools had opened in all the Muslim states of Central Asia. (*See also* **Central Asia; Colonialism; Socialism and Islam.**)

Resilient Religion

The most prestigious centers of Islamic culture and influence in Central Asia lie within the territory of Uzbekistan. Islam took root in the ancient cities of Bukhara, Samarkand, and Khiva in the 600s. Following the establishment of communist rule in the area in 1917, anti-Islamic policies prevailed. Despite harsh measures against the practice of Islam, a substantial number of Uzbek Muslims defied these policies by observing religious rituals and making pilgrimages to the graves of holy figures. With Uzbekistan's declaration of independence on August 31, 1991, the impediments to religious freedom were removed.

See *Law.*

Consensus

Conversion

The word *conversion* means "change or turn around." It was used first to describe the experience of people who became Christians. They saw themselves as undergoing an inner transformation, or change of heart, that inspired them to embrace Christianity. Muslims, however, believe that all people are born into Islam. The paths of some, or their parents' actions, lead them away from their faith. Therefore, conversion to Islam is not considered a change of heart, but a return to one's original condition.

The Conversion Process. Islam is defined as "submission." A Muslim is "one who submits or surrenders." This submission to God's will is shown through the public performance of the Five Pillars of Islam, which a convert undertakes as the core element of his or her conversion process. The person first recites the Profession of Faith in front of witnesses: "I bear witness that there is no god but Allah, and Muhammad is the messenger of Allah." Then he or she carries out the other pillars—prayer five times a day, giving money to the poor, fasting during the month of Ramadan, and pilgrimage to the holy city of Mecca.

Other acts have been associated with conversion to Islam. They are symbolic of the convert's desire to leave his or her past behind. Male converts are usually circumcised. Women adopt a conservative or modest form of dress, and many cover their hair. Most new believers adopt Muslim names and refrain from eating pork or drinking alcohol.

Spread of Islam. Islam has had a tradition of preaching since its beginning. According to the Qur'an*, the Prophet Muhammad was told, "Invite to the way of your Lord with wisdom and beautiful preaching; and argue with in ways that are best and most gracious." (surah 16.125) After Muhammad left Mecca and settled in Medina, the community of Islamic faithful grew rapidly. In the centuries following Muhammad's death, vigorous military campaigning by his followers extended the Islamic empire to include Spain, Central Asia, and India. At first, Arab Muslims found it difficult to place non-Arab Muslims within their social structure, but Islamic society soon accommodated large numbers of converts.

Two main groups existed within the early Islamic empire—the believers (Muslims) and the so-called "protected people." Because Christians and Jews had sacred scriptures of their own, they were not pressured to convert to Islam. They were free to practice their religion and to own property. Certain restrictions applied, however. Christians and Jews had to pay special taxes and aspects of their lives were controlled. They were subject to laws governing personal behavior, clothing, and means of transportation. They could not bear arms or construct buildings that were higher than those of Muslims. In effect, they had second-class status in the community and pressure to convert surely existed.

In addition to these differences in treatment, prohibitions on marriage between Muslims and non-Muslims and a desire for higher social status may have motivated some conversions. Economically, it was more advantageous to be a Muslim. Besides not having to pay the special taxes, Muslims had greater trading opportunities and fewer property restrictions.

* **Qur'an** book of holy scriptures of Islam

Muslims Worldwide

An estimate of the number of Muslims throughout the world ranges from 600 million to over 1 billion. Asia has the countries with the largest Muslim populations—Indonesia has 170 million Muslims, Pakistan 136 million, Bangladesh 105 million, and India 103 million. The Muslim population in the United States increased from about 500,000 in the 1970s to over 6 million by the end of the 1990s. The majority of American Muslims are first, second, or third generation immigrants. African Americans account for approximately 25 percent of American Muslims.

While many under Muslim rule converted to Islam for economic or social reasons, others were attracted to its practices and teachings. Beginning in the 1100s, Muslim traders and Sufi* missionaries had an enormous influence on the spread of Islam. They introduced the faith to people in sub-Saharan Africa, southern India, Indonesia, Malaya, and China.

Modern Converts. In recent centuries, emigration has contributed to the spread of Islam and the increasing number of Muslims worldwide. Furthermore, the Islamic principle of equality strongly appeals to people who have suffered discrimination or have felt alienated from the mainstream culture of their homeland. In the early 1900s, the Islamic faith took root among some African Americans who were weary of decades of oppression and the lack of a recognized cultural identity. At first, many African Americans were drawn to a form of Islam that encouraged racial pride through militancy and anti-white sentiment. More recently, however, many African Americans follow Sunni* Islam with its teachings of racial harmony. White and Hispanic Americans are also converting to Islam. They, too, are attracted by the concept of equality among believers, as well as the simplicity of Islamic traditions and the emphasis on community. (*See also* **Dietary Rules; Islam: Overview; Muhammad; Pillars of Islam; Rites and Rituals; Sufism.**)

* **Sufi** follower of Sufism, which seeks to develop spirituality through discipline of the mind and body

* **Sunni** refers to the largest branch of the Muslim community; the name derives from sunnah, the exemplary behavior of the Prophet Muhammad

Córdoba, Caliphate of

Córdoba is a city in southern Spain. The caliphate of Córdoba refers to the period from 756 to 1016 when the descendants of Umayyad princes ruled Spain.

In 711 Muslims annexed southern Spain, known as Andalusia, adding it to their growing empire. The empire was ruled by the Umayyad dynasty* from its capital in Damascus, Syria. When the Abbasids overthrew the Umayyads in 750 and seized control of the Islamic empire, one of the surviving Umayyad princes, Abd al-Rahman I ibn Mu'awiyah, fled to North Africa. From there he invaded Spain, overthrew the government of Andalusia, and set up his own state or amirate*. He immediately took steps to strengthen his kingdom by centralizing the government, building an army, and suppressing revolts. Córdoba became his capital city.

Internal conflicts in the 800s weakened the amirate, however, until Abd al-Rahman III ibn Muhammad came to power in 912. One of the greatest of the Spanish Umayyad princes, he gave himself the title of caliph* in 929. By taking this step, Abd al-Rahman presented himself as a powerful defender of Sunni* Islam and a rival of both the Abbasid dynasty and the Shi'i* Fatimid caliphate in Egypt. He reunited the country by waging war against northern Spanish rebels. During his rule, the Muslim conquest of Spain reached its fullest extent.

Under the caliph's patronage, Córdoba became one of the great Islamic cities. It became a flourishing center of Islamic culture, attracting scholars, scientists, artists, and writers from all over the known world. Abd al-Rahman encouraged the participation of non-Muslims as craftsmen, administrators, and scholars and allowed them to keep their own schools, libraries,

* **dynasty** succession of rulers from the same family or group

* **amirate** office or realm of authority of an amir

* **caliph** religious and political leader of an Islamic state

* **Sunni** refers to the largest branch of the Muslim community; the name derives from sunnah, the exemplary behavior of the Prophet Muhammad

* **Shi'i** refers to Muslims who believe that Muhammad chose Ali ibn Abi Talib and his descendants as the spiritual-political leaders of the Muslim community

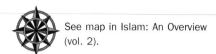

See map in Islam: An Overview (vol. 2).

and churches. An important Jewish culture flourished in Córdoba during this period. The caliph further added to the city's renown by building irrigation systems, expanding the mosque, and constructing a royal city. Córdoba continued to thrive under Abd al-Rahman's son, Hakam II, also a well-known scholar and patron of the arts and sciences.

After Hakam II's rule, the caliphs lost power, and by 1016, the Umayyad caliphate had ended. The country disintegrated into warring city-states and a series of figurehead caliphs occupied the throne for the rest of the century. (*See also* **Abbasid Caliphate; Andalusia; Fatimid Dynasty; Umayyad Caliphate.**)

Cosmetics

See *Body Decoration*.

Cosmology

* **monotheistic** refers to the belief that there is only one God

* **Qur'an** book of the holy scriptures of Islam

Cosmology is the study of the universe. Similar to other monotheistic* belief systems, Muslims believe that God created and rules the universe. Muslim cosmology, they believe, is based on God's teachings as revealed in the Qur'an*. Unlike modern cosmology, which studies only the observable universe, traditional Muslim cosmology considers both the physical and the spiritual worlds and seeks to understand God's purpose in creating and ordering the universe. Islamic cosmology, therefore, covers a wider range than modern cosmology.

God and the Cosmos. The Islamic concept of the cosmos is inseparable from the belief in the existence of God. The nature of the relationship between God and the cosmos has been one of the fundamental issues of Islam for centuries. Islamic cosmology defines the universe as "everything other than God," which is "everything in the heavens and the earth." God is considered the "lord of all worlds." The Qur'an, the most important source of cosmological knowledge, teaches that God created the world for a purpose, and the study of cosmology gives Muslims guidelines by which they can view life as the journey of the soul toward God.

Pre-Islamic Elements. Traditional Muslim cosmology contains some pre-Islamic elements, mainly from ancient Greek, Persian, and Indian teachings. One such element is the belief in cosmic harmony arising from the symbolic properties of numbers. It is based on the idea that the world has mathematical patterns and that there is significance to certain numbers; the number one, for example, signifies unity. Many religions attach mystical importance to certain numbers. From Chinese scientists, Muslim cosmologists adopted the magic square, in which the sum of all entries of any row, column, or diagonal is the same. Muslim scholars integrated these ideas into their God-centered perspective of Qur'anic cosmology.

Mutashabihat. Many of Islam's cosmological teachings come from the *mutashabihat*, verses of the Qur'an that may be understood in several ways.

For example, the Qur'an states: "God is the First and the Last, the Outward and the Inward." This teaches that the cosmos began at the command of the One God and will return to the One God at its end. It can also mean that the cosmos is contained or enclosed by God. Muslims use the image of two concentric circles to illustrate the idea of God as Outward and Inward. When God is viewed as the Outward, the inner circle represents the cosmos, while the outer circle represents Divine Reality. When God is viewed as the Inward, the inner circle represents Divine Reality, while the outer circle represents the cosmos. Muslim cosmology uses an expanded series of concentric circles to explain the entire hierarchy, or order, of physical and spiritual existence.

References to the dimensions of the universe appear in the Qur'an, which states that the cosmos contains seven heavens and seven earths, the Divine Throne and the Divine Footstool, the cosmic mountain Qaf, and the lote tree (marking the outermost point of the universe). The Qur'an describes opposite but complementary pairs: light and darkness, this world and the next world, paradise and hell, the origin and the return, spirit and body, sun and moon, day and night. Muslim scholars, such as Ibn Sina (died 1037), Abu Hamid al-Ghazali (died 1111), and the members of the secret brotherhood of philosophers and scientists known as the Brethren of Purity (flourished in the 900s and 1000s) used verses from the *mutashabihat* to make pre-Islamic cosmological concepts agree with Islamic teachings. The Brethren, for example, linked the ancient Greek scientist Ptolemy's theory of eight concentric circles with the Divine Footstool of the Qur'an. Muslim scholars also added a ninth circle and highest heaven to Ptolemy's theory to explain diurnal motion (the apparent movement of stars and planets in the course of each day). This last sphere, they believed, was the location of the Divine Throne.

Mir'aj. One of the most vivid descriptions of the cosmos in the Muslim tradition is of Muhammad's miraculous night journey (also known as the *mir'aj*, which means "ascent") from earth to heaven. The Qur'an states that the Prophet was transported from Mecca to Jerusalem, and then he was taken to the heavens until he came to the lote tree, before finally reaching the Divine Throne. Though the Qur'an does not offer more specific details, the hadiths*, the second most important source of knowledge in Islamic tradition and practices, give a rich account of the *mir'aj*. They describe how the angel Gabriel came to Muhammad at night, placed him on a winged beast called Buraq, and took him to Jerusalem. From there, Gabriel guided Muhammad up through the seven heavens, introducing him to the angels and prophets residing in each of them. Finally, they came to the tree that marked the end of the universe. Gabriel could go no farther than this point. From here Muhammad was transported alone on a silk carpet to the Divine Throne. There, Muhammad was shown the paradise God had prepared for the faithful and the hell prepared for sinners. The Prophet's journey, in cosmological terms, is seen as a symbol of the spiritual journey through all states of being in the cosmic hierarchy. The final goal of the journey is to go beyond the cosmos itself to reach the Divine Presence.

Influences of Cosmology. Cosmological teachings have profoundly influenced Islamic art, philosophy, and science. The principles of balance and order, for example, which are central to the Qur'anic view of the universe, influences Islamic notions of beauty and truth. The idea of an exact correspondence between the physical world (microcosm) and the greater universe

The Lote Tree

In ancient times, Arabs often planted a tree to mark the end of a road. The cosmic tree, or lote tree, which is also called the "tree of the extreme limit," marks the end of the universe.

Muhammad describes the lote tree as a large tree not resembling any of the other trees of paradise. The lote tree, which grows from a mysterious ocean of musk, covers all universes. Its trunk is an angel named Samrafil, and the top reaches so high that few can reach it safely. The tree has an infinite number of branches; the distance between each branch measures 500,000 light years. Every branch has an infinite number of leaves, and an angel sits on every leaf. Springs of water, milk, wine, and honey flow from the trunk.

* **hadith** reports of the words and deeds of Muhammad (not in the Qur'an, but accepted as guides for Muslim behavior)

Creed

* **alchemy** medieval chemistry, which sought to change base metals into gold

(macrocosm) is another key theme in Muslim cosmology and greatly influenced the medieval science of alchemy*. The concept of numerical symbolism of the alphabet, too, was closely linked with cosmological principles. (*See also* **Alchemy; Hadith; Qur'an.**)

Creed

* **Qur'an** book of the holy scriptures of Islam

The Islamic creed, called *aqidah*, as found in the Qur'an* is very simple. It consists of the five articles of faith: belief in God, angels, prophets, scriptures, and the Last Day (or Day of Judgment). These concepts were developed in more detail over the centuries. The first, third, and fifth articles—belief in God, his prophets, and the Last Day—are the principle articles of the *aqidah*. The second article—belief in angels as the servants and worshippers of God—evolved to correct the pre-Islamic notion that angels were the daughters of God. The fourth—belief in scriptures—is an important supplement to the belief in God's prophets. Thus, the belief in God, his prophets, and the Day of Judgment constitute the essential belief system of Islam.

* **salvation** deliverance from effects of sin

More elaborate statements of the Islamic creed developed because of internal and external conflicts in the early Muslim community. As questions concerning the beliefs arose, scholars began to produce creeds aimed at correcting errors and clarifying ideas. For example, questions arose as to whether faith and behavior are inseparably linked or if faith alone is crucial to salvation*. Would a Muslim who commits a grave sin automatically cease to be a Muslim? If faith is sufficient for salvation, is the importance of deeds diminished?

* **Sunni** refers to the largest branch of the Muslim community; the name derives from sunnah, the exemplary behavior of the Prophet Muhammad

* **Shi'i** refers to Muslims who believe that Muhammad chose Ali ibn Abi Talib and his descendants as the spiritual-political leaders of the Muslim community

* **imam** spiritual leader in Shi'i Islam, one who is regarded as directly descended from Muhammad; also, one who leads prayers

* **theology** study of the nature and qualities of God and the understanding of His will

The argument between the Sunni* and Shi'i* communities about the proper succession of imams* also contributed to the elaboration of the creed. In Shi'i doctrine, God alone chooses the imam. In Sunni doctrine, the Muslim community elects the imam. Other writings on the Islamic creed address such questions as the difference between God's attributes and God's being, divine justice, and free will.

Over time, Muslim scholars adapted doctrinal writings to address issues from Greek philosophy and from Christian theology*. By the middle of the 800s, various schools of legal thought began to develop around particular teachers who held slightly different views about Muslim beliefs and practices. Among the most influential of these was Abu Hanifah (died 767), whose *Al-fiqh al-akbar I* is considered the first formal statement of the Islamic creed. (*See also* **Abu Hanifah; Ibn Hanbal; Jafar al-Sadiq; Law; Malik ibn Anas; Qur'an; Shafi'i; Wahhabi.**)

Crusades

The Crusades were a series of expeditions that occurred primarily in the 1100s and 1200s, when European armies fought to gain control of Syria and Palestine. European Christians called this region the Holy Land because it contained the city of Jerusalem and other places associated with the life of Jesus Christ.

roue lozdonnerent que fu vne chofe monlt difficile .

Muslims had captured this territory from the Byzantine* Empire in the 700s but had permitted Christians and Jews safe access to pilgrimage sites in the region. After the Seljuk Turks rose to power in the 1000s and began to conquer other Byzantine territory, Emperor Alexius Comnenus asked western European rulers to help him defend his realm. Feeling a responsibility to aid the Byzantines, who were fellow Christians, Pope Urban II convened the Council of Clermont in France in 1095. Urban called Christians to go on an armed pilgrimage* to recover the Holy Land, promising spiritual rewards to those who joined the fight.

First and Second Crusades. Many European leaders answered the pope's call. Armies of trained soldiers, as well as large groups of peasants, left Europe for Palestine. This First Crusade (1095–1099) cost many European lives, but the crusaders also inflicted great casualties and massacred Muslim and Jewish civilians. The crusaders captured Antioch in 1098 and moved on to Jerusalem, which fell the following year. When the Muslim governor of Jerusalem surrendered, the crusader commander promised protection to its inhabitants. His troops disobeyed orders, however, and slaughtered the Muslims and Jews—men, women, and children— within the city.

Muslims and Christians fought over the Holy Land for hundreds of years in a series of campaigns known as the Crusades. This image from a 1462 Dutch manuscript illustrates the siege of Jerusalem during those wars.

* **Byzantine** refers to the Eastern Christian empire that was based in Constantinople

* **pilgrimage** journey to a shrine or sacred place

The First Crusade established crusader states in the Holy Land. Baldwin of Edessa, a French noble, became king of the new crusader state of Jerusalem in 1100. Additional crusader states were established in Mesopotamia, Turkey, and Tripoli. European settlers in these states captured and enslaved some of the remaining Muslims, but they permitted most to keep their lands, subject to a tax, and to continue practicing their religion.

At first, because of local quarrels among themselves, Muslim rulers in surrounding areas were relatively indifferent to the crusader states. The Europeans, however, soon began to encounter more forceful and organized resistance. After Muslim ruler Zangi of Mosul captured Edessa in 1144, Pope Eugenius III called the Second Crusade to defend the crusader states. Armies from Germany and France reached Jerusalem in 1148. There, they gathered a force of almost 50,000 men and attacked Damascus, held by the Turkish commander Unur. But Nur ad-Din, Zangi's son and successor, sent reinforcements to Unur and the crusaders retreated from Damascus in defeat.

Failed Prisoner Exchange. For the next 25 years the crusader states enjoyed a period of relative peace. By the late 1150s, however, Muslim forces began taking over neighboring territory. At the same time, internal conflicts divided the rulers of the crusader states. In the 1180s, Reginald of Chatillon, a European noble from Jerusalem, broke a truce with Muslim leader Saladin, Nur ad-Din's nephew, and attacked a caravan. Saladin then declared a jihad* against the crusader kingdoms. He achieved his first major victory in July 1187, at the battle of Hittin, killing Reginald and about 200 other captives and selling most of the foot soldiers into slavery. Jerusalem fell on October 2, 1187, and by 1189, Saladin controlled almost all of the kingdom of Jerusalem.

* **jihad** literally "striving"; war in defense of Islam

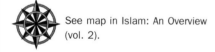

See map in Islam: An Overview (vol. 2).

Pope Gregory VIII, meanwhile, called for the Third Crusade, which reached the Holy Land in 1189. After Christian armies recaptured the city of Acre in 1191, one of the crusader generals, England's King Richard I "the Lionheart," negotiated a prisoner exchange agreement with Saladin. When Richard disagreed with the way the exchange was to be implemented, he refused to hand over his remaining captives and ordered them all killed. Richard went on to fight for control of Jerusalem but failed. The Third Crusade ended with a peace treaty in 1192. Jerusalem remained in Muslim hands, but pilgrims were allowed safe passage to holy sites.

Capture and Pillage. In 1202 the Fourth Crusade was organized against Egypt, which had become the new center of Muslim power. Merchants from Venice, who had agreed to help pay for the expedition, diverted it to Constantinople instead. After helping the Venetians recapture the port city of Zara from the Byzantines, the crusaders conquered Constantinople and pillaged the city. The event outraged the Byzantines and deepened the rift between the eastern branch of Christianity and the Roman church in western Europe.

Later Expeditions. Several other crusader campaigns occurred in the 1200s. Some were focused on Egypt, but they met with little success. One later crusade into the Holy Land became more of an attempt to gain control of the crusader states than to fight a holy war. At one point in the 1220s, Jerusalem was returned to Christian authority by a controversial peace treaty that lasted until 1244, when Muslims reconquered the city. Christian armies continued to have little success in the region. In 1291 Muslim forces recaptured Acre, the last crusader stronghold, completing the defeat of the Europeans and ending crusader rule. Plans for other crusades to the Holy Land never materialized, largely because of dwindling support and lack of funds.

Results of the Crusades. The Crusades proved largely unsuccessful for western Europe. Christian forces failed to accomplish their main mission of wresting the Holy Land from Muslim control. Although Christians saw the fight for the Holy Land as a sacred responsibility, the Crusades were marked by brutality and greed over land and the spoils of war. Muslims still consider the Crusades a symbol of Western aggression against Islam. (*See also* **Saladin; Seljuk Dynasty.**)

Da'wah

See *Missionaries*.

Day of Judgment

One of the five articles of the Muslim faith, called *aqidah*, is belief in the Day of Judgment. This term refers to the end of time, when all human beings will appear before God to account for their actions on earth. God will weigh their sins and good deeds and determine whether each person will be rewarded in paradise or punished in hell.

The Qur'an* does not specify when the Day of Judgment will come, saying that only God knows. The Islamic depiction of Judgment Day is similar to that given in the Bible. The day will be announced by the trumpet of the angel Israfil. Cataclysmic events will occur, including earthquakes, the moving of mountains, and the splitting open of the sky. The heavens will roll back and the sun will stop shining. Stars will fall to earth and oceans will boil over. The earth will crack open, and the dead will rise from their graves.

Although people will try to flee from God's power, they will all bow before Him and await His judgment. Each person's actions during life will have been recorded in his or her "book of deeds," which God will use to determine the individual's reward or punishment. If the book is placed in the person's right hand, the reward will be paradise. But if the book is placed in the person's left hand, the punishment will be the eternal fires of hell.

Islamic tradition—taken from the hadith* and other writings, but not mentioned directly in the Qur'an—says that Judgment Day will be preceded by a great cosmic battle fought between Satan's forces (led by false messiah* Dajjal) and the forces of God (led by the Mahdi, "rightly guided one," and Jesus). Dajjal, known as the deceiver, will spread corruption and oppression over the earth and will mislead humans with false teachings and miracles. The forces of God will fight to bring justice and true belief to all humanity.

Before the coming of Islam, Arabian belief in an afterlife was virtually nonexistent. When Muhammad first preached to the Arabian tribes about

* **Qur'an** book of the holy scriptures of Islam

* **hadith** reports of the words and deeds of Muhammad (not in the Qur'an, but accepted as guides for Muslim behavior)

* **messiah** anticipated savior to be sent by God

121

the Day of Judgment, many reacted with scorn and rejected his teachings. Nevertheless, he continued to preach the Qur'an's message of the complete power of God to resurrect and judge all people on the last day. The Day of Judgment symbolizes the ultimate and absolute power of God over human destiny, and it symbolizes the responsibility that individuals bear in following God's laws. The Qur'an teaches that God alone is the judge and master over both life on earth and the afterlife.

The Qur'an contains many poetic descriptions of both paradise and hell. It depicts hell as a fire having seven gates, which has led many theorists to believe that hell has seven levels, each for different categories of sinners. The Qur'an also describes the boiling waters, black smoke, and scorching wind of hell, and it states that those who are sent there will suffer eternally without any release. When their skin burns off, they will grow new skin so that their pain can continue indefinitely. Their thirst will be so great that they will drink foul liquids, only to become more parched. Boiling water will be poured over their heads, melting their insides, and iron hooks will drag them back if they try to escape.

In paradise, however, God's faithful will live in peace and contentment, enjoying gentle speech and pleasant shade in fragrant and harmonious gardens. They will eat delicious foods and drink from a clear, running stream. They will recline on couches adorned in rich fabrics and be waited on by servants. In addition, men will enjoy the attentions of the divine maidens called *huris*. Those who spend their lives doing good instead of evil; who are dutiful, truthful, and sorry for their misdeeds; who feed the poor and take care of orphans; and who have faith in the revelations of God will reach this paradise.

Islamic teachings about the afterlife emphasize the connection between one's actions in this world and one's fate in the next. Muslim traditions also point out that certain signs may foretell the coming of the Day of Judgment. In recent times, some scholars see the apparent moral degradation of contemporary society as a sign that the Day of Judgment is near. Others believe that humanity's significant social progress is a sign that the last day will arrive soon. (*See also* **Afterlife; Creed; Death and Funerals; Pillars of Islam.**)

Death and Funerals

* **Qur'an** book of the holy scriptures of Islam

The Qur'an* refers to death as "the certainty." For Muslims, death is the most important stage in the soul's progress toward God. For this reason, Muslims try to prepare themselves spiritually for it. In Islam, suicide is considered a grave sin.

When Muslims are near death, they are expected to repent their sins and, if possible, perform ritual ablutions, or purifications. Family and other loved ones should stay close to the dying person to pray for him or her and offer support. Those present at the deathbed should recite the *shahadah* (expression of faith) in the ear of the dying person so that he or she will remember it when questioned by angels. The dying person should recite it as well, if possible, without needing the encouragement of others. It is also desirable for the dying person to make a will distributing up to one-third of his or her property. When the person's death seems near, family members should recite surah* 36 from the Qur'an, which describes God's resuscitation of the dead on Judgment Day and encourages mindfulness of the Islamic faith.

* **surah** chapter of the Qur'an

The Qur'an provides no guidance on funeral rites. Muslims have developed customs concerning procedures during and after death. The family of the deceased is responsible for preparing the body for burial and for leading the funerary prayers. Muslims are required to bury their dead as soon as they are able, preferably before sundown on the day of death. As soon as the body cools, a close relative or a professional washer of the dead gives the body a complete washing in a ritually regulated manner. The body is typically washed three separate times, always in a respectful way that preserves the modesty of the deceased person. The washer plugs the body's openings with cotton, wraps the corpse tightly in a cloth shroud, and applies strong-smelling ointments, such as camphor. Throughout the cleansing process, the body should face Mecca. Some families place the deceased in a simple coffin. Sometimes, however, the body is placed in the earth without a coffin. If a Muslim dies as a martyr*, in childbirth, or as the result of an accident, the body is not washed at all, but is buried as it fell. If a man dies at the hajj*, his shroud must have no seams. If the deceased is a woman, her face must show through her coverings.

See color plate 6, vol. 3.

* **martyr** one who dies for his or her religious beliefs

* **hajj** pilgrimage to Mecca that Muslims are required to make once in their lifetime

The funeral service itself can take place in any appropriate, dignified location. Outside of the United States and other Western countries, it usually does not occur in a mosque. Whether the service is held inside or outside, the congregation stands throughout the ceremony. Bearers place the body in the grave, which should be deep enough to protect it from animals and to prevent unpleasant odors from escaping. Male relatives of the deceased enter the grave and arrange the body in its proper position. They place the body on its right side in a niche hollowed out of the grave wall, turn the head toward Mecca, and place the cheek on a stone or other support. The person who arranges the body in its final position recites the *shahadah* in its ear. After the men climb out of the grave, each member of the funeral party throws soil into the grave to fill it. Finally, a member of the party gives a blessing containing a summary of the key beliefs of Islam. Shi'i* Muslims also recite the names of the 12 holy imams*. Some family members mark the grave with a simple headstone, but tradition discourages the use of elaborate monuments.

* **Shi'i** refers to Muslims who believe that Muhammad chose Ali ibn Abi Talib and his descendants as the spiritual-political leaders of the Muslim community

* **imam** spiritual-political leader in Shi'i Islam, one who is regarded as directly descended from Muhammad; also, one who leads prayers

Traditional Muslims believe that the dreaded angels Munkar and Nakir visit the deceased in the grave and question him or her about the *shahadah* and other tenets of Islam. Satisfactory answers allow the deceased to wait in comfort until the Day of Judgment. According to tradition, if the person gives incorrect answers, he or she experiences various torments, such as feeling the crushing weight of the earth. The deceased remains in this intermediary state, called the *barzakh*, until the resurrection, when all the dead arise and rejoin their souls for God's judgment on the Last Day.

Muslims are encouraged to refrain from making loud expressions of grief at funerals because these are believed to increase the deceased person's suffering during the angels' questioning. Visiting the grave and offering prayers are considered worthy acts, but Muslim tradition specifies that mourning should be limited to three days. For widows, the period can last for four months and ten days.

Although all Muslim societies observe these basic funeral customs, many regional and folk practices also exist. Throughout the world, many Muslims include feasts in their rituals. Muslims in the southern Philippines sacrifice cows for the dead. In Java, Muslims place food offerings under the bed of the deceased during the first 40 days after the death. Family members in Iran may wrap the body in a cloth inscribed with quotations from the Qur'an. In Sudan, mourners place pebbles on top of the grave. In a custom with possible pre-Islamic origins, Muslims in Malaysia put betel nut scissors on the torso of the deceased to prevent demons and ghosts from stepping on it. In some parts of Egypt, Bedouin* women mourn by wailing in high-pitched voices. Lebanese mourners may bake special pastries as a sacrifice for the dead. In some places, including the United States, Muslims have adopted the custom of viewing the body in an open casket before the funeral. (*See also* **Afterlife; Day of Judgment; Shahadah.**)

* **Bedouin** nomad of the desert, especially in North Africa, Syria, and Arabia

Democracy

Democracy is government by the people, usually through elected representatives. In general, the spread of democracy throughout the world, which accelerated in the late 1800s and 1900s, has been associated with modern Western values. Muslims disagree about the proper role of democracy in Islamic countries, few of which have representative governments. Some argue that Islam is entirely compatible with democratic rule, while others insist that democracy is contradictory to Islam.

Perspectives on Democracy. Those who believe that Muslim societies should embrace democracy follow the basic philosophy of Egyptian reformer Muhammad Abduh (died 1905). According to Abduh, Islam encourages Muslims to form their governments on the basis of modern reasoning and by learning from the experiences of nations that have built successful systems.

Advocates of the liberal* Islamic view argue that the Qur'an* and hadith* clearly support the basic democratic principles of popular election, justice, and tolerance. The Qur'an, for example, states that God instructed the Prophet to consult with his advisers, even those whose counsel had led to defeat in battle. Islamic teaching also indicates that good Muslims should confer with one another about business and other matters. Some Muslims point to these principles as a basis for the election of representative leaders and government institutions, as in the case of Western democracies.

The concept of *maslahah*—seeking the public good—urges Muslim societies to do what is best for the people and avoid actions that may harm them. This concept establishes justice as a foundation of the political system. The Qur'an also forbids compulsion in religion, which is interpreted to mean a tolerance of religious and political diversity and the equality of Muslims and non-Muslims in civic rights and duties.

Conservative* Muslim scholars maintain that Islam as traditionally taught should be the only basis of government. Sayyid Qutb, a leading Egyptian ac-

* **liberal** supporting greater participation in government for individuals; not bound by tradition

* **Qur'an** book of the holy scriptures of Islam

* **hadith** reports of the words and deeds of Muhammad (not in the Qur'an, but accepted as guides for Muslim behavior)

* **conservative** generally opposed to change, especially in existing political and social institutions

tivist during the first half of the 1900s, also represented this view. For Qutb, many aspects of modern life, including Western institutions and beliefs, were evil and therefore inconsistent with Islam. He taught that the Islamic political system has three essential components: just leaders, obedient followers, and dialogue between the two groups. The *shari'ah**, he argued, is the source of all laws, both spiritual and worldly. For Qutb, the political system must enforce the *shari'ah* because the primary goal of Islam is the establishment of an Islamic state.

Hasan al-Turabi, an influential Sudanese political leader and follower of Qutb, argues that Western-style democracy is flawed because it grants ultimate authority to the people. The Qur'an, by contrast, declares that God has ultimate sovereignty. Furthermore, democratic systems are based on imperfect human reasoning and factional interests that prevent them from promoting real political equality, unity, and freedom.

Egyptian thinker Muhammad Imarah, by contrast, concludes that Islam and democracy are compatible. He argues that Islam distinguishes between religious and worldly matters. Therefore, religious and political authority should co-exist, but they should not be unified in one structure. In Imarah's view, a theocracy* is un-Islamic and oppressive, because it deprives people of their right to be involved in politics.

Historical Experience. The proportion of free democratic governments in Muslim countries is low compared to the rest of the world. A recent survey of government sources revealed that 121 (63 percent) of the world's 192 governments were electoral democracies. In the 45 countries with a significant or majority Muslim population, however, only 23 (about 51 percent) had democratically elected governments. Authoritarian regimes—led by kings, military officers, or former military officers—rule most Islamic nations. In these societies, security forces ensure the power of the state, and freedoms of assembly, speech, and the press are restricted.

The scarcity of democracy in Islamic countries may derive from historical experience. European nations controlled the region for several centuries. Even after the end of colonial rule in the 1950s and 1960s, these nations played an important role in the formation of many modern Muslim states. In the Middle East, for example, the British determined the political boundaries of Iraq and Kuwait, and they created the new country of Jordan. Such artificial borders caused ethnic, regional, and religious conflicts, and provided a weak basis for the legitimacy of rulers. As a result, repressive governments came to power in some emerging Muslim countries.

After achieving independence, many Muslim states imposed limits on the role of Islam in public life. Some governments, such as those of Egyptian president Gamal Abdel Nasser and Algeria's FLN party, adopted a modern, socialist* agenda. In the 1970s and 1980s, unrest generated by war and civil strife, discontent with growing state power, and poor economic conditions led to the rise of political movements based on strict adherence to Islamic principles. Generally, the Islamists oppose any attempts to secularize* society.

Governments in largely Muslim countries took various approaches to the Islamists' opposition. In some countries, such as Jordan, Islamist groups were permitted to participate in parliamentary elections. Other governments, such

Pro-Democracy Plan

In December 2002, the U.S. Department of State announced a new plan to foster democracy in Islamic countries. Noting that authoritarian regimes can create conditions for terrorism, State Department director of policy and planning Richard Haass said: "The United States will work more energetically than ever before to promote democracy in partnership with the people and governments of the Muslim world." The new initiative will provide resources intended to cultivate economic, educational, and political reform. Haass emphasized that Muslim societies themselves must create lasting change. They must also allow freedom of the press and respect for women's rights, as well as greater access to education for all their people.

* *shari'ah* Islamic law as established in the Qur'an and sunnah, the exemplary behavior of the Prophet Muhammad

* **theocracy** government headed by religious leaders and believed to be divinely guided

* **socialist** refers to socialism, the economic system in which the government owns and operates the means of production and the distribution of goods

* **secularize** to separate religion from other aspects of human life and society

* **fundamentalist** person who believes in a literal interpretation of scripture; Muslim who accepts Islam as a comprehensive belief system that can be applied to modern times

as those of Tunisia and Algeria, enforced rigid controls on the fundamentalists*, fearing that their desire to combine politics and religion would compromise individual rights and might win popular support. Indeed, when religious revolutionaries overthrew the government of Iran in 1979 and created an Islamic republic, many people were executed or imprisoned because they did not meet Muslim codes of modesty or morality. In 1989 Islamists organized a coup that seized control of Sudan with the promise of creating an Islamic democracy. Their treatment of non-Muslim minorities and Muslim opposition groups, however, has been deplorable. The non-Islamist regimes that had been replaced in Iran and Sudan also had poor records in terms of their treatment of minorities and in upholding basic human rights.

Future Trends. Issues that divide liberals and fundamentalists are likely to continue to affect the future of democracy in the Muslim world. Islamist parties have recently won electoral victories in Morocco, Bahrain, and Pakistan, and religious groups are gaining political strength in Egypt, Jordan, and Kuwait.

In some countries, support for a form of democracy that incorporates Islamic principles is growing. Turkey, one of the most secular Muslim countries, promoted the separation of religion and politics so vigorously that it banned religious-based political parties and even jailed their leaders. In November 2002, however, the Islamically-oriented Justice and Development Party won a parliamentary majority. Unlike fundamentalist groups elsewhere, the Justice and Development Party campaigned on a platform of economic reform rather than religious issues. This suggests that the party may retain a secular approach to government while incorporating Islamic principles. (*See also* **Algeria; Egypt; Fundamentalism; Government; Iran; Qutb, Sayyid; Turkey.**)

Dhikr

See *Sufism*.

Dietary Rules

* **Qur'an** book of the holy scriptures of Islam

* **hadith** reports of the words and deeds of Muhammad (not in the Qur'an but accepted as guides for Muslim behavior)

Islam has specific rules and recommendations about the consumption of food and drink. The Qur'an* and hadith* make many references to substances that are pure (*tahir*) and impure (*rijs, najis*), lawful (*halal*) and unlawful (*haram*). These dietary guidelines remind Muslims that they are part of a global community that shares certain values and responsibilities, regardless of their social standing. Islam teaches that by properly maintaining the physical body, a Muslim will have a healthy soul and spirit. A nutritious, balanced diet helps an individual to achieve this goal. Muslim dietary rules derive from pre-Islamic Arabian and Jewish dietary guidelines.

Basic Rules. The Qur'an urges Muslims to eat the good, lawful plants and animals that God has provided for them: "O' Believers! Eat of the good and pure that We have provided you with and be grateful to Allah, if you truly worship Him." Plant foods that are especially valued include dates, grapes, olives, pomegranates, and grains. Fish and beef are also recommended, as well as the meat of sheep, goats, and camels. Islam forbids Muslims to eat

Muslims are allowed to consume all types of meat except pork, as long as the animal was slaughtered according to Islam's strict dietary guidelines. Here, an Egyptian butcher displays his *halal*, or lawful, meats for sale.

pork and pork byproducts. Carrion (meat from an animal that was found dead), the flesh of carnivorous (meat-eating) animals, blood and blood byproducts, and food that has been consecrated to any being other than God are prohibited. Alcoholic drinks are also banned.

Meat is an acceptable food only when it is slaughtered properly. Ritual slaughtering and sacrifice—the killing of an animal for a sacred occasion—are required for cattle, sheep, goats, and fowl. These creatures must be killed in God's name by slitting their throats. Camels should be slaughtered by a stab wound in the upper chest. The Qur'an permits fishing and hunting wild animals as long as the prey is *halal*. Muslims may not eat anything that has been strangled, beaten, or gored to death, or animals that have died by falling. An animal that has been partially consumed by predators may be eaten only if it has actually been killed by ritual slaughtering or by a trained hunting animal.

Additional dietary rules apply to specific occasions. During the month of Ramadan, every able Muslim must abstain from food and drink during

* **hajj** pilgrimage to Mecca that Muslims are required to make once in their lifetime

* **heretic** person whose belief or practice is contrary to established religious doctrine

* **apostate** person who abandons his or her religious faith

* **atheist** person who denies the existence of God

Under the Influence

Although Islam's ban on the consumption of alcohol is strong, it has often been defied. Wine was a favorite beverage in royal courts and in public taverns. The Bektashi order, a popular Sufi order during the Ottoman Empire, used wine in religious rituals. Nonalcoholic intoxicants, including hashish and opium, were popular among peasants and city dwellers in many Muslim countries. Islamic judges condemned the use of such intoxicants, but with little success. In modern times, Islamic countries have taken harsh measures against alcohol and mind-altering drugs. Some, like Saudi Arabia, have outlawed alcohol not only for Muslims but also for non-Muslims. However, nonalcoholic beer and wines are consumed by many in these countries wishing to partake in the modern, Western party-culture. More secular countries, such as Egypt and Turkey, have passed strict antidrug laws but permit the controlled import, sale, and consumption of alcohol.

daylight hours. Pilgrims making the hajj* may not hunt or harvest any grain within the boundaries of the holy city of Mecca. During the two main feasts of the year following Ramadan and the hajj, however, Muslims must not fast. The hadith also provide guidelines for daily hospitality and acceptable table manners, such as remembering God at mealtime, taking food and drink with only the right hand, and sitting upright while eating.

Rules govern who can slaughter meat and from whom Muslims can accept food. Generally, any Muslim who is familiar with proper procedures can slaughter meat. The Qur'an also specifies that Muslims generally may accept food from Jews, Christians, and other groups that are guided by scripture. Some Muslim traditions suggest that if there is a doubt about the source of meat, a person need only say the name of Allah over it to make it acceptable. By contrast, food from known heretics*, apostates*, idol worshippers, and atheists* is forbidden.

Breaking dietary rules temporarily invalidates acts of worship such as prayer, fasting, and pilgrimage. Mere physical contact with pork, carrion, or wine can make a person or object impure, but this can be corrected by washing or by removing the forbidden substance. Violating the ban on intoxicating beverages and drunkenness, however, is a serious crime punishable by flogging. One hadith states that unrepentant Muslims will be denied the reward of drinking wine in the afterlife.

Contemporary Implications. Dietary rules have posed challenges for Muslims who live in Western countries. In the United States, for example, many prepared foods contain ingredients that make them unlawful for Muslims. Fast food restaurants often cook with lard, a pork byproduct. To avoid consuming such ingredients, many Muslims buy their meat and other foods from Muslim-owned markets. They also rely on food labels to ensure that products are *halal*. In areas with large Muslim populations, stores that cater to Muslim dietary guidelines have opened. Some farms permit Muslims to purchase and slaughter animals themselves.

Another issue for Muslims concerns whether it is permissible to work in stores or restaurants that sell alcohol or attend social functions where alcohol is served. Some argue that these practices are acceptable, and some Muslims even serve alcohol in their homes to non-Muslim guests. Others believe that such activities are wrong. Because some medications may contain traces of alcohol or other forbidden substances, Muslims are generally encouraged to avoid them unless the drug is needed to save a person's life. In general, any substances that might impair a person's faith and moral judgment should be avoided. (*See also* **Fasting; Ramadan.**)

Divorce

* **Qur'an** book of the holy scriptures of Islam

* **sunnah** literally "the trodden path"; Islamic customs based on the exemplary behavior of Muhammad

Islam permits divorce under certain circumstances. Traditionally, Islamic law has facilitated the divorce process for men while imposing significant barriers for women who want to end their marriages. Nevertheless, the Qur'an* and sunnah* emphasize the seriousness of divorce and view it as a last resort. The

Prophet Muhammad reportedly said: "Of all the permitted things, divorce is the most abominable [detestable] with God." An Islamic legal manual characterizes divorce as "a dangerous and disapproved procedure." Because the family is the foundation of Muslim society, the Qur'an encourages husbands and wives to do all they can to resolve their differences and stay together.

Arab Culture and Islamic Law. Before the rise of Islam in the early 600s, Arabs lived in a traditional patriarchal, or male-dominated, society. Men, as the head of the family, exerted complete control over their wives and children. According to custom, a man had the right to divorce his wife at any time and for any reason. A woman, by contrast, was considered the property of her husband and had only those rights that her husband allowed.

The Qur'an improved the status of women, noting that "women have rights similar to those [men] over them; while men are a step above them." The Qur'an further explained that rights are proportional to responsibilities and that men have greater responsibilities than women. As the *ulama* (Islamic religious scholars) developed laws to govern marriage, divorce, and inheritance, they incorporated Qur'anic principles. Although Islamic law extended some rights to women and limited the privileges of men, it did not change the preeminent position of the husband.

According to the Qur'an and Islamic law, a husband can repudiate, or disown, his wife without cause by a declaration known as the *talaq*. The power to exercise *talaq* requires neither judicial involvement nor the consent of the wife. The husband merely repeats the words "I divorce you" three times, once a month for three consecutive months. The three-month duration of the process imposes a waiting period during which the husband must continue to provide food, clothing, and shelter for his wife. The waiting period also gives the couple an opportunity to reconcile. If the two people have not resolved their differences by the end of the three months, the marriage formally ends. The husband remains free of any financial responsibility to the wife except for the *mahr* (money or property that the man had to pledge to legally validate the marriage). Some men agree to pay the *mahr* in two parts, half before the marriage and the other half in the event of divorce or death. In practice, many men bypassed the required waiting period by repeating the words "I divorce you" three times in rapid succession. Although it is considered sinful, this form of divorce is legal.

Islamic law denies women the right to end a marriage by repudiation but does permit them to initiate two types of divorce. *Khul* divorce, also known as divorce through ransom, allows a woman to buy herself out of a marriage by paying her husband an agreed-upon sum of money or by returning the *mahr*. *Tafriq* divorce allows a wife to petition a court for divorce on very limited grounds, such as the husband's impotence or desertion. In some countries, family law has expanded the grounds for *tafriq* divorce to include mistreatment, conflict, a physical defect on the part of the husband, failure of the husband to provide financial support, or the absence or imprisonment of the husband.

Aside from the obstacles that women encounter in trying to obtain a divorce, they have few rights regarding custody of their children after a divorce. Islamic law grants custody to the mother, but only if the children are very young. When the children reach a certain age, custody passes to the

Curbing Arbitrary Divorces

Islamic law allows a man to have as many as four wives if he can provide for them equally, but taking a second wife may lead to divorce. Instead of accepting the arrival of a second wife, the first wife may ask her husband to petition for divorce so that she can lawfully leave his household. Sometimes, a husband divorces his first wife in order to take a second wife. In a notable court case in India, a Muslim woman who had been married for 43 years was thrown out of her house after her husband repudiated her to take a second wife. Seventeen years later, the Mumbai (Bombay) High Court ruled that Muslim men must go through the court system and due process of law to obtain a divorce.

father, because he is considered better qualified to supervise their education. The age at which the father gains custody varies by country, but it is anywhere between two and ten for boys and seven to the onset of puberty or the time of marriage for girls. A mother may lose custody of the children in her care if she remarries.

Modern Reforms. With the exception of Turkey, which abandoned Islamic legal codes in 1926 and adopted a civil code, the most far-reaching reforms in family law in the Middle East have been implemented in Tunisia. The Tunisian Code of Personal Status, enacted in 1956, required men to register a *talaq* divorce in a government court and granted women equal rights to this type of divorce. Additional reforms in 1992 guaranteed child-support payments for divorced women and gave them the right to be considered legal guardians of their minor children along with the father.

In general, however, modern legislation regarding marriage and divorce has done little to correct the inequalities in Islamic family law between men and women. Some Muslims resent government intervention in what they regard as private family matters, and as a result, they ignore legal reforms. Furthermore, modern legislation tends to codify* Islamic law rather than to modify it. For example, in most Islamic countries today, the law requires that *talaq* divorces be registered in court. Nevertheless, husbands still retain their absolute right of repudiation on any grounds, as permitted by traditional Islamic legal codes. Because a woman does not have to be present when her husband repudiates her, some women do not even know that they have been divorced until they receive notification by regular mail, e-mail, or fax.

Islamist political movements have also limited reforms in family law. They often label advocates of change as secular* and anti-Islamic. Fundamentalist* groups have even reversed previous reforms. In 1975 Iran's Family Protection Act gave equal rights to divorce to men and women and granted the courts the power to make custody decisions in accordance with the best interests of the child. One of the first acts of the Ayatollah Khomeini's Islamic government in Iran was to reinstate a man's right to divorce at will and to give fathers and their relatives sole child custody rights. In December 2002 Iran's Guardian Council, which evaluate proposed legislation, approved a bill giving women greater rights to divorce their husbands. A woman may now file for divorce if she has her husband's approval or if she can prove that he is unable to provide for his family. (*See also* **Family; Law; Marriage.**)

Djibouti

See *East Africa.*

Druze

The Druze are the members of a group that began in the early 1000s as an offshoot of Ismaili Shi'ism*. Although the Druze believe in one God, most of their theology differs significantly from traditional Muslim beliefs and practices. Concentrated in Lebanon, Syria, and Israel, the Druze number about one million worldwide.

* **codify** to create a system of rules

* **secular** separate from religion in human life and society; connected to everyday life

* **fundamentalist** (adj.) generally refers to the movement that promotes a literal interpretation of scripture; in Islam, a movement that promotes politicization of religion to create an alternative public order

* **Shi'ism** branch of Islam that believes Muhammad chose Ali ibn Abi Talib and his descendants as the spiritual-political leaders of the Muslim community

In 1017 al-Hakim, the sixth caliph (leader) of the Fatimid dynasty of Egypt, announced that he was the earthly manifestation of God. Missionaries spread the message of al-Hakim's divinity throughout the empire. The followers of this new faith were named the Druze, after Muhammad al-Darazi, one of its most zealous disciples.

Within a few years of its founding, disagreements arose among the Druze missionaries. Darazi was assassinated and later labeled a heretic* by the Druze. In 1021 al-Hakim disappeared under mysterious circumstances. The new Fatimid government forced the Druze to leave Egypt, but the faith endured in the mountains of Syria-Palestine. Missionary Baha al-Din al-Samuki compiled the Druze teachings into six books known as *The Noble Knowledge*. The Druze stopped recruiting followers in 1043.

Since the end of the group's missionary endeavors, the Druze have maintained a strict rule of secrecy. The Druze teachings have been passed down to only a small number of chosen people, or *uqqal* (the enlightened), within the community of believers. The others, who are known as the *juhhal* (the ignorant), protect the religion through their loyalty to one another. The Druze also maintain secrecy in their dealings with outsiders. The Druze are permitted to hide their religious affiliation from non-Druze for the sake of self-protection or the safety of the community.

The Druze differ from traditional Muslims in several ways. The most important distinction is the belief that the revelations of al-Hakim, not the Prophet Muhammad, contain the ultimate truth. Furthermore, the Druze do not follow fundamental Islamic doctrine. They do not observe the Five Pillars of Islam, practice male circumcision, or permit polygyny*. The Druze believe in reincarnation*, which Muslims reject. Because of these differences, the mainstream Muslim community considers the Druze to be heretical.

* **heretic** person whose belief or practice is contrary to established religious doctrine

* **polygyny** practice of having more than one wife at one time

* **reincarnation** passing of a soul from the body of a deceased person to the body of a living one

East Africa

East Africa includes the countries of Djibouti, Eritrea, Ethiopia, Kenya, Somalia, Tanzania, and Uganda. Islam came to the region in the early 700s, eventually giving rise to an African-Arab civilization. Today Muslims are a political minority in most parts of East Africa, generally focusing their attention on religious and educational activities rather than on creating Islamic governments. In recent decades, however, some Muslim groups in East Africa have begun to fight for a closer connection between Islam and the state.

Islam Comes to East Africa

Arab and Persian traders and missionaries* brought Islam to East Africa beginning in the 700s. They arrived either by traveling up the Nile River or by crossing the Red Sea or the Indian Ocean. Eventually, the Muslim merchants settled in the coastal region of East Africa, intermarried with local people, and became the leaders in their communities. Converts to Islam adapted the beliefs and practices of this new religion to traditions of tribal religions. By the 1200s, trade between East Africa, Arabia, and the countries that border

* **missionary** person who works to convert nonbelievers to a particular faith

The East African country of Kenya has a relatively small but diverse Muslim population. Muslim men gather at this mosque in Lamu, Kenya, to meet, pray, and talk.

See map in Islam: Overview (vol. 2).

* **artisan** skilled craftsperson

the Persian Gulf was well developed. The cities along the coast, including Kilwa, Mogadishu, and Zanzibar, flourished with the export of copper, iron, cloth, ivory, gold, and slaves.

As the Bantu peoples of East Africa mixed with the Muslim population, they adapted their language to include many Arabic words. Eventually a distinctive language and culture, known as Swahili, developed. The term *Swahili* comes from the Arabic word *sawahili*, which means "of the coast."

Exploration and Colonization. By the early 1500s, Portuguese explorers engaged in the spice trade dominated the East African ports, and Arab merchants lost control of the region. Portuguese rule lasted until 1696, when forces from Oman conquered the area. Omani leaders restored Arab supremacy for a brief period, after which many of the coastal towns gained their independence from foreign powers. During the early 1800s, Oman recaptured the coast of East Africa, and the island of Zanzibar became the regional center of Muslim culture. The Arabs, who owned most of the land and controlled the government and law enforcement, comprised the social and political elite of Zanzibar. Smaller groups of Muslims from India managed the trade network. The majority African population, employed as artisans*, fishermen, and workers, held no real political power.

Zanzibar had a prosperous economy, which was based on a thriving slave trade and a growing demand for ivory and cloves. According to some estimates, slave traders sold as many as 50,000 Africans annually in the Zanzibar market. Slavery, which was not officially abolished in the region until 1873, caused extreme devastation across East Africa. Whole populations fled their ancestral lands to escape capture. Even after abolition, some slave trading continued into the early 1900s.

Commercial success in Zanzibar motivated Arab merchants to establish new trading routes and to build towns in the East African interior. In the process, they extended the influence of Islam, which until that time had been confined to the coastal cities.

At the end of the 1800s, European nations established colonial rule over Zanzibar, Tanganyika (present-day Tanzania), Kenya, Uganda, and other East African territories. Trade between the interior and the coastal cities increased, facilitating the spread of Islam. Exposure to Islam also grew because colonial administrators employed Muslims throughout the region as government officials, teachers, police officers, and soldiers. Furthermore, the use of Swahili in many regions of East Africa provided Muslims with a common language.

Independence and Conflict

After achieving independence from colonial rule in the 1900s, most of the territories of East Africa became secular* nation-states. Although Muslims accounted for a substantial segment of the population in these countries, they were still a minority, and Islam did not shape the political character of the new regimes*. Only in areas where Arabs constitute a majority or where Arab identity is particularly strong, such as Somalia, has Islam been incorporated into the national political system.

Zanzibar and Tanganyika Merge. East African states followed various patterns of development from colonialism to independence. In Zanzibar, which was controlled by the British, the ban on slavery weakened Arab power and eliminated a vital source of income. As a result, the island's African population made significant political and economic gains. World War II (1939–1945) fueled an independence movement and a political struggle between the Arab and African populations. The Zanzibar National Party, founded in 1956, emerged as an advocate for Arab interests. During the early 1960s, the Arab minority tried to oust the British and create an Islamic state. Arab parties gathered enough support from the African majority population to win elections in 1961 and 1963. After Zanzibar achieved independence (in December, 1963), however, African revolutionaries seized control of the government and established a socialist* regime hostile to Arab interests. In 1964 Zanzibar merged with Tanganyika, creating the new country of Tanzania. Muslims constitute more than 99 percent of the population of the island of Zanzibar, but only 35 percent of the population of mainland Tanzania.

In Tanganyika, Sufi* Islam had spread as a way to resist colonial rule. The Muslim brotherhoods became active in politics in the 1930s, and they later achieved considerable success in promoting Muslim interests at the national level.

Tanganyika gained independence in 1961, and Julius Nyerere (a Roman Catholic) became president. He worked to create a democratic political society, but his policies failed. Nyerere was president in 1964 when Tanganyika became Tanzania. He retired in 1985, and since then, Tanzania has been plagued by economic stagnation, unemployment, and conflicts among its Asian, Arab, and African communities. In recent years, reformist Islam—a version of the faith that emphasizes the teachings of the Qur'an* and sunnah* and rejects the integration of Islam and traditional African beliefs—has gained considerable influence in the country.

Muslim Nations. Djibouti and Somalia are almost entirely Muslim. Djibouti won its independence from France in 1977. Its population is 94 percent Muslim. Somalia, which gained independence from Great Britain and

* **secular** separate from religion in human life and society; connected to everyday life

* **regime** government in power

* **socialist** refers to socialism, the economic system in which the government owns and operates the means of production and the distribution of goods

* **Sufi** (adj) refers to Sufism, which seeks to develop spirituality through discipline of the mind and body

* **Qur'an** book of the holy scriptures of Islam

* **sunnah** literally "the trodden path"; Islamic customs based on the exemplary behavior of Muhammad

* **Sunni** refers to the largest branch of the Muslim community; the name derives from sunnah, the exemplary behavior of the Prophet Muhammad

* **guerrilla** unconventional warfare

Policies Affect Muslims Worldwide

The American anti-terrorist campaign in Afghanistan, unrest between Israel and Palestine, and the war between the United States and Iraq have affected Muslims throughout the world. In Kenya, Muslims have expressed resentment at the policies of Israel and the United States and solidarity with fellow believers in the Middle East. The turbulent events in international politics have strained relations between the minority Muslim population and the Christian majority. Muslim leaders complain of a long history of unfair treatment by the government. Christians worry that Kenyan Muslims will lend support to Islamic extremists.

* **radical** favoring extreme change or reform, especially in existing political and social institutions

* **mosque** Muslim place of worship

Italy in 1960, is a Sunni* Muslim nation, but its people are not Arabs. During the 1970s, the government of Somalia claimed a right to territory where ethnic Somalis lived in Kenya, Djibouti, and Ethiopia, but these states rejected Somalia's demands. In 1977 the French withdrew from Djibouti and revolution broke out in Ethiopia. Somalia decided to take advantage of the turbulent situation and began a guerilla* war against Ethiopia. The Soviet Union and Cuba—former allies of Somalia—chose to support Ethiopia. The war, which was inconclusive, sharpened the interest of Somalis in their Muslim identity. Somalia has been without a central government since 1991, when its ruler, Mohamed Siyad Barre, was deposed.

A Part of Ethiopia. Muslims comprise about half the population in Ethiopia, a nation that has a long history of conflict and cooperation between Muslims and Christians. During the late 1700s and early 1800s, the Christian rulers of Ethiopia felt threatened by the growing influence of Islam in the region. When Teodoros ascended the throne in 1831, he set out to abolish Islam. Teodoros established a lineage of rulers that culminated with Haile Selassie, who became emperor in 1930. The Italians invaded Ethiopia in 1934, forcing Haile Selassie to flee the country. With the help of the British, he returned to power in 1941. Haile Selassie remained at the head of the Ethiopian government until the early 1970s, when socialist revolutionaries overthrew him.

In 1978 Mengistu Haile Mariam formed the People's Democratic Republic of Ethiopia, which was supported by the Soviet Union and Cuba. Widespread uprisings followed. Muslims took this opportunity to express their dissatisfaction with the long-standing discriminatory policies of the Ethiopian government. Somali and Galla Muslims who lived in the Bale province rebelled, and other Islamic groups also revolted. Ethiopia, however, succeeded in suppressing the opposition and averting a Somali invasion.

Eritrea, which is almost equally divided between Muslims and Christians, has also been the site of conflict. In 1952 Eritrea (a former Italian colony) was made an autonomous, or self-governing, part of Ethiopia. Selassie tried to integrate its population into mainstream Ethiopia by banning Arabic and Tigriniya as its official languages. This and similar policies gave rise to a resistance movement in which both Muslims and Christians participated. Students, workers, and intellectuals led the movement. After Ethiopia formally took over Eritrea in 1962, fighting broke out between armed rebel groups and the government. Eritrea finally won its independence in 1993, but the country fought another war with Ethiopia from 1998 to 2000.

Kenyatta and Amin. Kenya, under the leadership of Jomo Kenyatta, won its independence from Great Britain in 1963. The Muslim population in Kenya, which accounts for about ten percent of the total, is particularly diverse and includes peoples of African, Asian, and Arab ethnicity. Muslims have had limited influence on the political development of the country, however, in part because they lack organization and are concentrated, in communities along the coast. In 1992 a radical* group established the Islamic Party of Kenya, but the country's Muslim leaders oppose this party.

Uganda, which won its independence from Great Britain in 1962, has a Muslim population of 16 percent. The colonial powers limited Muslim participation in the government and restricted financial support of mosques* and Islamic schools. During the early 1920s, Ugandan Muslims split over differences in the interpretation of religious traditions. This event impeded the development of a united Muslim community in Uganda and further weakened Muslim political influence. The situation did not improve until Idi Amin took power in 1971. A Muslim himself, Amin provided official support for Muslim interests. When he was deposed in 1979, many Muslims fled Uganda, and anti-Muslim groups destroyed many mosques and schools. Under succeeding regimes, Muslims have had very limited political influence. (*See also* **Colonialism; Slavery; Swahili.**)

Economics

Islamic ideas about economic practices date back to the Qur'an*. Although Muslims may disagree on some issues, they generally hold to the belief that all wealth and property comes from God. Although Muslim countries have adopted some Western economic models, they continue to adhere to religious principles in their financial dealings.

* **Qur'an** book of the holy scriptures of Islam

Islamic Economic Theory. Early Islamic thinkers had discussed specific economic issues, such as requiring fairness in trade, defining and distributing *zakat**, and prohibiting certain business practices. It was not until modern times, however, that Muslim scholars began to develop economic theories and a sense of the economy as a separate aspect of society. They sought to create a doctrine, separate from capitalism* and Marxism*, that would derive from traditional religious values.

* **zakat** charity; one of the five Pillars of Islam

The Qur'an, the life of Muhammad, and the sunnah* provide the foundation for Islamic economics. The Prophet's sayings and passages in the Qur'an emphasize modesty over extravagance in personal behavior. They promote the ideals of balance and compassion, calling for a society in which people help one another to meet their basic needs. For example, *zakat* ensures that Muslims share about 2.5 percent of their wealth with those who are less fortunate. The Qur'an says little about the operation of financial institutions, but it prohibits charging high interest rates on loans because that only increases the debt of the poor.

* **capitalism** economic system in which businesses are privately owned and operated and where competition exists in a free-market environment
* **Marxism** political philosophy that rejects capitalism and advocates a classless society
* **sunnah** literally "the trodden path"; Islamic customs based on the exemplary behavior of Muhammad

In the early 1900s, a movement to establish Islamic economic principles began in India. Muslims in that nation sought to protect their culture from outside influences. Sayyid Abu al-Ala Mawdudi, the leading promoter of Islamic economics, believed that a system based on Islamic values could help restore the role of religion in the lives of Muslims. He envisioned an economy in which people treated each other honestly and fairly, abiding by the principles of altruism* and brotherhood. The enforcement of *zakat* would spread wealth in an equitable way, he believed. He also interpreted the Qur'an as prohibiting all interest (not just high interest rates) and believed that such a prohibition would ensure fairness in lending practices. Mawdudi, however, said little about the practical aspects of finance and gave few concrete guidelines.

* **altruism** behavior that emphasizes the well-being of others

In contrast to Mawdudi and his contemporaries, the next generation of Islamic economic thinkers studied modern economic thought. They used advanced theories to promote ethical behaviors and to justify Mawdudi's ideas, primarily those regarding charity and interest. They believed that, in a region governed by Islamic values, people would naturally work hard, avoid extravagance, and treat others fairly.

By the beginning of the twenty-first century, Muslim economic scholars still had not produced a unified theory. Secular* approaches shape many economies in the Islamic world. Muslim scholars disagree on a range of issues, including the sharing of profits and losses, interest payments, property rights, and whether *zakat* adequately combats poverty. Some Muslim economists seek to ease traditional religious restrictions on financial transactions. They believe that minimal government interference in the market is best for economic development. Other Muslims favor a stronger policy to redistribute wealth. They oppose what they consider the inequalities and excesses of Western capitalism.

Islamic Financial Institutions. Islamic economic institutions have existed since the days of Muhammad. The Bayt al-Mal, or treasury, controlled tax collection and administration. It also managed the caliph's* finances, established programs for the poor, funded maintenance of roads and public buildings, and performed certain banking functions. In the 1800s, Islamic governments established agencies to manage *waqf** transfers.

Western institutions appeared in the Muslim world in the late 1800s, when colonial powers set up agencies to oversee economic functions. In many areas, new laws affected only dealings with foreigners and did not alter practices among Muslims. In Egypt, the British established special courts for non-Muslims that dealt with payment defaults* and deceitful trade practices. These courts generally ignored Islamic law when deciding such matters, and the Egyptian government finally abolished them after the revolution of 1952.

As Western economies became more complex in the second half of the 1900s, Muslim governments responded by creating many new economic institutions. Islamic states formed ministries to oversee planning, oil production, industry, tourism, and other activities.

Islamic financial institutions combine aspects of modern banking with religious principles. Because many people interpret the Qur'an as forbidding the charging of interest, banks charge membership fees instead. They issue debit cards, but not credit cards. Patrons may share in the bank's profits from investments if they are also willing to share the risks involved. Thus, bank members will profit if the bank makes money on its investments and lose if the bank investments fail.

Economic Development and Reform. Throughout its history, the Islamic world has experienced both poverty and prosperity. The past two centuries have brought great changes to Muslim economic development. Islamic nations vary widely in their level of wealth.

Islamic communities began to amass wealth in the 600s, reaching the peak of their prosperity during the Middle Ages*. By the 1100s, the Muslim world had begun to fall into a state of economic decline, a process halted by the rise of the Ottoman and Mughal Empires in the 1500s. In the late 1700s, however, Islamic economies sank once again. The Industrial Revolution in Europe and the United States helped Western nations strengthen their productive capabilities. Meanwhile, Islamic economies stagnated as Europe

* **secular** separate from religion in human life and society; connected to everyday life

* **caliph** religious and political leader of an Islamic state

* **waqf** donation of property for charitable causes

* **default** failure to repay a debt

* **Middle Ages** period roughly between 500 and 1500

flooded the world with mass-produced goods. By the early 1900s, Western powers had colonized many Muslim countries and had replaced their economic institutions with European ones.

As Islamic nations gradually won their independence from European domination, their economies changed. Independent Islamic governments took a more active role in their economic growth, promoting new industries, improving taxation procedures, and expanding banking practices. Using European technology and investment dollars, Muslim countries improved their infrastructures*. New ports, railroads, power sources, and irrigation systems were constructed. The building of these facilities, however, brought a high level of debt to the region. Muslim countries could not afford to repay their European lenders.

* **infrastructure** basic facilities and institutions that a country needs in order to function

The Islamic world currently consists of wealthy, middle-income, and poor nations. Many Muslim economies combine state ownership and central planning with free enterprise. Strong local banks that finance trade and investments characterize countries with solid economies. Wealthy nations include the oil-rich states of Kuwait, Saudi Arabia, Qatar, and Libya. Iran, Turkey, Albania, and Malaysia comprise the middle category, while Afghanistan, Egypt, Nigeria, Pakistan, and Bangladesh remain among the poorest nations in the Islamic world.

Islamic economies had grown slowly until World War II (1939–1945), when demand for oil soared. The petroleum industry brought significant economic development to Islamic countries. To increase their importance, these nations formed the Organization of Petroleum Exporting Countries (OPEC) in 1960. By 1970 Muslim nations were producing over 40 percent of the world's oil, as opposed to only 8 percent in 1940. Oil exports brought tremendous profits to the OPEC nations. The leaders of the oil-producing nations began spending money on technology, infrastructure development, and public services. Some Arab nations also began to invest in foreign markets.

The oil boom had a few financial drawbacks, however. Several Muslim nations neglected other areas of their economies. Agricultural production declined, and leaders lacked incentives to develop new industries. In the 1970s, OPEC raised the price it was charging for crude oil, driving Western nations to seek other oil sources. By 1991 OPEC's share of world production fell to 30 percent. Oil prices dropped, reducing the income of many Muslim states. Islamic nations scrambled to diversify their economies.

International Organizations. In the late 1900s, Muslims created economic institutions that reach out to Muslims internationally. Several Islamic organizations operate within the United States. These promote financial planning and business dealings between Muslims. They help Muslim immigrants maintain their religious values while fitting into mainstream capitalist societies.

The Organization of the Islamic Conference (OIC), for example, has over 50 member states. Islamic nations established the OIC in 1969 to promote economic solidarity. It seeks to unify efforts to protect the interests of Muslims worldwide. The OIC founded the Islamic Development Bank in 1973 to help impoverished Muslim nations and Muslims in non-Islamic countries. It works to prevent exploitation and to promote the efficient management of resources. (*See also* **Banks and Banking; Charity; International Meetings and Organizations; Mawdudi, Sayyid Abu al-Ala; Modernism.**)

Saudi Arabia's Oil Economy

The kingdom of Saudi Arabia has the largest oil reserves in the world, with the petroleum industry providing around 75 percent of national revenues. Since the mid-1990s, however, fluctuating oil prices have hurt the Saudi economy. Moreover, water shortages and a rapidly increasing population have increased Saudi reliance on agricultural imports. These developments, combined with a rise in government spending on education and social programs, left Saudi Arabia with a budget deficit in 2002. The Saudi government has taken steps to reduce its dependence on oil exports and to attract foreign investors.

Education

Education in the Islamic world varies considerably by country. Most Muslim schooling focuses at least in part on the transmission of Islamic traditions and values and on the use of the Qur'an* as a guide for public and personal behavior.

History

The Qur'an refers to education as the shaping of character in accordance with Islamic principles. The first Islamic communities mainly promoted the recitation of the Qur'an. During the late 900s, institutions of higher learning emerged to teach other subjects, such as Islamic law and the sciences. Western colonial* powers invaded Muslim countries during the 1800s and the early 1900s, altering educational systems and influencing many leaders to implement Western-style changes. In the early twenty-first century, many Islamic countries sought a return to a more traditional religious school curriculum.

Reading, Writing, and the Qur'an. Muslim educational systems had begun to emerge within a century after the death of the Prophet Muhammad. During the early years of Islam, children attended elementary schools called *kuttab.* Some also studied in groups in homes, mosques, libraries, and bookshops. The *kuttab* curriculum consisted mainly of reading, writing, and the recitation of verses from the Qur'an. Teachers emphasized memorization over analysis and interpretation. Arabic was the language of instruction, and because most students did not speak Arabic, this method of teaching did little to foster comprehension. Students learned the verses in that language by rote. To the disapproval of conservative* religious leaders, girls sometimes attended *kuttab*, and a few became teachers or scholars themselves.

During the 700s and 800s, older children and adults had opportunities to engage in advanced studies, and some selected a master to guide them in their moral and intellectual development. As in many other cultures, in both elementary and in higher learning, teachers had the right to administer corporal punishment, such as beatings. Many Muslims considered such measures essential for the formation of good character, and some adult students frequently received severe forms of discipline.

For students of all ages, mosques played a central role in the educational process. In many places, mosques operated informal schools, offering instruction on Islamic practices and theology*. Nearly all of these schools focused on the Qur'an. Some taught the basics of Islam and required students to learn verses; others dealt with more advanced topics of study.

Knowledge Base. Islam benefited from the learning of the past, especially the legacy of the ancient Greek civilization. The caliph* al-Mamun (ruled 813–833) founded an academy to translate works of science, philosophy, and medicine from Greek to Arabic. Muslims also made significant contributions in a range of academic disciplines. Andalusia, the southernmost region of Spain, was for several centuries the cultural center of the Muslim empire in the West. It attracted the leading scientists and scholars of the day. They made notable contributions to the fields of chemistry,

* **Qur'an** book of the holy scriptures of Islam

* **colonial** refers to the taking of land by a more powerful nation

* **conservative** person generally opposed to change, especially in existing political and social institutions

* **theology** study of the nature and qualities of God and the understanding of His will

* **caliph** religious and political leader of an Islamic state

Young Muslim women attend school in Algeria. Although their schooling still lags behind that of men and boys, increasing numbers of women and girls are gaining access to education.

medicine and surgery, mathematics, and philosophy. Christians and Jews studied with Muslims at the university of Córdoba, founded in 968. The Fatimid dynasty established al-Azhar, a mosque-university, in 978, and it remains one of the world's oldest institutions of higher learning. Between the 1000s and 1200s, Islam played an important role in the development of Western civilization by preserving and transmitting the learning of the ancient Greeks and made its own contributions in education as well.

Madrasahs. By the 1000s, many Muslim communities provided more formal schools intended for older students. Known as *madrasahs*, these schools functioned as residential colleges, replacing the mosque schools. They did not offer grades or degrees, nor did they have written examinations, grade levels, classrooms, graduation ceremonies, or desks. Students and teachers did not occupy fixed roles; those who studied in one class could teach in another, depending on the level of knowledge they had in a particular subject.

The Nizamiyah, founded in Baghdad, served as the first *madrasah*. Similar schools quickly spread across much of the Muslim world. Most emphasized *shari'ah**, or Islamic law, and applied it to the various subjects. Topics of study included theology, Arabic grammar, hadith*, and interpretation of the Qur'an. Many *madrasahs* also included secular* subjects, such as astronomy, medicine, geography, and literature. Teachers fostered dialogues between themselves and their students rather than enforcing rote learning. Women could not attend *madrasahs*, but a few studied the same subjects with private tutors.

Western Influence. After Napoleon invaded Egypt in 1798, and Western powers colonized other parts of the Muslim world, Islamic leaders began to adopt Western educational models in an attempt to modernize their

* **shari'ah** Islamic law as established in the Qur'an and sunnah, the exemplary behavior of the Prophet Muhammad

* **hadith** reports of the words and deeds of Muhammad (not in the Qur'an, but accepted as guides for Muslim behavior)

* **secular** separate from religion in human life and society; connected to everyday life

countries. They opened secular universities, recruiting instructors from Europe. They also established schools for naval and army engineering, Western medicine, civil administration, veterinary science, and other fields. Printing presses published translations of Western textbooks. At the same time, Muslim students began traveling to Europe to study at Western universities.

The Western presence in the Islamic world brought about changes in elementary education as well as in higher learning. Turkey, Egypt, and several other countries broadened the courses of study offered in at least some of their schools. Teachers de-emphasized memorization of the Qur'an and gave secular subjects a more important place in the curriculum.

Although European powers established schools for the children of the colonizers, they did not wish to grant Muslims access to the same level of education. Instead, they opened schools that would train the local population to become clerks and technicians who would help carry out the needs of the colonial regimes*. While European powers allowed *madrasahs* to operate, they gave these and other religious schools less funding and prestige than Western-supported programs. Students who attended religious schools had a disadvantage in the job market, as well. For these reasons, traditional religious education withered in many Muslim cities.

Because European nations interfered very little with some Islamic nations, such as Saudi Arabia, the Western influence affected some regions more than others. Moreover, while schools in the larger cities made changes, those in more remote and rural locations retained their traditional educational systems.

See color plate 13, vol. 1.

* **regime** government in power

Recent Trends

Many Islamic nations combine traditional religious principles with Western subjects and teaching methods. In many major cities, schools at all levels have the resources to attract good teachers and supply students with updated textbooks, laboratory equipment, and computers. Renowned Muslim universities include al-Azhar in Cairo, the University of Tehran in Iran, the Islamic University in Medina, Saudi Arabia, and the University of Indonesia in Jakarta.

Lacking Resources. Despite the success of some universities, many Islamic countries lack the resources to support their educational systems. In 1991 only about one-fourth of children in Bangladesh attended school, for example, and in the late 1980s, literacy rates in Oman and Senegal stood at 20 percent and 10 percent, respectively. Many primary school teachers are unqualified, having only a secondary school education and lacking knowledge of effective teaching techniques.

In many schools, teachers discourage students from asking questions or offering their ideas in discussions or in writing. To indicate mastery of the material, students often simply repeat lessons back to the teacher, which hinders the development of critical thinking skills needed for advanced study. Lack of modern learning materials and textbooks also hampers schools in some countries. Turkey, however, has made great strides in promoting education. An "Open University" broadcasts classes on television, and teachers receive instruction in subject matter and educational methods. Other countries have taken measures to acquire computers for their classrooms.

The education of women and girls still lags behind that of men and boys. Many schools are segregated by sex, and, in some areas, girls cannot continue their education beyond the elementary grades. Moreover, women who have the opportunity to continue in higher education may have to overcome the objections of friends or family, as well as consider the possibility that men may not want to marry them. Nevertheless, women and girls in many Muslim countries are rapidly gaining access to education.

Islamization. Since the mid-1900s, many Islamic leaders have called for a departure from secularism and a move toward a traditionally religious approach to schooling. This movement, often called Islamization, has taken shape from the ideas of conservative Muslims who see current Islamic societies and governments as heretical* and morally questionable. They believe that the reintroduction of religious schools will help reform society and lead to a greater emphasis on Islam in public life.

The movement toward Islamic schooling has succeeded in some countries. Beginning in 1980, for example, Iran abolished almost all traces of secularism in universities. The new regime fired professors who held secular or Western ideas, segregated the sexes, and required female students to wear traditional Islamic clothing. Similarly, courses of study changed as educators began teaching all subjects from an Islamic perspective. The reforms allowed for a greater emphasis on Islamic studies in general and on the Qur'an in particular. Moreover, the segregated system has provided more opportunities for women to receive higher education. In 2002 women comprised about one-half of the university students in Iran.

Other countries have not taken much initiative toward reform. This is especially true in countries that have diverse religious populations, such as Indonesia. Many Muslim-dominant nations, however, retain a secular system of education. In some of these countries, the Islamization movement has only led to minor changes in the schools.

In recent years, however, the call for Muslim academic reform has grown louder. Many Muslim states, for instance, have opened new universities that follow traditional principles. Their names, which usually contain the word *Islamic,* suggest their educational slant and purpose. Some Muslims applaud these changes. Others worry that this way of schooling will undo some of the progress they believe Muslim education has made during recent years. (*See also* **Azhar, al-; Madrasah; Universities.**)

Muslim Education in the West

Many Muslim parents in the United States, Canada, and western Europe seek ways to give their children an Islamic education. Public schools in these places often have policies, such as coeducation or a dress code for students, that make some Muslims uncomfortable. In addition, they fail to include Muslim values or the teachings of the Qur'an in the curriculum.

As a result, Muslims, like the members of other religious communities, have opened their own schools in Western countries. Some children attend private schools that combine studies of secular subjects with those of Islamic values, the Arabic language, and the Qur'an. Other children participate in after-school religious programs. In the United States, some Muslims send their children to Sister Clara Muhammad Schools, named after the wife of Elijah Muhammad, former leader of the Nation of Islam.

* **heretical** characterized by a belief that is contrary to established religious doctrine

Egypt

Home to one of the first civilizations in human history, Egypt has experienced a wide variety of religious influences. After Muslim armies conquered Egypt in the 600s, Islam became the force that shaped Egyptian life.

History

Throughout its history, Egypt has endured frequent invasions accompanied by changes in religious traditions and practices. Although the Muslims en-

* **secular** separate from religion in human life and society; connected to everyday life

* **Sunni** refers to the largest branch of the Muslim community; the name derives from sunnah, the exemplary behavior of the Prophet Muhammad

* **B.C.E.** before the Common Era, which refers to the same time period as B.C.

tered the region as yet another conquering force, Islam took root slowly in Egypt. The religion has inspired many changes in political and secular* traditions and has become the predominant faith among Egyptians. By the 1990s, around 90 percent of Egypt's inhabitants were Sunni* Muslims.

The Ancient Period. In ancient Egypt, rulers called pharaohs controlled religious and political life. Egyptians considered them to be directly related to the gods. In 525 B.C.E.*, however, the Persians invaded Egypt and dethroned the pharaohs. The Egyptians strongly disliked their conquerors, and welcomed Alexander the Great when he arrived with Greek and Macedonian armies nearly 200 years later. Alexander took control of Egypt without a fight and showed respect for the people's religious traditions. Ptolemy, one of Alexander's generals, took control of Egypt following Alexander's death in 323 B.C.E. Ptolemy's descendants ruled the region until Rome conquered the country nearly 300 years later. Egypt remained a part of the Roman Empire throughout the period when the Eastern Roman Empire evolved into the Byzantine Empire. During the period of Roman-Byzantine rule, Egypt became a Christian society with its own distinctive Coptic tradition.

* **C.E.** Common Era, which refers to the same time period as A.D.

Muslim Dynasties Emerge. Muslim forces captured Egypt in 642 C.E.*, possibly aided by those who were opposed to Byzantine rule. Initially, Islamic rulers did little to alter everyday life of the Egyptians. Arabic did not replace Greek as the official language of Egypt until the 700s. Muslims made no attempt to convert the Egyptians. They respected other religions and pledged to protect the Christian churches. Jews and Christians even served in the government under certain rulers. Non-Muslims, however, had to pay higher taxes than Muslims, even after they converted to Islam, which many people did.

Despite Muslim tolerance, turmoil occasionally erupted in Egypt during Islamic rule. Tribesmen and Coptic Christians sparked rebellions against the Muslim government. The largest uprising occurred in 829/830. The caliph* al-Mamun led an army from Iraq into Egypt to crush it. Afterward, Muslims imposed repressive measures on the Coptic Christians. Many Christians converted to Islam during this time.

* **caliph** religious and political leader of an Islamic state

In the centuries following the Muslim conquest, a series of Islamic dynasties emerged to control Egypt and other countries in the region. These included the caliphates* of the Umayyads, the Abbasids, and the military rule of the Tulunids and the Ikhshidids. In 969, the Fatimid dynasty took over Egypt, establishing itself as a rival to the Abbasid caliphate of Baghdad. The Fatimids ruled until the 1100s, when Abbasid forces regained control. Saladin, the Kurdish general who reconquered Jerusalem from Christian crusaders, was appointed to rule Egypt. Saladin founded the Ayyubid dynasty in Egypt. A century later, Turkish Mamluks, whom the Egyptians had imported as slaves to serve in their armies, rose to high positions in the government and slowly took control. After almost three centuries of Mamluk rule, the Ottomans conquered Egypt and most of the rest of the Arab world.

* **caliphate** office and government of the caliph, the religious and political head of an Islamic state

During the Ottoman Empire, Egypt served as a military, financial, and religious center. Cairo became one of the major cities in the Islamic world, and al-Azhar, the mosque-university founded by the Fatimids in the late 900s, prospered as a center of Islamic learning. Islamic religious scholars known as *ulama* gained economic and political stature and helped to maintain peace between Egyptians and their Ottoman rulers.

 See map in Middle East (vol. 2).

Over time, Islamic rule brought significant changes to Egypt. The succession of dynasties brought various forms of Islam to Egypt as the majority of Egyptians gradually converted from Christianity to Islam. The first Muslim conquerors brought Sunni, or orthodox, Islam to Egypt. The Fatimid rulers outlawed this faith in favor of Shi'i practices, but it returned during the reign of Saladin. Sufism* also gained in popularity among Egyptian Muslims. Sufis emphasized the power of love and the heart over intellectual teaching. Sufi leaders gained a large following. Although the *ulama* tried to persecute the Sufis, they reluctantly accepted Sufism when it became apparent that they could do little to diminish its popularity.

* **Sufism** Islamic mysticism, which seeks to develop spirituality through discipline of the mind and body

Colonial Era

Foreign powers invaded Egypt in the 1800s. For the first time in over a thousand years, the conquerors had no ties to Islam. The new regimes* disrupted Islamic culture and practice, and Egyptian Muslims realized that resistance would require superior strength and significant changes on their part.

* **regime** government in power

European Intrusion. By the third century of Ottoman rule, Egypt had fallen into disarray. Attempting to maintain such a large empire, the Ottomans had neglected Egypt and other Arab centers. Economic conditions declined while government corruption increased. In 1798 Napoleon Bonaparte of France led his armies into the region, where they remained and ruled for three years. Egyptian Muslims realized they could no longer count on the Ottoman military for protection. Religious leaders supported a military officer of Albanian origin named Muhammad Ali, who took the position of Ottoman governor in 1805. Muhammad Ali sought to transform Egypt into a modern state, embracing Western technology and developing centers of industry. He promoted education and social programs. Muhammad Ali tried to weaken the influence of Islam, however, turning on the *ulama*, whom he considered a hindrance to progress.

British Rule Begins. As Muhammad Ali's reforms increased Egypt's military and industrial strength, Britain began to perceive Egypt as a threat. The British government sent a naval force to Egypt. Unable to match Britain's strength, Muhammad Ali signed the Treaty of London in 1840. He agreed to reduce the size of his army and disband Egypt's war industries. Muhammad Ali's defeat increased the importance of Islamic religious scholars in Egypt, as people looked to them for guidance during trying times.

Having halted Egyptian industrialization, Britain moved to exploit the region economically. To support their textile factories, the British redirected Egypt's economy to cotton farming. Laborers suffered, and the local government became more corrupt. Egypt fell into debt to foreign nations. To protect their investment, the British established direct military rule over Egypt in 1882.

Resistance and Reform. Colonial rule led to economic and political chaos in Egypt and disrupted the traditional practices of many Muslims. In the late 1800s, the scholar Jamal al-Din al-Afghani became a leading advocate for Muslim resistance. He sought reform through modern ideas, stating that the principles of science, reason, and liberal* government did not vio-

* **liberal** supporting greater participation in government for individuals; not bound by traditions

143

late Islamic teachings. His actions and ideas inspired popular support for the resistance.

In the 1880s, an army officer named Ahmad Urabi led a military campaign for internal reform in Egypt. After the government arrested him, Urabi's followers continued the fight. Calling for an "Egypt for Egyptians," they demanded a new government with a constitution. Al-Afghani and his disciple Muhammad Abduh, supported the cause, as did many religious scholars. The British military, however, crushed the uprising and sent al-Afghani and Abduh into exile.

When Abduh returned, he focused his energies on social reform and modernization. As an educator, he worked to modernize the courts and the universities. As a senior legal officer, he promoted women's rights and modern banking practices in Egypt. Colonial influence, however, disrupted his campaign. An elite class, loyal to Britain, had emerged and had stripped power from the *ulama* and from Abduh.

* **inflation** sharp rise in prices due to an increase in the amount of money or credit relative to available goods and services

* **nationalist** one who advocates loyalty and devotion to his or her country and its independence

At the end of World War I (1914–1918), food shortages and inflation* gripped Egypt. A nationalist* movement emerged in the country, and Egyptians rose up in armed rebellions and strikes. The British loosened their control but did not give it up completely. They declared Egypt an independent monarchy in 1922.

Despite secular reforms, some Muslim leaders in Egypt still believed that a return to traditional Islam would lead to prosperity. In 1928, schoolteacher Hasan al-Banna founded the Muslim Brotherhood. This organization promoted Islamic ideals and rejection of Western influence. The movement quickly spread to other countries and gained popularity due to poor economic conditions throughout the Islamic world.

Al-Banna believed that colonizers had undermined the Islamic community and weakened Muslims spiritually. He wanted to rebuild Muslim life at the political, economic, and cultural levels. The Brotherhood initiated social programs that reached a large segment of the population. Al-Banna's organization also began a political campaign and launched attacks against British forces. By the 1940s, the Muslim Brotherhood in Egypt had more than 500,000 members and many supporters.

Modern Egypt

In 1952 the Muslim Brotherhood supported a revolt against British rule, and, two years later, Britain agreed to withdraw from Egypt. The end of colonial rule, however, did not bring religious harmony. Egyptians still argued about the role of Islam in modern life.

A New Leader. Aided by the Muslim Brotherhood, Gamal Abdel Nasser emerged as Egypt's new leader. In a move similar to that of Muhammad Ali, Nasser turned on his religious allies. He believed that the Muslim Brotherhood presented a threat to his leadership, and he drove it underground. Although Nasser did not oppose Islam, Egypt became more secular during his regime. The president emphasized a modern, socialist* agenda over religious rule.

* **socialist** refers to socialism, the economic system in which the government owns and operates the means of production and the distribution of goods

The Brotherhood continued to criticize Nasser for his lack of direction. One of their leaders, Sayyid Qutb, called for Muslims to take up arms against the government. Nasser ordered his execution and attempted to crush his Is-

A large crowd cheers Egyptian president Gamal Abdel Nasser after he announced he had taken over the Suez Canal Company in 1956.

lamist movement. In 1956, after Nasser tried to nationalize the Suez Canal, Israel (with support from Britain and France) invaded Egypt and occupied the Sinai Peninsula. Under pressure from the United States, Israel withdrew and Nasser's popularity soared. In the 1960s, however, Nasser faced a deep financial crisis, and, in 1967, Israel inflicted a humiliating military defeat on Egypt in the Six-Day War, taking occupation of the Sinai Peninsula. Support for Nasser gradually disappeared.

A Peacemaker Takes Over. Nasser died in 1970, and the following year, Anwar el-Sadat became Egypt's president. The emphasis on Islam rebounded and the Muslim Brotherhood returned to prominence. The group lacked a strong leader, however, and separated into moderate and militant factions. The moderates promoted charitable work and social action, such as building mosques and schools. The militants pursued change through political campaigns.

Although Sadat had an alliance with the Brotherhood, it unraveled in the late 1970s, especially after he signed a peace treaty with Israel in 1979. Many in the Muslim Brotherhood felt betrayed by his seeming support for Israel. They believed that Sadat had sacrificed larger Muslim goals for political interests. Sadat's popularity in Egypt fell, and in 1981, Islamic militants assassinated him.

Mubarak Succeeds. After Sadat's death, Hosni Mubarak succeeded to the presidency. He sought to reconcile the government with the moderate elements of the Muslim Brotherhood. Islam gained a greater official presence in Egypt as prominent Muslims gained seats in parliament and held positions in newspapers and publishing houses. Mosques expanded their functions to offer medical and social services at low prices, attracting a larger number of followers.

Peace With a Price

Soon after the founding of Israel in 1948, many Arab nations joined Egypt in opposition to the Jewish state. This solidarity remained strong for several decades. Then, in 1977, President Sadat traveled to Israel to begin peace talks with Prime Minister Menachem Begin. In 1979 President Jimmy Carter of the United States invited the two leaders to Camp David to help them resolve long-standing conflicts between their two nations. After heated debate, Sadat and Begin signed a historic treaty, ending a 30-year state of war. The following year, Anwar Sadat and Menachem Begin shared the Nobel Peace Prize for their courageous action. Although he gained international praise, Sadat had angered the Arab world. Egypt regained the Sinai Peninsula from Israel but suffered isolation from its former allies for years.

145

* **radical** favoring extreme change or reform, especially in existing political and social institutions

Radical* militant Muslims, however, still posed a threat to Egyptian stability. Led by members of the elite, these groups drew followers from the lower and middle classes. Although they lacked a unified agenda, radical groups often used violence to achieve their goals. Several factions sought to undermine Mubarak's administration and take over the government.

In the 1990s, a group called the New Islamic Current emerged in Egypt. Referring to themselves as the New Islamists, they advocated a reform agenda promoting democracy and pluralistic* ideals, such as respecting the rights of Egypt's several million Christians. The New Islamists attracted leading intellectuals and gained support from the general Muslim population.

* **pluralistic** refers to a condition of society in which diverse groups maintain and develop their traditional culture or special interests

Since the 600s, Islam has strongly influenced Egypt's history. Islamic intellectuals, political leaders, and ordinary citizens continue to search for ways to modernize the nation within Muslim traditions. (*See also* **Abduh, Muhammad; Afghani, Jamal al-Din al-; Fatimid Dynasty; Muslim Brotherhood**.)

Eid al-Adha

* **Qur'an** book of the holy scriptures of Islam

Eid al-Adha—the Feast of the Sacrifice—is Islam's most important annual festival. It commemorates the critical test of Abraham's faith. According to the Qur'an*, God ordered Abraham to sacrifice his son (identified as Ismail in Islamic tradition and as Isaac in Judaism) as an offering. When God saw that Abraham was prepared to obey the command, He intervened and substituted a ram. The celebration of this event begins on the tenth day of the twelfth month (Dhu al-Hijjah) when Muslims offer an animal sacrifice. Eid al-Adha is one of the ceremonies that pilgrims observe on the hajj*, but Muslims worldwide also enjoy this holiday.

* **hajj** pilgrimage to Mecca that Muslims are required to make once in their lifetime

Islamic law outlines the procedures that Muslims must follow during the feast. The animal to be sacrificed—a sheep, camel, goat, or cow—must be unblemished. Only an adult man, who can afford to pay for such an animal, can perform the ritual. The person slaughtering the animal must ensure that it is facing Mecca and then quickly cut its throat. Islamic law suggests that he should keep only one third of the meat for his own family and share the rest with the poor and other families.

Although the Feast of the Sacrifice commemorates a solemn occasion, the mood during Eid al-Adha (also called Eid al-Qurban) is cheerful and social. Muslims say special prayers during Eid al-Adha, and many families visit the graves of loved ones during the celebration. Families also visit friends and other relatives. Gifts and sweets are an important part of the celebration. Non-Muslim neighbors are often invited to join the activities surrounding the festival. (*See also* **Abraham; Dietary Rules; Fasting; Food and Feasts; Ismail**.)

Eid al-Fitr   See *Food and Feasts*.

Elijah Muhammad

1897–1975
Leader of the Nation of Islam

For more than 40 years, Elijah Muhammad (formerly Paul Robert Poole) was the leader of the Nation of Islam, a militant religious group that promoted the formation of a separate nation for African Americans. Born on a farm in Georgia in 1897, Poole moved to Detroit as a young man. In the early 1930s, he met Wallace Fard Muhammad, the leader of a black liberation movement called the Nation of Islam. Poole joined the movement and changed his name to Elijah Muhammad.

Although he had only a third-grade education, Elijah Muhammad quickly rose through the ranks of the organization. After Fard disappeared in 1934, Elijah Muhammad became the leader of the Nation of Islam. Under Elijah Muhammad's guidance, the Nation of Islam sought to address the problems of African Americans by helping them to develop economic independence and self-esteem. Over the next 40 years, black Muslims, as they were called, established more than 100 temples and numerous grocery stores, restaurants, and other small businesses nationwide. Elijah Muhammad's message of a separate black nation appealed to thousands of African Americans.

Despite his success, Elijah Muhammad was a deeply controversial figure. He taught his followers that blacks were superior to whites. The leaders of the civil rights movement in the United States argued that this philosophy endangered race relations during a critical period in U.S. history. The Muslim world also opposed Elijah Muhammad's teachings because the Nation of Islam was a separatist organization, not a community of believers. Furthermore, many black Muslims did not observe the five pillars, the cornerstone of Islamic practices. Toward the end of his life, however, Elijah Muhammad began to change some of the doctrines of the Nation of Islam to align them with traditional Muslim beliefs. Following his death, his son and successor, Warith Deen Muhammad, completed this process and transformed the movement into a more mainstream Islamic organization. (*See also* **Farrakhan, Louis; Malcolm X; Nation of Islam; Pillars of Islam; Warith Deen Muhammad.**)

Ethics

Ethics is a broad concept that refers to principles of right and wrong. People use ethics as a guide for one's own behavior and for evaluating the actions of others. Islamic moral codes, like all religious moral codes, stress the relationship between human beings and God. Muslims believe that moral standards come from God, and that they are therefore timeless and universal and should govern a person's conduct in all areas of his or her life.

Muhammad believed that morals develop with physical and mental maturity. In a hadith*, he stated that the actions of a minor go unrecorded by God until he or she reaches puberty. Muslim scholars believe that the soul develops in three stages. In the first stage, *ammara*, a person inclines toward

* **hadith** reports of the words and deeds of Muhammad (not in the Qur'an, but accepted as guides for Muslim behavior)

evil behavior which, if not controlled, leads him or her to spiritual ruin. An individual in the second stage, *lawwama*, recognizes evil, asks for Allah's forgiveness, and seeks to reform. In the third stage, *mutma'inna*, the intellect overcomes all evil tendencies and leads the soul to a state of contentment. A Muslim's *taqwa*, or piety, determines the stage that he or she reaches. Those who persist in unethical behavior lack *taqwa* and remain in the first stage.

Classical Discussions. Muslims have debated ethics for centuries. In the 1200s, for example, many scholars studied the "science of virtue." They focused on issues related to personal character and the cultivation of such traits as wisdom and tolerance. They tried to determine the feelings and thoughts that a "good" person would have, as well as the actions he or she would perform. Some scholars wrote about the ideals that they believed should guide such practices as politics, medicine, and business. They typically presented their views in the form of a story or a letter of advice to someone entering a particular field.

Three disciplines dominated classical Islamic discourse on ethics. Scholars developed the first *falsafah*, or philosophy, in the 900s. Early Muslim writers, such as Abu Nasr al-Farabi, viewed philosophy as a quest for personal excellence in moral character and intellect. Al-Farabi believed that anyone with enough intelligence and wealth could embark on this journey. Wisdom would come through deep contemplation and years of inner struggle. Unlike the Prophet Muhammad, who learned truth through divine inspiration, the philosopher toils to gain an understanding of moral law.

* **theological** refers to the study of the nature, qualities, and will of God

The second classical discipline, *kalam*, attempted to clarify religious teachings and took a theological* approach to ethics. Scholars in this field studied the nature of judgment. They stated that people make moral judgments by assigning praise to some and blame to others for various actions, and they thought that God's moral law provides the basis for such judgments. Some believed that God gave humans the capacity to choose between good and evil. Others, however, suggested that both moral or unethical actions occur according to God's will, and that humans can know the difference between good and evil only by reading and interpreting texts such as the Qur'an*.

* **Qur'an** book of the holy scriptures of Islam

The field of *fiqh* also includes discussion of ethics. *Fiqh* deals with law and the principles on which laws are based. Some scholars studied how people could understand and follow divine guidance. They considered the Qur'an and sunnah* the most important sources for comprehending God's law. They also described methods of reasoning, such as the use of analogy*, that could promote Islamic ideals and balance the notions of duty with concern for the general welfare.

* **sunnah** literally "the trodden path"; Islamic customs based on the exemplary behavior of Muhammad

* **analogy** comparison based on resemblance

Modern scholars routinely draw from earlier theories when writing about morality. Muslim *fiqh* scholars often make legal judgments based on precedents, or examples, set by medieval* ethicists. Their work sometimes reflects a dialogue between themselves and a scholar of the past. Shi'i and Sunni scholars both rely on precedents when deciding an ethical matter. Shi'i Muslims, however, place a greater emphasis on reason. They believe that a person can learn God's views on moral issues through rational thought.

* **medieval** refers to the Middle Ages, a period roughly between 500 and 1500

Medical Ethics. Ethics has many important applications in the Islamic world. It plays a prominent role in Muslim medical practice. Islamic medical codes dictate that a Muslim physician must believe in God and seek God's support. Doctors must maintain the same ethical standards in their private as well as their professional lives, and they must follow Islamic teachings both in the home and at work. A physician who lacks morals in his or her private life is considered unfit for professional practice, no matter what qualifications the individual has. The Qur'an encourages Muslim doctors to display humility, patience, and tolerance.

Muslim ethical codes impact medical practices in a variety of ways. For example, doctors must treat all those in need regardless of race or ability to pay. This practice reflects the Qur'an's call to care for and feed the poor with no thought of reward. Islam further holds that physicians do not have the right to take a human life. Doctors may not perform abortions unless the mother's life is threatened, and they may not practice euthanasia, or assisting in the death of a chronically ill person for reasons of mercy. Islamic ethics also concerns physical examinations of patients of the opposite sex. In such cases, the physician should seek the presence of a third party, if possible.

Muslim doctors must also follow ethical codes in their interactions with other physicians. Doctors may not accept payment for treating a colleague. They should avoid criticizing each other in front of patients or staff. Finally, Muslim doctors have a duty to study current medical research and to comply with the legal codes governing their profession.

Business Ethics. Ethics is an important part of Islamic business transactions. Islam teaches that Muslims have a duty to rise above corruption, despite the actions of others. Islamic law emphasizes fairness for consumers. Vendors must not sell defective merchandise. According to a hadith, an individual described as Allah's Messenger (Muhammad) forbids the sale of unripe fruits. If an individual purchases an item that does not have the advertised properties, he or she may cancel the sale.

Muslim businesses must conduct their operations in an ethical manner, and avoid racial discrimination. The Qur'an warns against engaging in businesses that conflict with Islamic values, such as those that promote gambling or drinking. When dealing with people in debt, professionals must consider that debt often drives a person to commit unethical actions, and treat the debtor with leniency. Debtors must also attempt to make timely repayments of their debts. (*See also* **Farabi, Abu Nasr al-; Medicine; Philosophy; Theology.**)

Ethics and Politics

After taking power in Iran in 1979, Ayatollah Ruhollah Khomeini became a symbol of oppression to many in the West. Among Shi'i Muslims, however, he was well-known for his teachings on government and ethics. Regarding the latter, he taught that prayer and spiritual discipline reveal God's mercy and goodness. With faith, a person comes to understand God's nature and moves away from sin. Khomeini believed that people have the potential to commit great good or great evil. He held that following Islamic values directs one to the pursuit of virtue and justice. Khomeini believed that a government should promote Islamic spiritual practice to help its citizens realize their potential for doing good.

Europe

Islam is currently one of the largest and fastest growing religions in Europe. Over 18 million Muslims live on the continent. Western Europe and southeastern Europe each contain about 9 million Muslims. Smaller Islamic communities have formed in many other European nations, such as Poland and Finland. France has the largest Muslim population in Europe. The 5 million Muslims in that country outnumber both Protestants and Jews.

Conquest and Reconquest. Islam has maintained a presence in Europe for over 1,300 years. In the 700s, Muslim armies conquered Spain along with parts of southern France and southern Italy. Around the 1100s, Christian armies from the West began driving the Muslims back. Initially, Christian rulers executed Muslims taken captive in battle. They later decided to sell Muslim war prisoners as slaves.

While Christian conquerors treated Muslim soldiers harshly, some allowed Muslims to practice their religion. This tolerance ended in 1492 during the Spanish Inquisition, when the Spanish monarchs launched a campaign to drive Muslims out of western Europe. Christian authorities persecuted both Muslims and Jews, and many people converted to avoid violence or death. The inquisitors, however, forced them to flee to North Africa. By the 1600s, few Muslims remained in western Europe.

In the 1400s, the Ottoman Turks expanded their Islamic empire into the modern Balkan states in southeastern Europe, which include Bosnia and Albania, among others. Ottoman forces occupied the Balkan Peninsula and pushed as far north as Vienna. Islamic rule inspired many conversions and established a strong Muslim presence in southeastern Europe. Its influence remained strong until the twentieth century, when nationalist movements sought to eject Muslims from the region. After World War II (1939–1945), communist rule further suppressed Islam in the Balkans.

Mass Migration. As the Muslim community dwindled in southeastern Europe, Islam became a major presence in western Europe. Muslims began migrating to Europe in the early 1900s, and their numbers increased after World War II. Muslims came to western Europe looking for work or as refugees. Many came to the continent from the former European colonies. Muslims who had cooperated with colonial regimes* moved to avoid retribution from the newly independent Muslim governments. For example, France accepted thousands of Algerian subjects after granting Algeria its independence in 1962.

Immigrants from the Islamic world poured into western Europe in the 1960s and 1970s. The growing European economies at that time needed cheap labor, and Muslims filled that need. Many moved to Europe to rejoin family members who had immigrated earlier. White-collar migrants and skilled laborers from former colonies established communities in France and the Netherlands. Students from Islamic countries came to study at European universities. After graduating, some decided to remain on the continent. More recently, a large number of Muslims moved to Europe to avoid political persecution. The Muslim population has also grown through the addition of converts, many of whom are European women married to Muslims.

Muslim communities in western Europe consist primarily of unskilled laborers, merchants, and lower-level office workers, although there are many college-educated Muslims who work as doctors or other professionals. Perhaps because Islamic communities in the Balkans have existed longer than those in western Europe, Muslims are spread more evenly through all levels of Balkan society.

Building Mosques. Islamic institutions are more firmly established in southeastern Europe than in western Europe. Only recently have Muslims in western Europe moved beyond renting a building for a temporary place of worship. With the help of national and international Islamic organizations, Muslim communities in western Europe have established permanent reli-

* **regime** government in power

gious institutions. In France, for example, Muslims support over a thousand mosques and prayer rooms.

The mosque is typically the center of Muslim community life. In addition to their traditional religious purposes, mosques serve a variety of social functions. European mosques are centers of religious education. About 15 percent of all Muslim children in western Europe receive regular religious instruction at a mosque. European Muslims also use mosques for weddings, funerals, and other social events. In Islamic countries, these ceremonies do not normally occur within the mosque. In addition, western European mosques sponsor sports, recreation, and youth activities. Some of these mosques contain shops that sell religious items and books.

A board of governors typically presides over a mosque. Board members oversee finances and maintenance. They also handle interactions with the surrounding non-Muslim society. For this reason, the governors must be familiar with the language, laws, and social customs of the host country. The board members also appoint the imam* of the mosque.

* **imam** spiritual-political leader in Shi'i Islam, one who is regarded as directly descended from Muhammad; also, one who leads prayers

Few Muslims in western Europe qualify for the position of imam. Governors' boards usually recruit them from the community's country of origin. Imams thus serve as the primary custodians of the religious and cultural values of the home country. They perform a wide range of spiritual and social duties. These include leading prayer services, counseling community members, performing ceremonial tasks, and conducting religious education. Imams in western Europe assume additional duties in the absence of other Islamic leaders, such as visiting Muslims in hospitals and prisons. Imams in Europe perform functions similar to those of a pastor or a rabbi, and Muslims in southeastern Europe have developed training centers for imams. Muslims in western Europe have worked to establish such schools, but their progress has suffered because of internal disagreements.

Promoting Muslim Interests. A variety of Islamic organizations seek to promote Muslim interests in Europe. They often compete with each other for influence in the local mosque communities. In the 1970s, European Muslims began to create organizations to oversee the mosques in their countries. These groups, however, sometimes came into conflict with the governments of their countries of origin. In response, some Islamic nations, such as Turkey and Morocco, created their own organizations to supervise the religious operations abroad. Other Muslim countries, such as Tunisia, make no effort to interfere with their former subjects in Europe.

Several international organizations have also sought to influence religious life in western Europe. A number of these groups, such as the Muslim World League, have established Islamic Centers in major European capitals. Muslim governments generally control these organizations through diplomatic representatives. Saudi Arabia plays a particularly active role in the operation of such organizations. International groups often struggle with local organizations for the loyalties of Muslims living in western Europe.

Fitting In. The experience of Muslims living in Europe has varied. Some actively seek to fit into their new country and embrace the dominant culture of their new home. Others seek acceptance while maintaining their traditional beliefs and practices. Still others reject assimilation* completely. They strive to maintain a separate Muslim identity within a foreign land.

* **assimilation** process of adapting s culturally to the larger population

Hope Amidst Calamity

The recent Yugoslavian civil war led to some of the worst atrocities ever experienced by Muslims living in Europe. The troops of Serbian leader Slobodan Milosevic murdered and raped tens of thousands of Muslim civilians living in Bosnia, Croatia, and Kosovo. NATO bombing destroyed much of Serbia's capacity to wage war. The alliance deployed troops to keep the peace and to protect the Muslim population in the region. In 2001 the Yugoslav government turned Milosevic over to the International Court of Justice in the Hague to stand trial for war crimes. Many Europeans and Americans, outraged by the attack on the Muslim community, showed their support by donating money to restoration projects.

* **ideology** system of ideas or beliefs

Muslims on the continent of Europe are generally free to practice their faith. In most nations, Muslims may take unpaid vacation days to celebrate their religious holidays. The European Commission on Human Rights has stated that a Muslim employee should have the right to attend Friday services if he informs his employer of that necessity. Except in Greece, however, European governments do not recognize Islamic law. Muslims may voluntarily abide by Islamic rules and set up their own religious courts for such matters as marriage, divorce, and inheritance, but these institutions have no validity in state courts.

Rights and Restrictions. Restrictions of religious rituals vary from country to country. For example, many nations allow Muslims to slaughter animals in accordance with Islamic law. Switzerland and Sweden, however, forbid this activity. Most western European countries allow Muslim girls to wear headscarves in the public schools. The French government, on the other hand, banned the practice until 1996. Since then, France and Belgium allow the governors of the schools to decide on the issue of headscarves.

European nations also vary in the civic rights they extend to Muslims. France and Germany, for example, withhold citizenship and voting rights from most Muslims. Great Britain, in contrast, grants full citizenship rights to Muslims who once lived in its former colonies, and some Muslims have been elected to political office.

Some European states extend official recognition to the Muslim community and to other religious groups. In Spain, for example, the Comisión Islámica de España (CIE) serves as the official representative of Muslims. It seeks to promote relations between Muslims and Spanish society at large. The CIE handles a host of issues including religious education; religious rights of soldiers, prisoners, and patients; and dietary rules.

Discrimination Continues. Government recognition has not always ensured the societal acceptance of Muslims. Many Europeans feel uneasy about the Muslims living among them. Events such as the 1973 Arab oil embargo, the September 11, 2001, attacks on the United States, and bombings committed by radical Algerian groups in Paris add to such feelings. Stereotyping by the media has further promoted negative opinions about Muslims, although many newspapers have printed articles detailing the history and peaceful aspects of Islam.

Although events in the Middle East have caused a surge of interest in Islam, groups promoting intolerance have gained in popularity in western Europe. Extremists promote racist ideologies* and blame Muslims for their country's problems. Some politicians, who welcomed immigrants in good economic times, now blame them for taking jobs from European citizens. Hate crimes and violence against Muslims have increased, with mosques and other Muslim-owned buildings as key targets. Some European politicians fear that supporting Muslim rights will erode their popular support. French presidential candidate Jean-Marie Le Pen advocated the expulsion of three million immigrants from France; support for his party, the National Front, continues to grow.

Muslims in southeastern Europe have faced even worse persecution. Religious and ethnic tensions have divided the region for decades. In the 1990s, civil wars broke out in Yugoslavia when Bosnia, Croatia, and Kosovo declared their independence from central government control. Forces from Serbia carried out a brutal campaign against Muslims in those regions. After heavy bloodshed, the North American Treaty Organization (NATO) sent a multinational force to end the massacre. (*See also* **Albania; Bosnia; Great Britain; Kosovo.**)

Family

The family is the foundation of Islamic society. It not only shapes a person's morals and ethics, but also his or her identity, determining social class, political affiliations, and cultural practices. The family also serves as the primary source of economic and emotional support. Despite the pressures of a rapidly changing world, family retains a central place in the lives of many Muslims.

History of the Islamic Family. Before the rise of Islam in the early 600s, Arabian families lived in a patriarchal, or male-dominated, society. The duty of a man was to support and protect his family, and the responsibility of a woman was to fulfill the roles of wife and mother. Children took their father's name and inheritance was passed down through the male relatives. Men considered women to be property, and no limitations on polygyny* existed. The practice of female infanticide—the killing of infant girls—was also widespread.

    Islam brought some changes to the structure of the family, particularly with regard to the status of women. The Qur'an* recognized women as human beings with legal rights and responsibilities, and it gave them the same

* **polygyny** practice of having more than one wife at the same time

* **Qur'an** book of the holy scriptures of Islam

Family has always been an important element of Islamic life. In this recent photo, an Iraqi family gathers during Ramadan, the holy month of fasting, to eat the traditional post-sundown meal.

Muslim Teens in America

The appeal of American popular culture poses a challenge for Muslim parents living in the United States. They expect their children to follow Islamic principles in both their private and public lives. Muslim teens, however, note the obvious discrepancy between the freedom that their non-Muslim peers enjoy and the restrictions parents place on their activities. While some Muslim teens attend public high schools, many are not permitted to date or to participate in certain social activities. These prohibitions are more strictly enforced for girls than for boys. To offset the frustration that might result from such limitations, some schools have started Islamic clubs. National organizations also sponsor opportunities for Muslim teens to meet others of their faith.

religious duties that men had. Furthermore, a woman could accept or reject a marriage partner. Infanticide was prohibited. Issues affecting the family, including marriage, divorce, and inheritance, became central to Islamic law, which was developed in the 700s and 800s.

Functions of the Family. In Western countries, the term *family* generally refers to a nuclear family consisting of one or two parents and their children. The word for *family* in Arabic, *ahl* or *ahila*, encompasses the nuclear family but may also include grandparents, uncles, aunts, and cousins.

The most important responsibility of the Muslim family is to guide children to an understanding of Islam. At the birth of an infant, the father whispers two prayers into the baby's ears. The infant is given a name, which may be derived from those of the prophets, their wives, or their companions, or may reflect an attribute of God. For example, the name Abd al-Aziz means "servant of the Almighty." Seven days later, a ceremony known as the *aqidah* takes place. The baby's head is shaved, and in traditional society, a sheep or goat is sacrificed. The meat is distributed among the poor, relatives, and neighbors. Through this ritual, the family expresses gratitude to God and happiness for the birth of a child. The family instructs the child in the traditions of Islam and celebrates various rites of passage that mark the transition to adulthood.

Islam encourages Muslims to marry and produce children. Marriage is a contract that the groom enters into with the bride or the bride's legal guardian. In a traditional Arab family, the father expects obedience from his wife and children. On a daily basis, the mother has the responsibility for caring for and disciplining the children. Islamic family law permits a man to have as many as four wives if he can provide for them equally. A husband has the power to divorce his wife without her consent and without legal proceedings. By contrast, a wife's right to end a marriage is restricted, but the laws differ from country to country.

Family loyalty is very important. Muslims are expected to place the family's well-being and reputation above their own desires and needs. In return, the family provides employment opportunities, financial and emotional support, shelter and care for the elderly and disabled, and education.

Effects of Colonialism. When Europeans took political control of Islamic areas in the late 1700s and early 1800s, they attempted to impose Western values on the people in the newly formed colonies. Their efforts backfired, and the Islamic family became a social, cultural, and religious refuge for its members. Eventually, the family became the focus of anticolonial resistance. Opposition groups emphasized Islamic religion and culture in the face of a common enemy—Western political and economic power with anti-Islamic goals.

Challenges to the Family. Since the 1950s and 1960s and independence from colonial rule, the state and other institutions have challenged the position of the family as the primary socioeconomic unit. Governments are assuming greater control of the economy, education, and employment opportunities in most Arab countries. As a result, many people have moved from rural areas to urban centers for vocational training and job opportunities.

Economic and political problems also threaten traditional family ties. High rates of unemployment have forced millions of men to relocate to Europe and elsewhere to search for work. The rising cost of living has caused women to take jobs outside of the home. Wars have also disrupted family life.

Despite these changes, the Islamic family is not disintegrating. In places where the family unit has been dispersed due to war, natural disaster, or economic need, the values and functions of the family have reemerged in different forms. Newcomers to a city make connections through family members. Young men living abroad, for example, often find jobs in the same factories or businesses as their sisters, cousins, or other relatives. Many Muslim men join religious brotherhoods or other groups in which they feel like one of the family. Women whose husbands work abroad often form close relationships with neighbors.

During the 1900s, some Muslim governments tried to address the inequality between husband and wife in Islamic family law. The rulers of the Ottoman Empire passed legislation that gave women certain rights to file for divorce. Many governments established a minimum age for marriage. Tunisia, Turkey, and Syria abolished polygyny. Nevertheless, the trend toward a strict interpretation of Islamic principles has substantially limited reform of family law in many Muslim countries. (*See also* **Divorce; Marriage; Rites and Rituals; Women; Women and Reform.**)

Farabi, Abu Nasr al-

870–950
Arab scholar

A prominent intellectual, Abu Nasr al-Farabi became known in Muslim countries as the second father of philosophy (after Aristotle), the father of Islamic logic, and the father of political science. He grew up in a small village near Farab in Turkistan, a region of Central Asia. Al-Farabi became a *qadi* (judge), but abandoned his profession to move to Baghdad in 901, where he taught and devoted himself to a life of learning.

Al-Farabi mastered numerous languages during his academic career. He became an expert in science, medicine, mathematics, music, and poetry, as well as other subjects. His achievements caught the attention of the amir* of Aleppo, who made him a member of his inner court.

* **amir** military commander, governor, or prince

Al-Farabi became best known for his philosophical writings. He believed that philosophy and prophecy are essentially the same. Prophecy, however, comes in bursts of divine revelation, while philosophy involves years of intense study. Al-Farabi prized reason above enlightenment, stating that it enabled people to perceive truth in its purest form. Religious scholars strongly opposed al-Farabi's ideas, and the prominent legal scholar Ibn Taymiyyah issued a fatwa* banning the study of philosophy.

Al-Farabi wrote over 100 books on a wide variety of topics. He made many contributions to the field of logic and political philosophy. One of his most famous books describes the properties of the "virtuous city," in which citizens share and protect their resources. Al-Farabi valued peace, and believed that conflict between states reflected a lack of philosophical thought in government. Scholars consider al-Farabi one of Islam's greatest philosophers. (*See also* **Ethics; Philosophy.**)

* **fatwa** opinion issued by Islamic legal scholar in response to a question posed by an individual or a court of law

Farrakhan, Louis

1933–
Black Muslim leader

* **calypso** style of music that originated in the West Indies

* **Sunni** refers to the largest branch of the Muslim community; the name derives from sunnah, the exemplary behavior of the Prophet Muhammad

* **mosque** Muslim place of worship

Louis Farrakhan heads the Nation of Islam, a militant religious group in the United States that promotes the development of African American society. Its primary goal is to develop economic independence and pride among African Americans. Although Farrakhan's sharp criticism of American society has provoked controversy, his leadership has enabled the Nation of Islam to gain visibility and support.

Born in the Bronx, New York, in 1933, Louis Eugene Wolcott was raised by his West Indian mother in Boston. After attending Winston-Salem Teachers College for two years, he worked as a calypso* singer and guitarist. In 1955 Malcolm X recruited Wolcott to the Nation of Islam, a black nationalist movement led by Elijah Muhammad. Wolcott later received the Muslim name Abdul Farrakhan and served as an apprentice to Malcolm X.

In 1964 Malcolm X left the movement and converted to Sunni* Islam. Farrakhan denounced his former teacher and became the national representative of the Nation of Islam and the head minister of its mosque* in Harlem, a largely African American neighborhood in New York City. He established a newspaper, *Final Call*, to build the group's following.

After Elijah Muhammad died in 1975, the black Muslim movement split. Farrakhan's group retained the name of Nation of Islam and the organization's focus on African American unity and independence. Farrakhan promoted the development of black-owned businesses and family values. Under his leadership, the Nation of Islam helped fight crime and drug abuse in urban ghettos.

Louis Farrakhan taught that whites, especially Jews, were responsible for the oppression of African Americans. His views came under public scrutiny

Louis Farrakhan, current head of the Nation of Islam, has long been an outspoken proponent of African American unity. Although his negative views toward whites and the United States have caused much controversy, Farrakhan's supporters praise his work to rid urban ghettos of crime and drug abuse.

when, during the 1984 presidential campaign, Farrakhan drew a firestorm of criticism from Jewish voters after he praised Adolf Hitler, the German leader who ordered the killing of six million Jews during World War II.

In 1995 Farrakhan attracted media attention for his role in organizing the Million Man March in Washington, D.C. Seeking to reform America's image of black men, he called for African American men to gather at the nation's capital to show their unity and support for family values. Jews and Christians protested Farrakhan's involvement in the march. He also drew opposition from African American women, who were excluded from the event. Despite the disapproval, Farrakhan's stature grew after several hundred thousand men participated in the march.

Farrakhan's supporters regard him as a hero for helping the disadvantaged. To his opponents, he is racist, sexist, and violent. Some even consider him a traitor for his friendship with Libyan dictator Mu'ammar al-Qaddafi and other militant Islamic leaders and for his verbal attacks on the U.S. government. With the persistent growth of urban poverty, Louis Farrakhan's message continues to strike a responsive chord among some segments of African American society. (*See also* **Elijah Muhammad; Malcolm X; Nation of Islam.**)

Fasting

Fasting is a common practice in many religions. It generally refers to the voluntary abstention from eating for a period of time. Islamic tradition encourages numerous days of fasting. The most important fast, during the month of Ramadan, is one of the Five Pillars of Islam (obligations required of all healthy adult Muslims) and lasts an entire month. Other fasts include Ashura, a day-long fast similar to the Jewish Day of Atonement, and a six-day fast during Shawwal, the month after Ramadan. Expiatory fasting, or *kaffarah*, is fasting that atones for sins or for neglecting one's duties. Some Muslims also choose three additional fast days each month or fast on Mondays and Thursdays.

The Qur'an* instructs all Muslims to participate in the great fast of Ramadan, the ninth month of the Islamic calendar. During this period, Muslims abstain from food and drink each day from dawn to sunset. The month is an occasion for spiritual reflection, prayer, and discipline. Muslims at this time thank Allah for their blessings and for forgiving their sins. The great fast is also a special time to respond to the needs of the poor.

During Ramadan, Muslims awaken before sunrise to eat their first meal of the day. They do not eat or drink again until after sunset. At dusk, Muslims eat a light meal. Later in the evening, families often gather together to share a larger meal.

Muslim countries have developed a variety of local customs connected to Ramadan. In many parts of the Islamic world, the fast is a festive time. Communities often decorate their streets with lights and ornaments. In some areas, Muslims serve special foods that are not eaten any other time of the

* **Qur'an** book of the holy scriptures of Islam

year. During the last ten nights of the month, Muslims commemorate the Night of Power, when Muhammad received God's revelation. At the end of Ramadan, Muslims hold a great celebration, the Festival of the Breaking of the Fast (Eid al-Fitr). In some countries, this three-day celebration is a national holiday. Family members and friends gather to exchange gifts and eat heartily.

Islamic law excuses certain people from the Ramadan fast. Those exempted include children younger than adolescents, the sick, the elderly, travelers, and women who are pregnant, nursing, or who have just given birth. As they have done for centuries, Muslim legal authorities still issue judgments on the subject of fasting. Many of their rulings concern issues related to modern life, such as whether receiving inoculations or intravenous medication breaks the fast.

Muslim societies strongly encourage participation in the Ramadan fast. In countries ruled by Islamic law, breaking this fast can result in punishment. These penalties differ from country to country and have included verbal reproaches, floggings, and fines. (*See also* **Dietary Rules; Food and Feasts; Pillars of Islam; Ramadan.**)

Fatimah

ca. 605–633
Daughter of Muhammad

Fatimah, daughter of the Prophet Muhammad and wife of Muhammad's cousin Ali ibn Abi Talib, is revered among Muslims for her religious devotion and exemplary life. Born in Mecca around 605, Fatimah was one of the six children of the Prophet and his first wife Khadija, and she was the only child who produced a line of descendants.

Fatimah accompanied her father on his flight from Mecca to Medina in 622. Soon afterward she married Ali. Fatimah bore two sons, al-Hasan and Husayn ibn Ali, and two daughters, Zaynab and Umm Kulthum.

After the Prophet's death, the Muslim community faced disagreement about who should succeed him as caliph*. The majority followed Abu Bakr, but Fatimah supported Ali's claim to this position. In 656, more than 20 years after Fatimah's death, Ali was elected fourth caliph of the Muslim community. He is considered to be the first imam* of Shi'i Islam. Muslims who follow the Shi'i tradition believe that the succession of imams must come from the Prophet's own descendants, and they refer to Fatimah as the "Mother of the Imams."

Unlike the Prophet's third wife A'ishah, who took an active role in political affairs, Fatimah lived a relatively quiet life, spending her time fulfilling her domestic duties. Muslims honor Fatimah for her virtue and consider her a model daughter, wife, and mother. Indeed, many believe that she lived a life without sin. Fatimah died just a few months after her father. She is the only woman included among the Fourteen Perfect or Pure Ones in Shi'i tradition. Her descendants went on to found the Fatimid dynasty (909–1171). (*See also* **Ali ibn Abi Talib; Caliph; Fatimid Dynasty; Husayn ibn Ali; Muhammad.**)

* **caliph** religious and political leader of an Islamic state

* **imam** spiritual-political leader in Shi'i Islam, one who is regarded as directly descended from Muhammad; also, one who leads prayers

Fatimid Dynasty

The Fatimid dynasty*, members of the Ismaili sect of the Shi'i* Muslims, rose to power in North Africa in 909. Although they eventually extended their control as far as Iraq, they failed to achieve their goal of destroying the Abbasid caliphate*. The Fatimid dynasty ended in 1171.

From the beginning, the Fatimids sought to end the power of the Abbasids. Claiming to be descendants of the Prophet Muhammad through his daughter Fatimah, they believed that they alone held the right to rule the Islamic community. At first, revolutionary Ismaili ideas spread to parts of North Africa through a network of secret cells. Ismailis established a mission in Yemen, and in 893 launched a propaganda* campaign among Berber* tribes in the mountains of Algeria. These tribes, traditionally hostile to the Aghlabid governors appointed by the Abbasids, joined the Ismaili cause. They defeated the Aghlabids in 909 and proclaimed a new Fatimid state. The first Fatimid caliph, al-Mahdi, founded a new capital at al-Mahdiyah in Tunisia. For the first 50 years of their reign, the Fatimids held power in North Africa and Sicily. Internal and external conflicts, however, preoccupied the new rulers. They faced troubles with neighboring Muslim rulers and with rebellious Berber tribes. In addition, they had taken over regions that were involved in a war against the Byzantines* in Sicily and Italy. Despite these challenges, the Fatimids launched three expeditions in the early 900s to take control of Egypt. Although these early efforts failed, in 969 Fatimid armies succeeded in conquering the Nile Valley. They went on to the Sinai region and through Palestine to southern Syria. The Fatimids built the city of Cairo, which became their capital, and moved the caliphate there, establishing themselves as rivals of the Abbasid caliphate in Baghdad.

In Egypt, the Fatimids established a court that was renowned for its splendor and for its military and naval power. At its peak, the Fatimids controlled North Africa, Sicily, the Red Sea coast of Africa, Syria, Palestine, Yemen, and the holy cities of Mecca and Medina. In addition, the Fatimid caliph presided over a network of missionaries* who operated in lands still under Abbasid rule. These missionaries sought to convert Sunnis* to the Ismaili faith and encouraged revolution against the Abbasids. The Fatimids expanded trade between Red Sea ports and Asia, and they even sent missionaries as far as India.

Between 1057 and 1059, the Fatimids succeeded in taking power in Iraq after a dissident* general changed sides and decided to support the Fatimid caliph. Yet the Fatimids were not able to provide military backing for his movement, and the Seljuk Turks expelled him from Baghdad. From that point on, the Fatimids struggled to maintain power. Political dissent in Egypt, along with economic problems brought on by drought, plagues, and famines, weakened support for the Fatimid regime. The Crusades* also contributed to the decline of the dynasty. Because Muslims needed to maintain a unified front against the invading crusader armies, the radical* ideas of the Ismaili sect were seen as a threat to Muslim unity. By the reign of al-Mustansir (reigned 1036–1094), Egypt was enveloped in violence and political turmoil.

In 1073 the Fatimid caliph invited Badr al-Jamali, an able military commander, to enter Cairo and bring order to the city. In one night, his forces

* **dynasty** succession of rulers from the same family or group

* **Shi'i** refers to Muslims who believe that Muhammad chose Ali ibn Abi Talib and his descendants as the spiritual-political leaders of the Muslim community

* **caliphate** the office and government of the caliph, the religious and political head of an Islamic state

* **propaganda** information presented in a way to influence people or further a cause

* **Berber** refers to a North African ethnic group that consists primarily of Muslims

* **Byzantine** refers to the Eastern Christian empire that was based in Constantinople

* **missionary** person who works to convert nonbelievers to a particular faith

* **Sunni** refers to the largest branch of the Muslim community; the name derives from sunnah, the exemplary behavior of the Prophet Muhammad

* **dissident** disagreeing, especially with an established political or religious system

* **Crusades** during the Middle Ages, the holy wars declared by the pope against non-Christians, mostly Muslims

* **radical** favoring extreme change or reform, especially in existing political and social institutions

massacred all of the leading generals and city officials. Badr al-Jamali assumed military, religious, and administrative power. He restored order and improved the economic situation. When the caliph al-Mustansir died in 1094, Badr's son al-Afdal chose his successor. Rejecting al-Mustansir's own choice of his elder son, Nizar, al-Afdal picked the weaker younger son, Ahmad. Most of the Ismaili mission refused to accept this new caliph and broke off relations with Cairo. A new Ismaili movement under Hasan-i Sabbah, known as the Assassins, arose and declared its support for Nizar. By 1130 civil war consumed the entire Fatimid state. The last four caliphs had little power or influence. After the death of the last caliph in 1171, Saladin, who had emerged as the new power in Egypt, seized control, and the Fatimid caliphate formally ended. (*See also* **Assassins; Caliphate; Egypt; Ismaili.**)

Fatwa

* **theology** study of the nature and qualities of God and the understanding of His will

A fatwa is a formal legal opinion issued by an Islamic legal scholar, or mufti. The scholar usually gives a fatwa in response to a question from an individual. Muftis base these decisions on their interpretations of *shari'ah*, or God's law. Fatwas cover a broad range of issues, including theology*, law, and philosophy. Though not legally binding, fatwas often influence judges in their decisions.

Muftis and Their Role. Muftis are usually private individuals of high moral character and intellectual ability. Some have held official public positions and have formally advised courts. Some muftis receive salaries from the state, while others go unpaid, accepting gifts and support from *mustaftis*, or questioners.

* **Qur'an** book of the holy scriptures of Islam

* **sunnah** literally "the trodden path"; Islamic customs based on the exemplary behavior of Muhammad

When issuing fatwas, muftis cite the Qur'an*, the sunnah*, or another accepted authority. They should never allow personal opinion to bias their responses and should consult other scholars if they are unsure about an issue. *Mustaftis* come from all levels of society, and include men, women, laborers, scholars, and heads of state. Questioners typically accept their fatwa if it seems competent and based on tradition. Fatwas of the highest caliber contain detailed examples of *ijtihad*—formal, reasoned, interpretation. Occasionally, a mufti will issue a fatwa on his own initiative.

Muftis and the practice of issuing fatwas stemmed from the need of the early Islamic community to learn and to follow Muslim principles. Before the development of universal schooling and literacy, only a few people studied the Qur'an and related texts. Muftis served as spiritual guides for both the people and the state, and established Islamic law as a unifying force. They ranged from local scholars who issued informal fatwas to powerful officials who influenced public policy. Some people had to travel to find a mufti, and others had to choose among several. Those dissatisfied with a response could seek out a second fatwa, and people embroiled in a dispute often questioned different muftis. Opposing sides in court sometimes bring competing fatwas to support their cases. Muftis have even engaged each other in "fatwa wars" over larger doctrinal issues.

Form and Content. Muftis nearly always issue fatwas in written form. Many go unrecorded, written directly on the slip of paper containing the question. More elaborate fatwas exist in archives or in published collections. They vary in length from single word responses to book-length treatises. They also vary in scope. A minor fatwa may deal with the application of a single law. A major fatwa could legitimize a nation's new economic policy. Other fatwas deal with such issues as contracts, punishments, rituals, and foreign rule.

The way in which a question is worded strongly affects the answer. Many *mustaftis* wrote questions to highlight certain facts or to elicit a particular response. During the Ottoman Empire, officials revised questions so that muftis could answer them with brief statements. Questions should pertain to actual events and not hypothetical situations. *Mustafis* should omit personal names and locations, making the questions as generic as possible.

Fatwas from different regions vary according to language, conventional formulas, and rhetorical* style. Treatises suggest proper wording for openings and closings, stock phrases such as *Allahu a'lam* (God knows best) that appear at the end of most fatwas, and special terms of address. They also discuss the organization of the texts and advise against leaving blank spaces to avoid alteration or addition.

* **rhetorical** refers to rhetoric, the art of speaking or writing effectively

Muftis have issued fatwas for a variety of reasons. During the Ottoman Empire, for example, fatwas sanctioned declarations of war and peace, as well as domestic reforms and laws on such subjects as taxation and criminal justice. The legitimacy of the sultan* also hinged on the advice of muftis. A fatwa led to the deposition of Sultan Murad V in 1876 on the grounds of insanity. Fatwas also encouraged religious tolerance. When the Ottomans questioned Sufi* practices, muftis confirmed the legitimacy of Sufi music and dancing while condemning the intolerance of critics.

* **sultan** political and military ruler of a Muslim dynasty or state

* **Sufi** refers to Sufism, which seeks to develop spirituality through discipline of the mind and body

During colonial times, fatwas became important tools for mobilizing the population. They defined Islamic territory and advised Muslims when to wage war against unbelievers and when to emigrate from a seized land. In 1891 an Iranian mufti prohibited smoking for as long as the British had the monopoly on tobacco. In the late 1930s, the Muslim Brotherhood of Egypt and other groups published leaflets demanding that every Muslim fight a jihad, or holy war, for Palestine. In Iran, Ayatollah Khomeini issued the most famous fatwa in recent times, calling for the execution of author Salman Rushdie in 1989 for his book, *The Satanic Verses*, which Khomeini considered an attack on Islam.

Modern print and electronic media has greatly widened the potential impact of fatwas. These decisions exert a strong influence on public and legal matters throughout the Islamic world, and Muslims continue to rely on muftis for spiritual guidance. (*See also* **Ijtihad; Justice; Law; Religious Scholars.**)

Food and Feasts

Customs involving food and feasts serve as an important part of most religions. For Muslims, following Islamic dietary rules and restrictions and participating in religious celebrations serve as acts of worship that help to unify the Islamic community.

The feast of Eid al-Fitr, one of the most widely observed Islamic celebrations, marks the end of fasting during the holy month of Ramadan. Thousands of Muslims gather in Strasbourg, France, for an Eid al-Fitr celebration, shown here.

* **Qur'an** book of the holy scriptures of Islam

* **hadith** reports of the words and deeds of Muhammad (not in the Qur'an, but accepted as guides for Muslim behavior)

Rules and Customs. In Islam, acceptable food and drinks are referred to as *halal*, meaning lawful; impure products are *haram*, or prohibited. Both the Qur'an* and hadith* provide guidelines to indicate which foods and drinks are classified as *halal*. Muslim scholars refer to the Qur'an and other traditional sources to decide whether certain dietary practices agree with Islamic law.

According to the Qur'an, God forbids the eating of pigs, blood, animals found dead, and animals over which the slaughterer invokes any name other than Allah (God). The Islamic holy book also prohibits the consumption of alcohol and foods sacrificed to idols. Muslim teaching further bans the eating of dogs, reptiles, carnivorous mammals, insects, and rodents. It urges Muslims to avoid eating animals that have not been slaughtered according to Islamic law. Moreover, believers may not consume foods that contain substances designated as *haram*. Examples include gelatin, which typically contains pig parts, and vanilla, which is extracted with alcohol.

Cows, sheep, and chickens must be slaughtered according to *halal* regulations, which call for slitting the throat of the animal with a sharp instrument and the draining of the blood before the head is removed. The name of Allah should be recited over the animal. Some Muslims play a taped recording of the Qur'an.

In addition to providing food guidelines, the Qur'an also encourages Muslims to eat a nutritious, balanced diet. It recommends a selection of beef, fowl, fish, grains, milk, fruits, and vegetables. The Qur'an further calls on Muslims to avoid waste and excess when eating. Muhammad extolled the benefits of moderation. He cited the belly as an individual's worst weakness. To help Muslims avoid gluttony, he taught that they should stop eating before they became full. He recommended filling one-third of the stomach with food and one-third with water, leaving the last third empty.

Muhammad also delivered rules for proper eating etiquette. He stated that, before eating, Muslims should wash their hands and praise Allah. They should eat using only their right hand. At the end of each meal, Muslims should give thanks to God and praise God for the food, the ability to swallow it, and the ability to allow it to exit. He entreated Muslims to wash their hands after meals.

Over the years, Muslims have addressed many questions regarding their dietary regulations. Islamic scholars do not always agree on certain issues. For example, some traditionalists believe that Muslims should not eat food prepared by Christians or Jews. Reform-minded scholars, however, allow this practice, stating that Christians and Jews are People of the Book and that the Qur'an permits marriage among the groups. Islamic authorities also disagree on whether Muslims should take medications that contain traces of alcohol or other forbidden substances. Most hold that patients may take such drugs only if they need them in order to survive and have no recourse to substitutes. Scholars also ponder whether Muslims may work in places that serve alcohol, whether they may attend events involving intoxicating beverages, and whether they may serve alcohol to their non-Muslim guests.

Setting Muslims Apart. Since the religion's founding, Islamic teachings about food have served a variety of functions. For example, Muhammad used dietary rules to help distinguish Muslims from Arabia's many warring tribes and to help unite them in faith. In places like India with strict social castes, Muslims of all classes ate together and followed the same customs. This practice reinforced their sense of community. Though influenced by Hebrew law, Islamic dietary customs also set Muslims apart from Jews. The Qur'an's ban on alcohol serves as the most profound distinction. (Jewish people use wine in many rituals and feasts.)

Muslims believe that their religion's teachings on food result in physical benefits, which in turn aid in spiritual development. For example, the balanced diet recommended by the Qur'an promotes growth, strength, and healing. Fully removing the blood from a slaughtered animal decreases the amount of harmful bacteria the meat may contain. Following Muhammad's teaching on moderation reduces health problems related to obesity. Moreover, the Prophet's rules promote hygiene and combat the spread of disease.

Celebrating Religious Occasions. In addition to observing various dietary practices, Muslims use food to celebrate holidays. Religious gatherings form an important part of Islamic worship, and feasts serve as major components of most Islamic festivals. Such events promote a sense of community as Muslims gather with family and friends.

The two most widely observed feasts are the Feast of the Breaking of the Fast of Ramadan (Eid al-Fitr) and the Feast of Sacrifice (Eid al-Adha). The former begins with the first sighting of the moon on the last day of the Ramadan fast and lasts for three days. Before the festivities, Muslims make contributions to charitable organizations. During this festival, school is cancelled. Muslims serve special foods and sweets to their guests and give gifts to the children. The final day of Eid al-Fitr involves great feasting and celebration.

The Feast of Sacrifice takes place at the end of the hajj—the annual pilgrimage to Mecca—and is observed by both pilgrims and nonparticipants. During this three-day holiday, Muslims commemorate Abraham's faith in God when God commanded him to sacrifice his son. Muslim families sacrifice an unblemished animal and consume one-third of the animal's meat dur-

Ramadan Feasting

Although many see Ramadan as a time of fasting, it involves many food traditions. After sundown, Muslims recite a short prayer, then break their fast with dates in the manner of Muhammad. This begins a night usually spent visiting friends or socializing in cafes. Regardless of their activities, many Muslims hold an *iftar* (evening meal) involving such courses as lentil soup, apricot juice or other fruit drinks, stuffed grape leaves, chicken with rice, and savory pastries. After completing a prayer, Muslims enjoy tea and sweets such as *qatayef,* fried pancakes stuffed with cheese or walnuts and dipped in syrup. Muslims also participate in *suhour,* a meal taken before dawn. *Suhour* may include sweet tea, porridge, fruit, eggs, bread with olive oil, and unsalted cheeses.

ing the feast. They give the rest to the poor. Muslims who do not make the hajj visit mosques and the graves of their ancestors instead. As with Eid al-Fitr, they also visit relatives, exchange gifts, and eat sweets.

Muslims observe many other feasts as well as the two major ones. Newly wedded couples hold a *walimah,* or wedding feast, attended by family, friends, and neighbors. The feast of Mawlid an-Nabi celebrates Muhammad's birthday. On Lamu Island off the Kenyan coast, *mawlid* serves as the main holiday of the year and involves week long Qur'an recitation competitions. Muslims hold another feast on the Night of the Middle of Sha'ban, the month before Ramadan. Muhammad taught that, on this night, God records each person's actions for the coming year, as well as who will be born and who will die. During Ramadan, Muslims celebrate the Night of Power, the night on which Muhammad received the teachings of the Qur'an, with a feast. Many believe that God forgives their sins on this night.

Foods and feast traditions serve as an integral part of religious life for Muslims around the world. The faithful go to great lengths to ensure that the food they buy at stores and at restaurants does not contain *haram* substances. Supermarkets in the United States increasingly sell meat slaughtered according to Islamic law. North Carolina, a state that raises chickens for sale, exports *halal* birds to some Muslim countries. In areas of the United States with small Muslim populations, Islamic lobbyists continue to press for a greater availability of food prepared in accordance with Islamic dietary guidelines. (*See also* **Abraham; Calendar, Islamic; Dietary Rules; Eid al-Adha; Fasting; Ramadan.**)

Fundamentalism

Fundamentalism generally refers to an uncompromising devotion to a particular faith. Originally, *fundamentalism* was the term applied to a specific Christian experience, especially strong in the United States, which developed in response to modernism in the 1800s. Fundamentalism, however, has since formed a part of every major faith in response to problems associated with modernization. The fundamentalists of some religions believe in the literal and absolute truth of their holy scripture. They reject alternative views of their religion and fear that secular, or nonreligious, forces will weaken or eliminate their faith. To avoid this, they stress the traditional elements of their religion.

Generating Controversy. Use of the term *fundamentalist* to describe some Muslim groups is controversial. Some say that the term connotes ignorance and backward thinking, and as such, is insulting to legitimate Islamic reform movements. Others argue that there is no exact translation for the term in Arabic or other major Muslim languages. By the 1980s, however, Arabic writers began to use the term *usuliyah,* a new Arabic word that is based on the Arabic term *usul,* which means "fundamentals."

Roots of Islamic Revivalism. Throughout history, Islamic activist movements have promoted a return to the fundamental principles of their religion. The call for revival took on a special sense of urgency in the 1800s when European powers colonized much of the Islamic world, bringing Western influences to the region. Many Muslims perceived colonial rule as a threat to the survival of their faith.

In the late 1800s, reformers Jamal al-Din al-Afghani and Muhammad Abduh established the Salafi, a movement to reform and renew Muslim life. Both men believed that rigid traditionalism had obscured the original message and was responsible for the decline of Islam. Advocating that reform was necessary to counteract European dominance, they adapted traditional Islamic teachings to modern life, reshaping Muslim education, law, and politics. Salafi principles spread to many Muslim nations in the 1900s.

Modern Islamic Revivalism. Reformer Sayyid Qutb (1906–1966) is considered the founder of the modern Islamic revivalist movement. He called on Muslims to actively fight against secularism, and a religious resurgence swept across the Islamic world in the 1970s. The movement drew support from diverse segments of society, ranging from illiterate and unemployed people to well-educated professionals. Following Qutb's advice, many Muslims withdrew from mainstream society, returned to traditional styles of dress, and became more devoted to prayer and fasting.

The term *fundamentalist* has been applied to a wide array of Muslim people, groups, and governments in recent times. Saudi Arabia's so-called fundamentalist government is pro-Western, while in Sudan, the fundamentalist movement supports distinctly anti-Western views. In Afghanistan, the ultra-orthodox Taliban elevated the *ulama** to positions as government leaders and removed women from public life.

* *ulama* Islamic religious scholars

Islamic groups vary widely in their goals and methods. Many practicing Muslims are part of nonviolent political and social movements within mainstream society. They seek to improve society through the building of schools, health clinics, or mosques. Others have used radical means to achieve their goals. In Iran, for example, Ayatollah Khomeini supported popular demonstrations that brought an end to the Iranian monarchy in 1979. Some militant (or extremist) groups, such as al-Qaeda, have also engaged in violence to further their cause. (*See also* **Abduh, Muhammad; Afghani, Jamal al-Din al-; Qaeda, al-; Qutb, Sayyid; Salafi; Taliban.**)

Games and Sports

Islam has long recognized the value of physical activity and recreation as a way to relax the mind and refresh the body. Until recently, however, physical education and organized sports were generally ignored in Muslim countries, and women who aspired to be athletes faced many obstacles. Today Muslims compete in regional, national, and international sporting events. In some parts of the Islamic world, women have opportunities to become active sports participants.

Historical Snapshot. Muhammad endorsed several sports and games as beneficial for his followers. These activities included horseback riding,

Football, called soccer in the United States, is a growing sport in Islamic nations. The Saudi Arabian football team, shown here, poses in International Stadium in Yokohama, Japan, before the start of the 2002 World Cup finals.

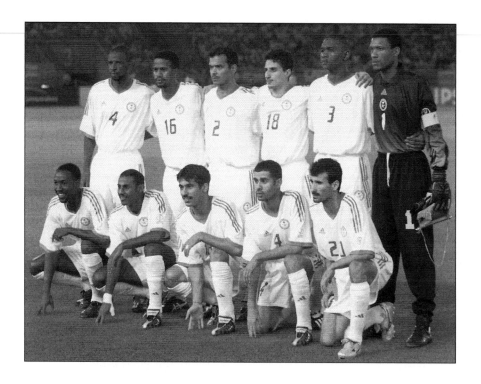

* **hadith** reports of the words and deeds of Muhammad (not in the Qur'an, but accepted as guides for Muslim behavior)

See color plate 10, vol. 1.

wrestling, spear play, swimming, chess, and backgammon. According to the hadiths*, Muhammad also encouraged people to learn the art of archery and to engage in footraces. It is reported that he even raced with his wife A'ishah. He warned archers, however, against shooting at chickens for target practice, because he believed that humans should not have fun at the expense of other living creatures. In addition to the health benefits of these activities, some of the sports the Prophet recommended proved to be useful for combat training.

Early Muslims included games in some of their rituals. In the 600s, for example, the followers of Muhammad used Egyptian ball-and-stick games during spring celebrations.

Historically, certain factors have limited the popularity of sports among Muslims. The hot and arid climate in many parts of the Islamic world is not conducive to year-round outdoor physical activity.

During the colonial era, European nations introduced physical education programs to their Muslim colonies. Based on French and British models, these programs focused on gymnastics, military drills, and calisthenics—rhythmic exercises performed without equipment. Physical education programs at the elementary school level encompassed a wide range of activities. Secondary schools, by contrast, offered limited choices. Physical education was not part of the secondary school curriculum, and so teachers and parents gave it little importance. Interested students could, however, participate in sports after regular school hours.

Beyond Spectators. In recent years, Muslim schools have placed a greater emphasis on physical education programs. Such programs are broad in scope and required in many nations. All scholastic levels, from primary to university, now include physical education classes. Islamic universities in Algeria, Egypt, Iraq, Iran, and elsewhere offer training for teachers of physical education.

The popularity of sports varies among Muslim cultures, but athletic pursuits have generally made great gains. Some governments fund, organize, and administer sports clubs to identify talented individuals and to provide training for them. Muslim nations have also created federations to develop various sports and prepare teams for international athletic events. Soccer, volleyball, gymnastics, swimming, tennis, and fencing are among the popular sports at this level of competition.

For years, Muslim countries have participated in the Olympic Games, and many athletes have excelled at individual sports, such as track and field and weightlifting. Islamic nations have also made advances in team sports, such as soccer. The men's soccer team from Nigeria won the gold medal for that sport at the 1996 Summer Olympics. Turkey, Saudi Arabia, Nigeria, and Tunisia qualified for the first round of the 2002 World Cup soccer playoffs.

Traditionally, cultural restrictions limited opportunities for Muslim women to participate in sports. Although Muhammad encouraged his followers to play games and engage in physical activity, Muslims generally believed that a woman's place was in the home. In recent years, however, this situation has changed. Girls now receive physical education instruction in school. Women regularly compete in local, regional, and national sporting events. A modest but growing number of Muslim women contend for Olympic medals. When competing in public, Muslim women usually wear sport dresses and headscarves.

In 1993, the first Muslim Women's Games were held in Tehran, Iran. This Olympic-style event, held every four years, gives athletes from Islamic countries the opportunity to participate in an international competition while adhering to regulations about appropriate clothing. Women wear full traditional Islamic dress for the opening ceremonies, which are open to male spectators, coaches, officials, and media representatives. For all other events, only women may be present. The games feature competition in badminton, basketball, chess, handball, swimming, volleyball, and karate. (*See also* **Education; Women.**)

Out of the Living Room

When Islamic revolutionaries seized control of the government of Iran in 1979, they instituted a law prohibiting women from socializing with men to whom they were not related. This meant that women could watch sports on television in the privacy of their own homes, but they could not attend public sporting events. Recently, an Iranian soccer club decided to bypass this restriction and permit women to attend men's soccer matches. Mahdi Dadras, manager of the Paykan Club in Tehran, noted that the presence of women in the soccer stadium boosted his players' morale.

See *Architecture.*

Gardens

Gasprinskii, Ismail Bey

**1851–1914
Crimean Tatar reformer**

Ismail Bey Gasprinskii was born in a small village on the Crimean Peninsula, in what is now the southern Ukraine. His family had served in the Russian military for generations. As a teenager, Gasprinskii attended a military academy in Moscow before spending three years abroad, living in Vienna, Paris, and Istanbul. Returning to Russia, Gasprinskii taught Russian to Crimean Muslims and, from 1878 to 1882, he served as mayor of the Crimean city of Bakhchisaray.

Gasprinskii was an ethnic Turk who dedicated his life to helping Muslims overcome cultural and economic obstacles. He wrote widely about the problems facing Turkish Muslims in Russia. In 1883 he started a newspaper called *The Interpreter*. Appearing in Turkish and Russian, it became one of the most influential Turkish newspapers in Russia. Gasprinskii used his newspaper to urge Russian Turks to adopt new, more modern, ways of thinking.

Gasprinskii's ideas inspired the Jadidism (modernism) movement. He encouraged Muslims to borrow from European traditions in order to restore their own culture and unify all Muslims. He believed that technology was necessary for advancement and he advocated education that included science, mathematics, and other practical subjects. He also promoted greater equality for women.

Despite his calls for change, Gasprinskii remained committed to the basic principles of Islam. Gasprinskii also believed that a common Turkic language would strengthen Russian Muslim society. He worked to promote literacy* and greater involvement in public affairs.

* literacy ability to read and write

While some Muslims questioned whether Gasprinskii's ideas were well suited to Islam, Gasprinskii reached a wide audience through his travels and his writings. His ideas influenced Muslim communities in Russia, Turkey, and Egypt. (*See also* **Central Asia; Modernism; Women and Reform.**)

Gaza

See *Palestine.*

Ghazali, Abu Hamid al-

1058–1111
Theologian, legal scholar, and mystic

* **theologian** person who studies the nature, qualities, and will of God

* **vizier** Muslim minister of state

* **Sufism** Islamic mysticism, which seeks to develop spirituality through discipline of the mind and body

Few individuals in the history of Islamic learning have had as profound an influence as medieval theologian*, legal scholar, and mystic Abu Hamid al-Ghazali. His major work pulled together the various strands of the Islamic sciences so well that scholars ever since have admired it. Born in 1058 in Tus, in the province of Khurasan in northeast Iran, al-Ghazali gained distinction in the court of the Seljuk vizier* Nizam al-Mulk. At age 34, he became a professor of law at the Nizamiyah college in Baghdad. After teaching for several years, however, al-Ghazali suddenly lost his faith in purely intellectual matters and suffered what the modern world would call a nervous breakdown. He became paralyzed and even lost his ability to speak. After leaving his position at the college, he spent 11 years traveling, meditating, and reflecting. By the time he returned, he had found the object of his search—in the practice of Sufism*.

In his autobiography, *Deliverer from Error*, al-Ghazali explained that conventional theologians, philosophers, and teachers all claimed to possess the truth but in reality wasted time in pointless discussions. In al-Ghazali's view, only the Sufis walked the right path. The Sufis combined knowledge with action, had sincerity of purpose, and actually experienced the serenity and contentment that comes from God's illumination of the human heart. With this new understanding, al-Ghazali set out to identify and analyze the circumstances that helped or hindered a person seeking to live a good life. His search resulted in his best-known work, *The Revival of the Religious Sciences*, which integrates all the major components of Islam: theology, law, ethics, and mysticism. Al-Ghazali sought to simplify the understanding of Islam. He believed that to be a good Muslim it is not necessary to understand the more complex matters that interest theologians. It is enough, he insisted, simply to believe the teachings of God as told to the Prophet and recorded in the Qur'an.

Al-Ghazali was also interested in social reforms. In his works, he criticized Muslim scholars who focused too heavily on abstract matters while ignoring the practical needs of the common people. He also condemned the wealthy for their lack of concern for the poor.

A popular and respected thinker during his lifetime, al-Ghazali's enlightened approach to his subject, his sincerity and objectivity, and his progressive tone ensure the lasting appeal of his work. He is one of the writers whose work has received much attention from Western as well as Muslim scholars. (*See also* **Philosophy; Sufism; Theology.**)

Ghazali, Zaynab al-

1917–
Founder of Muslim
Women's Association

* **hadith** reports of the words and deeds of Muhammad (not in the Qur'an, but accepted as guides for Muslim behavior)

* **Qur'an** book of the holy scriptures of Islam

Zaynab al-Ghazali, an influential writer and teacher on the subject of women's rights and duties in Islam, was born in Egypt in 1917. She attended public school through the secondary level and also studied religion at home, obtaining certificates in hadith*, preaching, and the Qur'an*. Her father encouraged her to become an Islamic leader, and for a short time, al-Ghazali supported the Egyptian feminist movement. Nevertheless, she soon abandoned this affiliation, believing that Islam itself guaranteed women's rights.

In 1936, when she was only 18 years old, al-Ghazali founded the Muslim Women's Association. She claimed that the organization had three million members at its height. Al-Ghazali gave weekly lectures on Islamic values. The association published a magazine, operated an orphanage, provided assistance to poor families, and mediated family disputes.

The Muslim Women's Association took a political stance, insisting that Egypt adopt Islamic law. Hasan al-Banna, the founder of the Muslim Brotherhood, recognized that al-Ghazali's group had similar goals to those of his organization. He asked al-Ghazali to merge the association with the Muslim Sisters, the women's branch of the brotherhood. Al-Ghazali initially rejected this idea, but yielded in 1949, when she realized the importance of all Muslims uniting behind al-Banna. During the 1950s, the government of President Gamal Abdel Nasser suppressed the Muslim Brotherhood. The Muslim Women's Association worked with the Muslim Sisters to help families who had lost relatives and property as a result of the persecution.

During the 1960s, al-Ghazali helped the Muslim Brotherhood to reorganize. As a result of her activities, she was arrested in 1965, and sentenced to 25 years of hard labor. In the book about her prison experience, *Days from My Life*, al-Ghazali describes being tortured and writes that she endured suffering with more strength than most men. She was released from prison in 1971 by President Anwar el-Sadat.

Al-Ghazali has continued to write and teach. She believes that Islam permits women to participate in all aspects of public life, as long as these activities do not interfere with their first and most sacred duty: to be wives and mothers. In her opinion, women should submit to their husbands and stay at home while their children are young. Al-Ghazali's own life seems to contradict this. She divorced her first husband because he interfered in her Islamic activities and threatened to divorce her second husband for similar reasons. When asked about this discrepancy, al-Ghazali says that her case is special because she did not have any children. This gave her the freedom to devote her energies to the Islamic cause. She notes that she remained obedient to her husband. Al-Ghazali has become a model for the increasing numbers of women who have embraced the Islamic movement since the 1970s. (*See also* **Egypt; Muslim Brotherhood; Women and Reform.**)

Government

* **Qur'an** book of the holy scriptures of Islam

* **hadith** reports of the words and deeds of Muhammad (not in the Qur'an, but accepted as guides for Muslim behavior)

* **secular** nonreligious; connected to everyday life

* **shari'ah** Islamic law as established in the Qur'an and sunnah, the exemplary behavior of the Prophet Muhammad

See color plate 4, vol. 3.

The nature of government and its relationship to Islam are among the central issues in modern Islamic thought. The Qur'an* and the hadith* contain little instruction regarding political systems. Islamic scholars, therefore, have disagreed about the proper role that government should play in Muslim societies and the type of government that is compatible with Islamic values. Some argue that secular* governments are appropriate for Muslim communities, while others believe that Islam requires the establishment of political institutions that operate according to the *shari'ah*.

Changing With the Times. The modern Arabic term for government, *hukumah*, refers to the group of individuals who exercise the authority of the state. In classical Arabic usage, the word *hukumah* meant the dispensation of justice, whether given by a mediator, judge, or ruler. By the 1000s, the term had taken on stronger political significance and referred to the function of *hakim* (a provincial governor). Over time, the meaning of *hukumah* expanded to include administration, rule, and political authority. The word's current meaning derives from the 1800s, when Muslim societies became increasingly interested in European forms of government.

In its early years, the Islamic community made decisions based on the principle of consensus, or agreement. The various tribes met to discuss problems and cooperated to enforce social order and security. As the Muslim empire grew, however, new methods of government became necessary. Muslim societies, adopting models from Byzantine and Persian cultures, became more autocratic, meaning they invested power in a single person.

According to Islamic legal tradition, rulers and other officials had an obligation to govern in accordance with *shari'ah*. Subjects, in turn, had to obey their rulers. This did not mean that most Muslim rulers systematically enforced or observed *shari'ah*. It simply meant that rulers received their authority from religion. In fact, the state itself did not exist as an institution with legal authority. Over the past 150 years, political analysts have distinguished between *hukumah* and *dawlah* (state), reflecting a process of political and legal secularization in the Muslim world.

Various Perspectives. During the 1800s, officials, diplomats, and writers from Muslim countries began to promote European principles of government. Much of the interest in this area was generated by the teachings of Ottoman scholar Mehmet Namik Kemal (1840–1888). Kemal attempted to blend elements of traditional Islamic thought with modern European ideas. He considered such

issues as the origins of government, popular sovereignty and majority rule, the separation of powers, and the benefits of a written constitution.

Since Kemal's time, secularists, reformers, and conservatives have debated the nature of government in Muslim society. Egyptian religious scholar Ali Abd al-Raziq (1888–1966) represented the secular viewpoint. Abd al-Raziq taught that Islam, properly understood, demands no particular form of government and no specific political institutions. The historical caliphate*, in his view, had no basis in scripture or tradition. Its apparent religious legitimacy, he wrote, was based on a misunderstanding of the Prophet's own mission, which was purely spiritual. Abd al-Raziq's teachings raised many objections. Traditional legal scholars protested his secular interpretation, insisting that the *shari'ah* acts as a check on the power of the government and protects the people from arbitrary rule.

* **caliphate** office and government of the caliph, the religious and political leader of an Islamic state

Reformist thinker Muhammad Rashid Rida (1865–1935) advocated Islamic rule within a modern political environment. Contrary to classical teaching, Rida viewed the caliphate as a largely spiritual institution. Through the caliph's lawmaking authority as chief religious scholar, he guarantees that the civic government has an Islamic basis as well as a flexible body of law. The caliph himself has no direct governmental responsibilities. Rida is sometimes credited with originating the concept of the modern Islamic state.

Another influential voice in the debate about Islam and government was that of Islamic revivalist Sayyid Abu al-Ala Mawdudi (1903–1979). Mawdudi noted that God possesses supreme authority, and therefore, Muslims who serve in earthly governments are God's representatives. Mawdudi saw secular democracy as un-Islamic because its authority derives from human beings rather than from God. He defined an alternative "theodemocracy" with the people being God's representatives. Although Mawdudi did not make specific recommendations about government, he emphasized the activist and totalitarian nature of the state. To express God's absolute sovereignty, the institutions of the government must have unlimited power. In Mawdudi's

Presidential/Parliamentary-Democracy	Traditional/Constitutional Monarchy	Authoritarian and Military-ruled	Single or Dominant Party
Albania	Bahrain	Azerbaijan	Egypt
Algeria	Brunei**	Kazakhstan	Iraq
Bangladesh	Jordan**	Kyrgyzstan	Maldives
Burkina Faso*	Kuwait**	Guinea	Mauritania
Chad*	Malaysia**	Libya	
Djibouti	Morocco**	Pakistan	
Ethiopia	Oman	Sudan	
Gambia	Qatar	Syria	
Guinea-Bisseau	Saudi Arabia	Tajikistan	
India		Tunisia	
Indonesia		Turkmenistan	
Iran*		Uzbekistan	
Ivory Coast			
Lebanon*			
Mali			
Niger			
Nigeria			
Senegal			
Sierra Leone			
Tunisia			
Turkey			
United Arab Emirates			
Yemen			

(*) with features of authoritarian rule; (**) constitutional monarchy

Note: The governments of Afghanistan, Comoros, Eritrea, and Somalia are currently in transition.

This chart shows the type of government in selected countries with large Muslim populations. Some Muslim countries have been able to balance electoral democracy with Islamic values. Other countries have more authoritarian regimes. About half of the countries with a majority Muslim population have democratically elected governments.

* **fundamentalist** generally refers to the movement that promotes a literal interpretation of scripture; in Islam, a movement that promotes politicization of religion under modern conditions to create an alternative public order

view, there is no difference between state, government, and society—all are part of the larger Islamic order and guided by the *shari'ah*.

The ideas of Hasan al-Turabi (born 1932), a prominent Sudanese Islamic leader, reflect some of the principles of Western political systems. Al-Turabi advocates an Islamic government that would play a limited social role. He has expressed considerable willingness to adopt political institutions from the West as long as they are not explicitly forbidden by *shari'ah*. Indeed, al-Turabi claims that he prefers Western democracies to Islamic dictatorships.

Al-Turabi's role in Sudanese politics seems to contradict his theories on government, however. During the mid-1980s, he headed the National Islamic Front (NIF), the political party of the fundamentalist* Muslim Brotherhood. In 1989 the NIF supported a military coup that brought an Islamist regime to power. Although al-Turabi was not the official ruler of the country, his party wielded considerable influence, effectively transforming Sudan into a police state. The people of Sudan suffered significant human rights abuses, including torture and the denial of freedoms of speech, assembly, and religion.

During the mid-1990s, al-Turabi became the speaker of parliament. In December 1999, however, President Umar al-Bashir dissolved parliament. Two years later, he imprisoned al-Turabi and some of his supporters on charges of undermining the state. Today the National Congress Party (formerly the NIF) and the military rule Sudan.

Conservative Muslim scholars insist that Islam should be the only basis of government. Sayyid Qutb, a leading Egyptian activist during the first half of the 1900s, dismissed Western beliefs and institutions as entirely incompatible with Islam. In his view, *shari'ah* is the source of all laws, both spiritual and worldly. For Qutb, the political system must enforce the *shari'ah* because the primary goal of Islam is the establishment of an Islamic state.

The Islamic Experiment. The modern notion of Islamic government has faced its most visible test in Iran, where since 1979 the country's religious leaders have actually attempted to create an Islamic state. Shi'i* religious leader Ayatollah Ruhollah Khomeini (1902–1989) inspired a revolution against the secular policies of Muhammad Reza Shah Pahlavi when he promoted the idea that Islam requires the establishment of political institutions that can enforce *shari'ah.* He also believed that religious scholars should play a leading role in such a government. Although Khomeini did not elaborate on the structure of an Islamic government, he distinguished it from both a republic based on popular sovereignty and a constitutional monarchy. Unlike these forms of government, the Islamic state recognizes the ultimate sovereignty of God and works to implement God's law in the world.

Although the revised Iranian constitution of 1979 allowed for the separation of powers among the executive, legislative, and judicial branches of government, in effect Khomeini became the sole authority in the country. Since Khomeini's death, more moderate elements have attempted to introduce limited liberal reforms. These, however, continue to provoke controversy.

Democracy and the Future. Fewer than one-quarter of the countries with majority Muslim populations have democratically elected governments. Those with competitive democratic systems, such as Bangladesh and Indonesia, are among the largest Muslim societies. Authoritarian regimes—led by kings, military officers, or former military officers—rule many Islamic nations. In these societies, security forces support and ensure the power of the state, and freedoms of assembly, speech, and the press are severely restricted. Autocratic governments have provoked increased criticism since the late 1990s. Critics point out that poverty, illiteracy, unemployment, and cultural stagnation are more likely to occur where democratic movements are suppressed. They also argue that such conditions foster terrorism among those with extremist views. They call for Muslim societies to adopt democratic reforms in order to remedy these problems. Traditionalists, however, warn Muslims not to imitate Western systems but to support forms of government that uphold Islamic values.

Some Muslim countries have been able to successfully balance electoral democracy with Islamic values. After Turkey became a republic in 1923, the government instituted secular laws based on parliamentary democracy. Committed to modernization and westernization, the authorities eliminated Islam from all areas of public life. Although official policies about Islam grew more liberal over the years, a ban on religious-based political parties remained in place. Nevertheless, the Islamist-oriented Justice and Development Party won a parliamentary majority in 2002. The party's appeal, however, stemmed as much from its platform of economic reform as from its Islamic identity. (*See also* **Democracy; Law.**)

See color plate 5, vol. 3.

* **Shi'i** refers to Muslims who believe that Muhammad chose Ali ibn Abi Talib and his descendants as the spiritual-political leaders of the Muslim community

From Tribal Council to Military Junta

Although relatively few Muslim countries have representative governments, democratic institutions have deep roots in Islamic culture. The people of pre-Islamic Arabia had a *majlis*—a type of tribal council. The term later came to signify the place where the caliph or sultan would listen to the concerns of his subjects. Today, *majlis* refers to an institution that deals with matters relating to the public interest. In Turkey, Iran, and most Arab countries, the *majlis* is equipped with legislative authority. During the mid- to late 1900s, the military leaders of various countries, including Sudan, overthrew their governments. Once in power, they created all-powerful institutions that they called *majlis*.

Great Britain

Great Britain has a long and complex relationship with the Muslim world. British colonial policy has affected Islamic cultures in Asia, the Middle East, and North Africa. In addition, Britain has attracted large numbers of Muslim immigrants. An ally of Israel and the United States, Britain also maintains close ties with Arab nations and other Islamic cultures. The country continues to play an important role in affairs central to Muslim interests.

Contact With the Muslim World

* **Middle Ages** period roughly between 500 and 1500

* **Crusades** during the Middle Ages, the holy wars declared by the pope against non-Christians, mostly Muslims

British contact with Muslim states began during the Middle Ages*. The Crusades* brought many Europeans to Jerusalem, a holy city for Muslims, Christians, and Jews. In 1189 the English king, Richard I (Richard the Lion-Hearted), led an army on the Third Crusade in an attempt to take control of Jerusalem. Although Richard failed to gain control of the holy city, the Muslim sultan Saladin admired him for his courage. According to legend, Saladin sent fruit to the English king when he lay sick with a fever.

The British made contact with other Muslim empires as well. By the late Middle Ages, English merchant ships had established trade routes with Arab countries along the Mediterranean Sea. Muslim merchants controlled the flow of goods from Central Asia and southern Asia, supplying the British with textiles, glass, porcelain, and especially spices. Such items found markets throughout western Europe. Around the same time, European ships first sailed all the way around Africa, establishing a sea route to Asia. European trading companies established bases in Morocco and other African countries. In some places, these companies became so powerful that they actually collected taxes from the local people and acted as their rulers. During the 1750s, the British East India Company assumed control over Bengal, a section of India's vast Mughal Empire.

Conquest and Partition of India. What began as a trading relationship between England and India soon developed into a commercial and political empire. By 1803 the British had moved north to Delhi, a city in northern India. They continued to expand their territory until they controlled most of the region that is present-day India, Bangladesh, and Pakistan. The sale of exports from these regions helped to support the Industrial Revolution in Britain and greatly increased British wealth. Indeed, the Indian subcontinent came to be known as the "Jewel in the Crown" of the British empire.

Both Hindus and Muslims wanted political power, but often clashed among themselves. In 1905 the British government announced that it would divide the large state of Bengal into two new regions. The eastern state had a Muslim majority, and the western section remained largely Hindu. Although the division of Bengal provoked much controversy, it gave Muslims the opportunity to argue for increased political opportunities. The All-India Muslim League emerged in 1906 as the leading advocate for greater political power. When the British reunited Bengal in 1911, the Muslim elite felt as if the British had taken away their hard-won rights. Muslims continued to press for reforms that would give them greater political influence.

As Indians struggled for independence in the mid-1900s, the British government made plans to withdraw. Two world wars had crippled Britain's economy and depleted its military resources. Unable to maintain a peaceful rule in India, it decided to prepare the region for self-rule. British leaders accepted the Muslim League's argument that a single united India would not serve the interests of Muslims. In 1947 they once again divided the region into two parts. India became a secular state with a Hindu majority and the territories of Pakistan and East Pakistan (now Bangladesh) formed a Muslim-majority state. The partition created hardships for both Hindus and Muslims. Approximately 10 million people migrated between the countries, and conflicts led to massacres on both sides that killed as many as one million people.

Dominion in Africa and the Gulf States. Britain also exerted considerable influence in the Persian Gulf and in North Africa. France and Egypt opened the Suez Canal in 1869, a strategic waterway that provided easy passage to and from Egypt for trade ships. Egypt, however, fell into debt and sold its shares in the canal to Britain. When Egypt could not repay the remaining debt, France and Britain took joint financial control of the country. Claiming that civil disorder in Egypt required military intervention, Britain bombed Alexandria in 1882 and occupied the country. In 1914 Britain formalized the arrangement by declaring Egypt a British protectorate*. Increased unrest and demands for independence, however, forced Britain to grant Egyptian independence in 1922.

Britain also claimed power in the Red Sea and Persian Gulf regions. Britain's interest in the Persian Gulf stemmed mainly from its desire to protect its trade route to India. By the end of the 1800s, British leaders had persuaded the rulers of several Gulf states, such as Kuwait and Qatar, to grant Britain control of their foreign relations. When the Ottoman Empire dissolved at the end of World War I, Britain also gained control of Iraq and Palestine. British rulers hoped to turn Iran, with its rich petroleum reserves, into a British protectorate. Although this goal was never achieved, Britain maintained a strong commercial presence in Iran based on oil export. British power in North Africa and the Middle East began to dissolve after World War II (1939–1945). Britain had incurred too much debt during the war to be able to maintain effective foreign rule, and the weakened British forces could not defend themselves against local resistance movements. Even so, Britain maintained a presence in the Gulf region until the early 1970s.

Palestinian Conflict. After World War II, Britain faced a complex problem in Palestine. During the early 1900s, Jewish people had immigrated to the region from Europe to escape from persecution. They believed in Zionism, the idea that the Jewish people have a historical claim to a state in Palestine. In 1917 Britain issued the Balfour Declaration, which stated that it favored the establishment of a Jewish national homeland in Palestine, provided that this action did not interfere with the rights of others living in the region. After World War II, however, the British refused to increase the number of Jews who could immigrate to Palestine, even though many Holocaust survivors had nowhere else to go. Palestinian Jews rose up against the British, asking other nations for support. The Arabs also took up arms against their colonizers. The British government made plans to remove its forces from the region.

Unable to present a partition plan acceptable to both the Arabs and the Jews, Britain set May 14, 1948, as the deadline for its withdrawal and asked

* **protectorate** country under the protection and control of a stronger nation

Political Gains

Although Islamist political parties have not gained popular support in Britain, individual Muslims have earned positions in government. In the city of Bradford, for example, the number of Muslim councilors increased from 3 in 1981 to 11 in 1992. Bradford elected a Muslim lord mayor—Britain's first—in 1985. In 1994 voters in Waltham Forest elected Britain's first Muslim woman mayor. By the end of the 1990s, Muslim local councilors across Britain numbered about 150. At the national level, Muslim candidates have also been successful. In 1997 the first Muslim member of Parliament, Muhammad Sarwar, was elected. The Labor Party appointed three Muslims—Lord Ahmed, Baroness Uddin, and Lord Ally—to the House of Lords as life peers.

the United Nations to help resolve the conflict. The U.N. mandated the partition of Palestine into two states—one for Jews and one for Arabs. Israel proclaimed its independence on the date of the British withdrawal, and Arab armies invaded the new Jewish nation. The two forces battled for several months, until the U.N. helped to create new borders for Israel. Jordan occupied the West Bank (of the Jordan River), which was supposed to be part of the Palestinian state called for by the U.N. Many Palestinian Arabs fled to surrounding areas as refugees. Many Muslims denounced Britain for aiding the Zionist cause. While Britain remains an ally of Israel, British leaders also support Palestinian rights and the establishment of an independent Palestinian state.

Muslims in Great Britain

In the early 1800s, the Muslim community in Britain consisted mainly of Bengali and Yemeni seamen recruited by the East India Company. These sailors found themselves without work when their ships docked in England and settled in the port cities of London, Cardiff, and Glasgow. In 1889 Britain's first known mosque appeared in Woking, a town in southern England. The Muslim population remained stable until after World War II, when Muslims began immigrating to Britain in greater numbers.

Settlement Patterns. Devastated by World War II, the British needed to rebuild the nation's industries. The government welcomed unskilled and semi-skilled workers from overseas, especially from countries that had been part of the British empire. During the 1950s and 1960s, South Asians flocked to industrial cities, such as Bradford, Leeds, and Manchester. Many settled in London as well. The majority of Muslim immigrants were men who planned to work and save money before returning to their homeland and families. Few mosques or religious services existed for them at this time. Muslims performed their daily prayers in private, often beside their factory machines at work.

In the late 1960s and 1970s, the British economy stabilized, and new immigration laws limited the numbers of immigrants from South Asia. Many who had arrived earlier, however, had decided to stay. The existing laws allowed their families to join them in Britain, increasing the Muslim population and strengthening Islamic communities. At the same time, some East African nations, such as Uganda, underwent Africanization movements and expelled their Indian minority populations. Tens of thousands of these displaced Indians, many of them Muslims, settled in Britain. In 1963 Britain had only 13 registered mosques. By 1970 this number had increased to 49, and by 1990 it had grown to 452. By the early 2000s, there were more than 600 official mosques in Britain, as well as more than 200 unregistered mosques. In addition, the British government recognizes some 950 Muslim organizations operating in Great Britain. These serve a diverse Muslim population that is estimated at around 1.5 million.

Social Issues. British Muslims have faced considerable discrimination and prejudice in recent years. Negative stereotypes have led to what some have called "Islamophobia," or bias against Islam. Many factors contributed to the rise of anti-Islamic feelings, including the notorious Rushdie affair. In 1988 British author Salman Rushdie won a prestigious literary prize for his novel *The Satanic Verses*. Many Muslim groups objected to the book's content because they believed that it insulted Muhammad and Islam. They demanded that Rushdie and his publisher be prosecuted under Britain's blasphemy laws. British courts rejected this demand, and on January 14, 1989, a group of Muslims in Bradford publicly burned copies of the book. Later that year, Iran's Ayatollah Khomeini issued a fatwa* calling for Rushdie's death. Many people began to associate Islam with intolerance. Throughout the late 1980s and 1990s, various assaults on Western targets have linked Islam in the public mind with intolerance and terrorist activities.

* **fatwa** opinion issued by Islamic legal scholar in response to a question posed by an individual or a court of law

Because the British government considers Muslims a religious rather than an ethnic group, it does not include Muslims in the Race Relations Act, which protects ethnic minorities, such as Jews and Sikhs*. Many Muslims have lobbied for laws protecting religious minorities. In 1996 the Runnymede Trust, an independent charity concerned with race and ethnicity, established the Commission on British Muslims and Islamophobia. It strongly urged the creation of legislation to protect Muslims against violence and discrimination based on religion. Other issues that concern British Muslims include the right to take time off from work to perform daily prayers; the right to have *halal** foods available in schools and the military; the right of Muslim men in the military to wear beards; the right of Muslim women to wear headscarves to work; and the right to follow Islamic laws regarding family matters, such as marriage, divorce, and burial.

* **Sikhism** religion of northern India that promotes rejection of caste and idolatry

* *halal* permissible; acceptable under Islamic law

Other issues focus on education. Muslims have pressed for the right to send their children to single-sex schools when available. They have also demanded that girls be permitted to wear headscarves in school and to cover their bodies during physical education classes. Muslims also demand sensitivity to their religious values regarding sex education, religious education, and aspects of art and performance activities in public schools. Some Muslim organizations have called for public support for separate Islamic schools.

The media have also made efforts to dispel negative stereotypes of Islam. The BBC World Service has instituted a policy to avoid linking the terms "extremist" or "terrorist" with Islam. In 1999 the Broadcasting Standards Commission released guidelines that urge producers to practice sensitivity in their choice of language and images when discussing religion. In addition, some Muslim-controlled media have emerged, including the monthly newspapers *Q-News* and *The Muslim News.* At least 15 radio stations have received licenses for limited Islamic broadcast. (*See also* **Arab-Israeli Conflict; Colonialism; Egypt; Europe; India; Jerusalem; Mughal Empire; Rushdie, Salman; Trade.**)

Gulf States

The countries bordering the Persian Gulf, known as the Gulf states, include Bahrain, Iran, Iraq, Kuwait, Oman, Qatar, Saudi Arabia, and the United Arab Emirates. Since ancient times, the Persian Gulf has served as the primary trade route for the people who live along its shores. The strategic location of the region has fostered cultural interaction between the societies of the Middle East and the civilizations of Africa, India, China, and even Europe. The discovery of oil in the early 1900s brought tremendous wealth to the Gulf states and renewed its international political importance.

Gulf States

The Gulf States consist of eight countries that border on the Persian Gulf. One of these countries, the United Arab Emirates, is a federation of seven small states. Oil is the most important natural resource in the region, and since the early 1900s, oil production and export have accounted for much of the region's wealth.

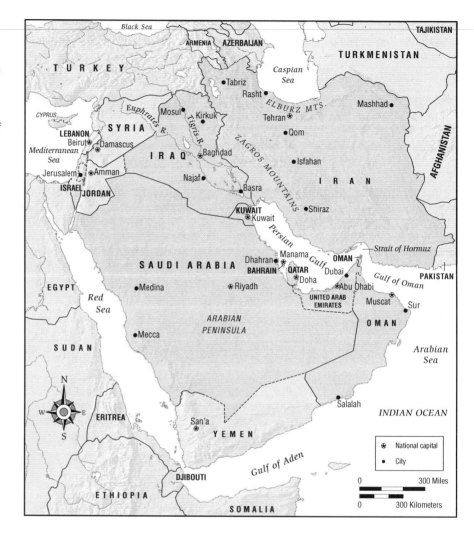

* **Sunni** refers to the largest branch of the Muslim community; the name derives from sunnah, the exemplary behavior of the Prophet Muhammad

* **Shi'i** refers to Muslims who believe that Muhammad chose Ali ibn Abi Talib and his descendants as the spiritual-political leaders of the Muslim community

* **B.C.E.** before the Common Era, which refers to the same time period as B.C.

* **C.E.** Common Era, which refers to the same time period as A.D.

The countries covered in this entry share several characteristics. The Gulf states have historically been a stronghold of Islam, and their people are mostly Arabs and Sunni* Muslims. In general, the tribe acts as the basic unit in these societies, and as a result, most political and economic activity is connected to relationships between families and clans.

Fight for Equality. Bahrain is an archipelago, or group of several islands, in the Persian Gulf. Shi'i* Muslims account for 70 percent of the population, and Sunnis make up 30 percent. The Bahraini royal family and many from the merchant class follow the Sunni branch of Islam.

Archaeological relics discovered on Bahrain Island date back to 2000 B.C.E.*. At that time, the area was a thriving trading center connecting the southern region of Mesopotamia (present-day Iraq) with South Asia. Historical records indicate that the people of ancient Bahrain had contact with Assyria, Persia, Greece, and Rome. Bahrain may have been under Arab rule when it became part of the Persian Empire during the 300s C.E.*. Muslim forces conquered the archipelago in the 700s, and Arab dominance endured until the arrival of the Portuguese in 1521. In 1602 the Persians recaptured Bahrain and maintained control of the region until 1783 when Ahmad ibn al-Khalifah seized power. The al-Khalifah family has ruled Bahrain since that time.

The shipping lanes of the Persian Gulf made it an area of strategic importance among foreign powers during the 1800s. British authorities attempted to protect their interests in the region by intervening in the political affairs of the Gulf states. Beginning in 1820, Great Britain and Bahrain signed a series of treaties that eventually gave Britain authority over Bahrain's foreign policy.

Widespread discontent within the Shi'i community led to riots on the islands in 1923. In the wake of the riots, agents of the British government deposed Bahrain's ruler. Sunnis opposed to British intervention in the islands' internal affairs demanded restoration of the former ruler and the creation of an advisory council to assist him in governing the country. During the 1930s, Shi'is demanded proportional representation on municipal and educational councils.

Issues regarding political equality sparked violence between Sunnis and Shi'is in 1952. Meanwhile, nationalists* worked to channel popular discontent against the British administration and away from religious matters. In 1971 Bahrain succeeded in gaining full independence from Great Britain.

Shi'i anger resurfaced in Bahrain after the Iranian revolution (1978–1979). Throughout the 1980s, radical* groups steadily gained strength, but the government successfully limited the political activity of both moderates and extremists. Relations between Shi'is and Sunnis in Bahrain remain volatile. The Sunni minority, to which the royal family belongs, still maintains a tight grip on power and wealth in the country, while the majority Shi'i community continues to demand more representation in government.

Unrest at Home and Abroad. Kuwait lies between Saudi Arabia and Iraq on the Persian Gulf. Its population is overwhelmingly Arab and Muslim. Among the followers of Islam, 70 percent are Sunnis and 30 percent are Shi'is. About 15 percent of Kuwaitis identify themselves as Christian, Hindu, or Parsi.

The ancient civilization of this desert nation dates to 2000 B.C.E. Like Bahrain, Kuwait had contact with many diverse cultures. The Greeks even built a temple to the goddess Artemis on Faylakah Island in Kuwait Bay. During the early 1700s, a group of families of the Anizah tribe of central Arabia migrated to Kuwait in search of good grazing lands and water. In 1710 the settlers founded Kuwait City, and in 1756 they chose Abd Rahim of the al-Sabah family as shaykh, or chief, of the community. Since that time, members of the al-Sabah family, who adhere to the Sunni branch of Islam, have ruled Kuwait in conjunction with upper class merchants.

Great Britain became involved in Kuwait in the late 1800s, when it tried to prevent Germany and the rulers of the Ottoman Empire from gaining influence in the region. In 1899 Kuwait and Britain reached an agreement allowing Britain to control Kuwait's foreign affairs. The country became a British protectorate* in 1914, and during the early 1920s, the British established its borders with Saudi Arabia and Iraq. Kuwait achieved full independence in 1961. Shortly thereafter, Iraq claimed that Kuwait properly belonged to it. The League of Arab States rejected Iraq's assertion and recognized Kuwait's independence.

Domestic affairs also became tumultuous, as tensions between the majority Sunnis and minority Shi'is escalated in the 1970s. In 1979 activists seized control of Iran and established an Islamic republic. The Ayatollah Khomeini, Iran's political and religious leader, encouraged Muslims throughout the Islamic world to take similar action against their governments. Shi'i groups staged a series of demonstrations in Kuwait City. A war between Iran

* **nationalist** one who advocates loyalty and devotion to his or her country and its independence

* **radical** favoring extreme change or reform, especially in existing political and social institutions

* **protectorate** country under the protection and control of a stronger nation

and Iraq that began in 1980 also threatened Kuwait's security. Growing discontent among Shi'is led to violence in the mid-1980s. The government launched a campaign of intimidation and surveillance of suspected militants and dissolved the popularly elected National Assembly.

By 1990 the Kuwaiti government agreed to form a council charged with studying the past and future role of the parliament. Within several months, however, Iraq invaded the country. The Iraqis were expelled in 1991, and the following year, Kuwait reorganized its National Assembly and held elections. Anti-government Islamic candidates—both Sunni and Shi'i—won enough seats for a majority. They advocated amending the constitution to make *shari'ah** the basis of Kuwaiti law. Today the government uses *shari'ah* as a source for developing law and procedure, especially in personal matters.

Desert Storm. After experiencing relative success in the Iran-Iraq War, Iraqi armed forces invaded and occupied Kuwait on August 2, 1990. Saddam Hussein, the president of Iraq, had been angered by Kuwait's demand that he repay the millions of dollars they had given him during the war with Iran. He also disagreed with Kuwait regarding claims to some oil fields. The invasion set off an international conflict. The governments of Kuwait and Saudi Arabia appealed to foreign powers for support. To force Saddam Hussein to withdraw his army, the United Nations imposed strict trade sanctions* on Iraq. Fearing that Iraq would attack Saudi Arabia and seize that country's valuable oil reserves, the United States and its European allies sent troops to the region. Saudi Arabia, Egypt, and other members of the Arab League joined the coalition and contributed troops to the campaign. On January 16, 1991, the United States led an air offensive against Iraq, marking the beginning of the Persian Gulf War.

By the end of February 1991, the allies had defeated Iraqi forces and had declared a cease-fire. The presence of U.S. troops in Saudi Arabia, a consequence of the war, angered Islamic militants. Believing that this was the beginning of an American occupation, they cited the presence of the U.S. military as justification for terrorist attacks against American interests in the region.

A Distinctive Brand of Islam. Oman occupies the southeastern coast of the Arabian Peninsula, at the site where the Persian Gulf meets the Arabian Sea. More than 75 percent of Omanis are Arab and almost all are Muslims. Most belong to the Ibadi, a sect* that is neither Sunni nor Shi'i. There is also a sizeable Sunni minority in Oman.

Ancient cultures inhabited Oman at least 10,000 years ago, and Arabs migrated to the region centuries before the founding of Islam. The two main rival families, from northern and southern Arabia, were often at war. Omani tribes converted to Islam in the 600s. By 751 the people had begun to follow the teachings of a group known as the Ibadi, a subsect of Khariji Islam. Imams*, elected to govern tribal affairs, ruled the country until 1154, when a dynasty of kings was established. The imams reasserted their political authority in the early 1400s and eventually regained control of Oman.

Civil war between descendants of Oman's founding families broke out again in the early 1700s. In 1744 both sides elected Ahmad ibn Sa'id al-Busa'idi as imam, ending the war. Members of the Bu Sa'id family created a lasting dynasty, serving the country under the title of sultan*. For almost 200 years, the tribes of the northern interior, who had continued to support an

* **shari'ah** Islamic law as established in the Qur'an and sunnah, the exemplary behavior of the Prophet Muhammad

* **sanction** economic or military measure taken against a nation that acts in violation of international law

* **sect** religious group adhering to distinctive beliefs

* **imam** spiritual-political leader in Shi'i Islam, one who is regarded as directly descended from Muhammad; also, one who leads prayers

* **sultan** political and military ruler of a Muslim dynasty or state

elected imam rather than the sultan, sought to overthrow the dynasty. Peace was restored in 1959, when the last Ibadi imam was forced into exile.

In 1970 Qabus ibn Sa'id ousted his father, Sultan Sa'id ibn Taymur, and began implementing modern reforms. Until that time, Oman was underdeveloped and relatively isolated from the larger Islamic world. Under the leadership of Qabus ibn Sa'id, the country expanded its educational system and established a network for mass communication. These changes led to a more open discussion of religious doctrine and practice among Muslims who follow different branches of the faith.

Shaykhs Versus Imams. Qatar, located on a peninsula that juts north into the Persian Gulf from the Arabian mainland, is 95 percent Muslim. Almost all Qatari Muslims follow the Hanbali school of Sunni Islam, which is related to a conservative religious movement known as Wahhabism. Since the late 1800s, Qatar has been ruled by shaykhs*, but the country's religious leaders exercise considerable influence over judicial and educational affairs.

The first written mention of Qatar, which was originally settled by nomads from central Arabia, dates from the 900s. Today, the majority of the population consists of immigrant workers from Pakistan, India, Iran, and other areas.

During the 1700s, the al-Khalifah family moved to northwestern Qatar. Persia, threatened by their potential power, invaded Qatar in 1783. The al-Khalifah defeated the Persians and eventually became the rulers of Qatar and the independent state of Bahrain. In 1867 war broke out between the shaykhs of Bahrain and their subjects on Qatar. Tensions subsided the following year, when Great Britain intervened and installed Muhammad ibn Thani al-Thani as ruler of Qatar. He returned the favor by granting Britain authority in Qatar's foreign affairs. The Qataris managed to avert Ottoman rule during the last decades of the 1800s, and in 1916 Qatar became a British protectorate. After oil was discovered there in 1940, Qatar rapidly modernized. The country planned to become one of the United Arab Emirates in 1971, but chose instead to remain independent.

United Front. During the late 1800s, the rulers of the Trucial States, a federation of seven states on the Persian Gulf, gave Great Britain the right to control their foreign policy. In 1971 six of these states—Abu Dhabi, Ajman, Dubai, Fujayrah, Ash Shariqah, and Umm al-Qaywayn—formed the United Arab Emirates (UAE). The seventh state, Ras al-Khaymah, joined the UAE the following year.

Muslims comprise 96 percent of the population. The majority identify themselves as Sunnis; only 16 percent follow Shi'ism. Although the UAE's native people are Arab, most of its residents consist of immigrants from South Asian countries, such as Bangladesh and Iran. Indigenous Arabs account for 25 percent of the total population.

The UAE operates as an alliance, but the ruler of each member state retains control of taxation, national security, and certain resources within its jurisdiction. The 1971 constitution gives highest federal authority to the Supreme Council of Rulers, a body consisting of the union's seven amirs*. All decisions need approval from at least five members, including Abu Dhabi and Dubai, which are the largest of the emirates. The ruling families share a commitment to both Sunni Islam and the Maliki school of law, which favors relatively strict interpretations of the Qur'an* and hadith* but also tolerates flexibility in applying the law for the benefit of the entire community. (*See also* **Iran; Iraq; Saudi Arabia; Wahhabi.**)

Riches From the Sea

Although Gulf state economies are now closely linked to oil, in earlier times fishing and pearl diving provided great wealth. The waters of the Persian Gulf were famous for high-quality pearls. Divers took enormous risks to bring pearls up from the sea bottom. Attaching themselves to a rope, they dove off the side of the boat, descending into deep waters with only the air they could hold in their lungs. Divers worked from sunrise to sunset, risking attacks from sharks and stingrays. In addition, because of the pressure at the sea floor, many divers injured their eardrums. Kuwaitis were especially famous as pearl divers, and the business provided private wealth as well as government income. After the Japanese discovered a way to make artificial pearls in the early 1900s, pearl diving in the Gulf region declined.

* **shaykh** tribal elder; also, title of honor given to those who are considered especially learned and pious

* **amir** military commander, governor, or prince

* **Qur'an** book of the holy scriptures of Islam

* **hadith** reports of the words and deeds of Muhammad (not in the Qur'an, but accepted as guides for Muslim behavior)

Hadith

Hadith are reports of the words and deeds of the Prophet Muhammad and other early Muslims. After Muhammad's death, his companions carefully noted all of his teachings and actions, which they studied as the ideal model for Muslim behavior. They recounted these teachings to other Muslims so that the memory of the Prophet's life and works might influence the community of believers. Hadith (the word may be used as singular or collective) are a central part of Muslim culture. After the Qur'an*, they are the most important source of guidance for Muslims.

Providing Clues About Early Islam. As preserved for subsequent generations, hadith take the form of short, unconnected pieces, each of which is preceded by a list of its authoritative transmitters, or those who reported the text. Hadith cover many topics relating to both faith and daily life. In addition to such religious subjects as prayer, purification, and pilgrimage*, hadith also address business transactions, inheritance, marriage and divorce, crime, judicial practices, war, hunting, and wine. Using direct language and a conversational style, each chapter of hadith contains anecdotes about how the Prophet dealt with these matters. Muslims use these stories for guidance in dealing with every aspect of their own lives. The hadith are also admired as examples of the richness of Arabic prose from the early Islamic era.

Throughout the history of Islam, the Qur'an and hadith have functioned together to shape the life of the Muslim community worldwide. Hadith provide the basic sources for the biography of the Prophet, filling in details about his personality, family life, and career. Hadith also help Muslims to interpret the Qur'an by explaining the circumstances in which portions of the sacred book were revealed, by supplying the meanings of obscure verses and words, and by providing examples in which the Qur'anic texts were applied to situations in daily life. By the early 800s, hadith had also become officially accepted as one of the sources of Islamic law.

Checking the Sources. Hadith were gathered and transmitted orally for two centuries before being collected in written form and codified*. Compilers searched widely for hadith, carefully recording reports exactly as received from recognized experts. They verified the chains of authority and transmission as far back as possible, often to Muhammad himself. These chains of transmission were assessed for their authenticity by examining the number of transmitters, their credibility, and by the continuity of the chains. The nature of the text was also examined. Reports that seemed illogical, exaggerated, or contradictory to the Qur'an were considered suspect.

In the 800s, an authoritative version of hadith was developed. It contained six large collections, which take their titles from the names of their compilers: al-Bukhari (died 870); Muslim ibn al-Hajjaj (died 875); Abu Daud al-Sijistani (died 888); Ibn Majah al-Qazwini (died 887); Abu Isa al-Tirmidhi (died 892); and Abu Abd al-Rahman al-Nasai (died 915). Sunni* Muslims accept these volumes as the most authoritative texts and also respect the collections of Malik ibn Anas (died 795) and Ahmad ibn Hanbal (died 855). Shi'i* Muslims use these same collections but recognize only some of the Prophet's companions as valid authorities. They consider hadith from

* **pilgrimage** journey to a shrine or sacred place

* **codify** to create a system of rules

* **Sunni** refers to the largest branch of the Muslim community; the name derives from sunnah, the exemplary behavior of the Prophet Muhammad

* **Shi'i** refers to Muslims who believe that Muhammad chose Ali ibn Abi Talib and his descendants as the spiritual-political leaders of the Muslim community

descendants of Muhammad through Ali ibn Abi Talib and Fatimah, as well as those from later imams*, to be fully authoritative. From the standpoint of their particular beliefs, Shi'i Muslims consider four hadith collections as particularly important—those of Muhammad ibn Yaqub al-Kulayni (died 940), Muhammad ibn Babuyah al-Qummi (died 991), and two collections of Muhammad al-Tusi (died 1068).

Studying the Hadith. By the time the hadith collections had been completed, a science of criticism had developed. Scholars focused on the reliability of the original sources and the accuracy of the transmission from oral to written form. Awareness of possible fabrication, or invention, and false teachings has long been a concern, and it has become a major issue in academic circles since the 1900s. A great deal of literature emerged dealing with many aspects of the hadith, including historical context, the study of difficult words, and explanations of contradictions. While there are some new perspectives based on recently discovered material, Muslims generally depend on hadith treatises* and commentaries of past centuries.

Some reform-minded scholars have recently suggested that the refusal of many Muslims to engage in a rigorous examination of hadith literature is blind conformity to the ways of the past. Some writers have composed thoughtful restatements of the ancient manuals, demonstrating a sensitivity and awareness to modern problems. Although this has provoked some controversy, reformists have refrained from attacking the hadith themselves but have simply urged Muslims to be more thoughtful in their acceptance of material attributed to the Prophet.

Since the 1990s, hadith scholars have been using computer technology to improve access to the vast amount of material in hadith collections. Specialists have created CD-ROMs that contain some 75,000 hadith, as well as their translations into ten languages. (*See also* **Ablution; Hajj; Law; Muhammad; Prayer; Qur'an.**)

600,000 Traditions

Collecting hadith became one of the most respected occupations in the early Muslim community. The teacher al-Bukhari reportedly spent more than 16 years traveling from his native Bukhara, in Central Asia, to Egypt. On his long journey he consulted with more than one thousand Arab leaders. After hearing more than 600,000 stories of the Prophet, al-Bukhari selected about 7,000 and recorded them in his book *Sahih* (which means "true" or "valid"). Although some of the material in *Sahih* is repetitious, there are still over 2,700 separate hadith that cover such topics as the creation, paradise, hell, ritual purification, and prayer.

* **imam** spiritual-political leader in Shi'i Islam, one who is regarded as directly descended from Muhammad; also, one who leads prayers

* **treatise** long, detailed essay on a particular subject

Hair and Beards

Islamic teachings about hair and beards emphasize not only cleanliness and good hygiene, but also modesty and Islamic values. Women's hair is held to be powerful and thus dangerous; its beauty, texture, and fragrance can attract and arouse men's interest. Observant Muslim women therefore wear a *hijab** to cover their hair when they leave their homes. Many Islamic teachings also recommend the removal of a woman's bodily hair, particularly her pubic and underarm hair.

Islam shares its views of hair with the two other major faiths that emerged in the Middle East, Christianity and Judaism. All three religions focus on the power of hair and its potential danger to the established social order. In Judaism and early Christianity, women hid their hair from all but their husbands. The three religions emphasize men's authority over women and the need to control women's sexual lives, often symbolized by the restraint of a women's free and flowing hair. The "hair dances" of the Arabian Penin-

* *hijab* refers to the traditional head, face, or body covering worn by Muslim women

sula—in which women swing their long, flowing manes of hair before an all-female audience—provide an acknowledgement of the equation of women's hair with sexuality, freedom, and power.

Pre-Islamic* folk traditions about the power and significance of hair persist throughout parts of the Middle East and Asia in the practice of burying or hiding shorn hair clippings. Islam does not frown upon the dyeing of hair, and many Muslim men as well as women use henna* to color their hair and beards. The Islamic legal scholar Ibn Taymiyah (1263–1328) noted the practical functions of this use of henna, stating that the Qu'ran* and the sunnah* teach Muslims to be visibly distinct from nonbelievers and that one way to accomplish this is to dye the hair and beard.

Islam condemns the selling and buying of hair and the production of wigs made from human hair. A part of the human body, hair should not be used as an item for trade. In the past, women seeking to thicken or lengthen their hair were advised to use animal wool for this purpose. Wig makers received scornful words from Muhammad.

Muslim men are encouraged not to cut their beards to a length of less than one fist-width. Numerous traditions indicate that the Prophet urged devout Muslim men not to imitate the *kuffar* (unbelievers) by cutting their beards or trimming them too short. Instructions on personal hygiene call for Muslim men to keep their mustaches neatly trimmed but not to remove their beards, which distinguish men from women and Muslims from nonbelievers. Hadith* teachings state that men without beards cannot head the *ummah* (Muslim community) or lead prayers. Beards have traditionally served as symbols of authority in the Middle East, even in pre-Islamic times. In ancient Egypt, for example, it is said that Queen Hatshepsut wore an artificial, gilded beard to assert her status as a ruler. (*See also* **Body Decoration; Clothing; Hijab; Ibn Taymiyah; Women.**)

* **pre-Islamic** refers to the Arabian Peninsula or to the Arabic language before the founding of Islam in the early 600s

* **henna** reddish dye that comes from the leaves of the henna plant

* **Qur'an** book of the holy scriptures of Islam

* **sunnah** literally "the trodden path"; Islamic customs based on the exemplary behavior of Muhammad

* **hadith** reports of the words and deeds of Muhammad (not in the Qur'an, but accepted as guides for Muslim behavior)

Hajj

See color plate 15, vol. 3.

The hajj is an annual pilgrimage to Mecca in Saudi Arabia—the birthplace of the Prophet Muhammad and the most sacred site in the Islamic world. The pilgrimage takes place during the second week of Dhu al-Hijjah, the final month of the Islamic lunar calendar. Every adult Muslim with the physical and financial means to travel is required to perform the hajj at least once during his or her lifetime. Each year, about two million Muslims from virtually every nation of the globe gather in Saudi Arabia for this important event. It is the largest and most culturally diverse assembly of humanity to gather in one place at the same time.

The hajj differs significantly from other pilgrimage traditions, such as those in Christianity and Hinduism. In other religions, the idea of a pilgrimage is important but voluntary, and pilgrims can visit any of several holy sites. The hajj, however, forms an essential part of the Muslim faith as one of the Five Pillars of Islam. Islamic tradition requires that all pilgrims gather at the same place to simultaneously worship together. Although Muslims may choose to visit other shrines and may make a pilgrimage to Mecca at other times of the year, these do not take the place of the hajj.

Rituals of the Hajj. The sequence of the rituals performed during the hajj was set by Muhammad shortly before he died. The rituals are meant to symbolically reenact events from the life of the Prophet Abraham and his family. Before the hajj begins, all male pilgrims put on special clothes called *ihram*, consisting of two white sheets or towels covering the upper and lower parts of the body. The *ihram* symbolizes the equality and humility of all Muslims before God, regardless of race or economic class. Women are not required to wear a special garment, but must conform to rules of modesty and good taste. Many pilgrims keep their *ihram* for several years after making the hajj, and some use it as a burial shroud.

See map in Middle East (vol. 2).

The hajj begins with the *tawaf*, a ritual that is performed at least twice—immediately after arriving in Mecca and just before departing the city. To perform the *tawaf*, pilgrims walk around the Kaaba (House of God) seven times. The Kaaba is the cube-shaped structure believed to have been built by Abraham and his son Ismail. It is now surrounded by the Great Mosque. This ritual imitates the angels circling God's throne in heaven. After the *tawaf*, pilgrims immediately perform the *sa'y* by running back and forth seven times between two small hills near the Kaaba. This ritual recalls Hagar's frantic search for water for her son Ismail after they were abandoned in the desert. After the *sa'y*, most pilgrims bathe and relax at the nearby well of Zamzam, which appeared miraculously to save Hagar and Ismail from death. Many pilgrims drink from the well and sometimes carry home bottles of water for friends unable to make the hajj themselves.

The culmination of the hajj is the procession on the ninth day of the pilgrimage to the plain of Arafat just outside Mecca. The pilgrims erect tents in the valleys and surrounding mountains. From just after noon until sunset they pray and converse with one another. Many believe that God is most attentive to prayers on this site and during this time. Some pilgrims climb the sides of the Mount of Mercy, where Muhammad delivered a famous sermon, but most remain in their tents to protect themselves from the harsh desert sun. Just after sunset, the pilgrims break camp. As they leave the valley, they converge on the narrow mountain pass of Muzdalifa, where they spend the night in the open. Though Muzdalifa offers no modern comforts, many pilgrims consider this one of the most inspiring parts of the hajj. The next day, the pilgrims continue to the valley of Mina, where they set up another enormous tent city.

At Mina, two rituals reenact Abraham's test of faith when God demanded the sacrifice of his son Ismail. First, pilgrims hurl seven pebbles at tall stone pillars that represent the devil who tried to tempt Abraham to disobey God. This ritual results in some of the most energetic moments of the hajj, giving the pilgrims a sense of release, but pilgrims must be careful to avoid the flying pebbles. After this, each pilgrim makes an animal sacrifice, or *qurban*, commemorating the ram that God accepted in Ismail's place. They consume part of the meat in a feast and give the rest to the poor. Muslims worldwide celebrate this day as Eid al-Adha.

For the next few days, the pilgrims travel back and forth between Mina and Mecca—often via special pedestrian tunnels cut through the mountains. They repeat the stonings, *tawaf*, and *sa'y*. The hajj ends on the 12th or 13th day of Dhu al-Hijjah.

The hajj celebrates the reunion and the renewal of the entire Muslim community. It is the most powerful reminder of Islam's ideals of unity and human equality. Many Muslims choose to make the hajj near an important turning point in their lives, such as marriage, retirement, illness, or approaching death.

Pilgrims From Around the World. In recent years, critics have charged that the organization of the hajj has become too political. In the 1980s, the government of Iran demanded that the pilgrimage be removed from Saudi supervision. The Organization of the Islamic Conference (OIC), however, defeated this demand and has tried to defuse political tensions surrounding the hajj.

In order to help manage the large influx of pilgrims, the OIC in 1989 endorsed a quota system limiting the number of pilgrims from each nation outside of Saudi Arabia. No more than 1,000 pilgrims per one million residents of a country are now permitted to go. Exceptions are made for countries with minority Islamic populations, such as South Africa, the United States, and various western European countries. Here higher percentages are allowed in order to help these Muslims strengthen their relationship with the rest of the Muslim community. The quota system, however, had been disadvantageous to the countries of the Arab world, especially Yemen and the states that surround the Persian Gulf. For example, 30 years ago, Muslims from Arab-speaking countries accounted for 60 percent of all hajj pilgrims, whereas today they make up only about 20 percent of the world total.

In the last ten years, the largest number of hajj pilgrims has come from Indonesia, Pakistan, Turkey, Iran, Egypt, India, Nigeria, and Bangladesh. In countries with minority Islamic populations, the greatest number has been from the United Kingdom, Russia, and the United States. Meanwhile, the percentage of female pilgrims has risen steadily, from 33 percent in the 1970s to nearly 46 percent in the first years of the twenty-first century. Generally speaking, women in modern urban areas are more likely to make the pilgrimage than those in rural and isolated regions. Countries such as Afghanistan, Yemen, and Bangladesh have a low percentage of women making the hajj, all below 20 percent. In several countries, such as Indonesia, Malaysia, and Lebanon, however, women constitute the majority of hajj pilgrims. (*See also* **Abraham; Ismail; Kaaba; Mecca; Muhammad; Pillars of Islam; Saudi Arabia.**)

Halal

See *Dietary Rules*.

Hamas

Hamas is the acronym of Harakat al-Muqawamah al-Islamiyah (Movement of Islamic Resistance), the most important Islamic organization in the Israeli-occupied territories of the West Bank and Gaza Strip. Established in 1987, this militant group seeks to destroy Israel and to establish an Islamic state in Palestine, the general term for the region. The Arabic word *hamas* also means "zeal."

During the late 1970s, a new type of Islamic activism appeared in Palestine. Associated with the Egyptian-based Muslim Brotherhood, this movement inspired its followers to work for the elimination of Western influence and for the renewal of Islam in society. Members of the brotherhood preached in mosques* and encouraged attacks on unveiled women and the destruction of taverns and cinemas. Initially, the Muslim Brothers confined their political activities to opposing the Palestinian communist party. By the mid-1980s, members of the Muslim Brotherhood and other small groups in the occupied territories called for jihad* against Israel, claiming that Muslims had a religious duty to fight for the return of the land in the West Bank and Gaza that Israel had occupied since the 1967 Arab-Israeli War. The Palestinian *intifadah* (uprising) broke out in 1987—a spontaneous, popular resistance to Israel's continued occupation of the region.

As the resistance movement grew, Dr. Abd al-Aziz al-Rantisi and Shaykh Ahmad Yasin founded Hamas groups in the Gaza Strip in December 1987. Soon thereafter, the Muslim Brotherhood formally adopted Hamas as its "strong arm." The charter of Hamas explains that anti-Israeli activity is part of jihad. It also rejects the legitimacy of the state of Israel and claims that military action is the only option for the liberation of Palestine.

Hamas considers itself a complement of the Palestine Liberation Organization (PLO), the official representative of the Palestinian people. The two groups differ on key issues, however. For Hamas, neither Palestine nor any part of it may be relinquished. The PLO, by contrast, has recognized Israel's right to exist alongside a Palestinian state. Hamas objected when the PLO entered a peace agreement with Israel in 1993. Hamas responded by intensifying its attacks against Israelis, including civilians. As the PLO and Israel took measures to punish Hamas, PLO chairman Yasir Arafat also appointed Hamas members to leadership positions in the Palestinian Authority in order to give them a voice in the political process. In September 2000, peace talks between the PLO and Israel collapsed, provoking a second *intifadah* and increased violence against Israelis.

Hamas claims that 30 to 40 percent of the Palestinian people are members of its organization and that most of its budget supports education and other social welfare projects. The Israeli government has banned the movement. (*See also* **Arab-Israeli Conflict; Jihad; Muslim Brotherhood; Palestine Liberation Organization.**)

* **mosque** Muslim place of worship

* **jihad** literally "striving"; war in defense of Islam

See map in Israel (vol. 2).

See *Dietary Rules*.

Haram

Harem

In its most common usage, the term *harem* refers to the section of a house where a Muslim leader's wives live. More broadly, a harem serves as the quarters restricted to female members of a family. The term also refers to the women themselves. The purpose of a harem is to protect women from inappropriate contact with men. Closely linked with the term *haram*, meaning forbidden, the word conveys a sense of sacredness and inviolability. Only husbands and relatives may enter this part of the home.

Harem

The harem is a room or section of a house where traditionally the female members of a household lived and where they were protected from contact with men. As women became more educated and customs changed, the practice of enclosing women in a harem declined.

* **concubine** woman who lives with a man without benefit of marriage and whose legal status is below that of a wife

* **dynasty** succession of rulers from the same family or group

* **Qur'an** book of the holy scriptures of Islam

Harems existed in the Middle East long before the rise of Islam. Pre-Islamic rulers in Egypt, Persia, and Assyria often had large harems in their royal courts. These consisted of wives, concubines*, female attendants, and other attendants who served as court officials. Rulers added wives from prestigious and influential families to their harems to forge political alliances. Some of these women played public roles. Others jockeyed for position from within the harem to gain power for themselves or their sons. Internal struggles within a harem had major political consequences, sometimes leading to the downfall of a dynasty*.

As the new Muslim community conquered these older societies, the new rulers adopted the concept of harem. This was justified by parts of the Qur'an* requiring actions that ensure modesty and chastity. Muslims and Arabs of all classes kept harems. In homes of the wealthy, wives had their own servants and suites of rooms. Families of average income also placed their women in seclusion. Even poorer households maintained separate, though more cramped, quarters for women.

Among the nobility, the practice of enclosing women in a harem served as a sign of status, showing that the family did not need its women to work for a living. Poorer women often had no choice but to earn money in the fields, as clerical workers, or as domestic servants. In Islamic countries, female workers wore veils in order to separate themselves symbolically from the world of men.

In the twentieth century, the harem system declined in popularity. Polygyny* became less common as women became more educated and joined the workforce as professionals. Some conservative Muslims continue the practice of maintaining harems, however, and radical groups in such places as Saudi Arabia call for a return to the seclusion of wives and daughters and an end to employment for women outside the home. (*See also* **Women.**)

* **polygyny** practice of having more than one wife at the same time

Harun al-Rashid

ca. 764–809
Fifth Abbasid caliph

* **caliph** religious and political leader of an Islamic state

Harun al-Rashid, the fifth and most famous Abbasid caliph*, was the son of al-Mahdi, the third caliph. As a teenager, Harun helped lead two successful military campaigns against the Byzantine Empire before receiving the title *al-Rashid* (one following the right path). After al-Mahdi died in 785, Harun's half-brother, Musa al-Hadi, became the fourth caliph. A year later, after al-Hadi mysteriously died, rumors circulated that Harun's mother, al-Khayzuran, had murdered the fourth caliph so that her son could rule.

Harun appointed the Barmakids, a powerful Iranian family, as administrators of the Abbasid empire, and his childhood tutor Yahya became his chief minister. The empire prospered under Harun's rule. Industry and trade expanded and wealth flowed into Baghdad, the capital. Harun extended diplomatic ties with the Holy Roman Empire and China, and his grand palace included a court that numbered in the hundreds.

Harun accomplished much during his reign. He built the first hospital and observatory in Baghdad and supported education, music, and poetry. In popular myth, the caliph was thought to disguise himself so that he could walk through the streets unnoticed to learn more about his subjects.

In 803 Harun turned against the Barmakid family, executed his former allies, and seized their property. Many historians believe that Harun had grown jealous of the Barmakid family's power and wealth. Harun's next administrators were less capable. Revolts increased and some provinces broke away from Baghdad. Harun sought to prevent further strife by dividing the empire between two of his sons. The empire, however, plunged deeper into civil war and Abbasid power declined in the decades following Harun's death.

The splendor of Harun's palace and luxury of his court had been previously unmatched. He became a legendary figure among Arabs and several stories in the famous book *The Thousand and One Nights* reflect the glory of his reputation. (*See also* **Abbasid Caliphate.**)

Health Care

Islamic teachings encourage Muslims to protect and restore their health, but they do not specify particular types of treatment. As a result, health care practices in the Islamic world encompass elements of various cultures and traditions.

Early Healing Traditions. Early Islamic medical practice centered on the teachings of the Qur'an* and hadith*. These works discussed a wide range of topics, including the healing power of honey, the medicinal properties of wolf's bile, and whether it was acceptable to use forbidden substances (*haram*) if they have the power to restore a person to health. Over time, the "Medicine of the Prophet," as collections of Muhammad's sayings, deeds, and attitudes on the subject became known, incorporated natural, herbal medicines. Common medical procedures included cauterization (burning or destroying tissue) and bloodletting. Such practices were believed to be helpful for a wide variety of disorders.

Reflecting the influence of pre-Islamic communities, Muslims also used magic or faith-based remedies. Spiritual healers diagnosed and treated illnesses attributed to supernatural forces, especially the evil eye and spirit beings known as the *jinn*. They used charms, amulets, and magic to combat these powers.

Many different cultures informed the health care practices of Islamic communities throughout the world. Muslims integrated the medical traditions of the ancient Egyptian, Indian, Persian, and Syrian civilizations. Beginning in the 800s and continuing through the Middle Ages*, Greek medicine experienced a revival in Muslim countries. Scientists in the Muslim world built on this classical heritage and made significant contributions to medieval medicine. The medical tradition of the time viewed health as a state of bal-

* **Qur'an** book of the holy scriptures of Islam

* **hadith** reports of the words and deeds of Muhammad (not in the Qur'an, but accepted as guides for Muslim behavior)

* **Middle Ages** period roughly between 500 and 1500

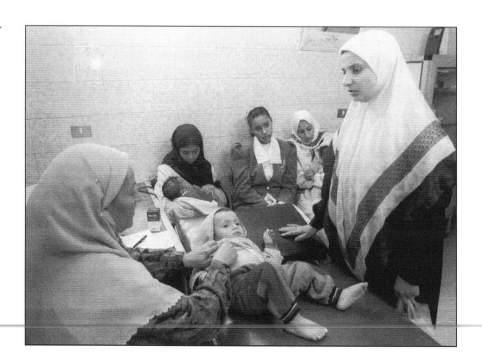

Clinics funded by Islamic charities offer medical care to the poor. In this clinic in Cairo, Egypt, a doctor performs a routine checkup on an infant.

ance among four "humors"—blood, phlegm, yellow bile, and black bile. These substances were characterized by four primary qualities: heat, cold, moisture, and dryness. All diseases and health problems, including psychological disorders, were explained in terms of imbalance among these humors and qualities. Remedies were intended to restore balance and health.

Combining Biology and Chemistry. In addition to pre-Islamic and ancient healing traditions, Islamic health care practices reflect the political experience of Muslim countries. European colonization in the early 1800s brought Western biomedicine* to the Islamic world. Western governments often imposed their medical practices on their colonies in an attempt to control the local population. In the North African city of Tunis, for example, the French colonial government sought to reduce the power of Muslim doctors by restricting licenses to practice to Europeans only. Despite the colonizers' efforts to promote biomedicine, most of the Muslim population continued to rely on traditional forms of health care.

The dominance of biomedicine came about differently in Egypt. Muhammad Ali, ruler of Egypt in the early 1800s, believed that a state-sponsored public health program would combat epidemics and reduce infant mortality, which would, in turn, stimulate the economy. Ali invited European doctors to train Egyptians. A group of state-sponsored health care providers, including both men and women, launched vaccination campaigns to fight disease. The British occupation of Egypt in 1882 thwarted Ali's efforts, however. Colonial authorities introduced a Western form of medicine to the country. Furthermore, they privatized medical education and established English as the language of instruction.

Modern Health Care. Today, the health policies of Muslim nation-states are based on the principles of biomedicine, which serve as the foundation of medical education, research, and public health programs. Nevertheless, traditional medical practices predominate in many Islamic communities. Outside of major cities, traditional healing may be the only available form of health care, and in some areas, it is simply preferred.

For many Muslims, religion, magic, and medicine remain closely related. Prevention is central to health care in Islamic societies. Many Muslims believe that the word of God, either written or oral, can ward off evil, including sicknesses associated with the spirit world. Traditional healers (practitioners of natural medicine) and spiritual healers (practitioners of supernatural medicine) attend the sick in Muslim countries. The lower classes also depend on paramedics—trained medical professionals who are not physicians—to provide health care.

During the mid-1900s, Islamic political groups promoted a form of health care that combined religion and biomedicine. The Muslim Brotherhood sent physicians into disadvantaged rural areas of Egypt to engage in public health education. Having defined poverty as a primary cause of poor health, the group operated charity clinics but also advocated wealth distribution based on Islamic principles.

In recent years, Muslims have established clinics in places such as Jordan, Sudan, and Egypt. Financed by private commercial and financial enterprises, the clinics offer affordable high-tech medical care. Advocates view the Islamic alternative to health care as a way to address unmet needs at a

* **biomedicine** type of medicine based primarily on biology and biochemistry (the chemical compounds and processes occurring in organisms)

AIDS Awareness

Intravenous drug use and unsafe sex are the two most common ways that people contract HIV/AIDS. Although the incidence of HIV/AIDS in Muslim countries is low by international standards, Iran's health community has launched an aggressive campaign to combat the disease. Television ads explain how the disease is transmitted and recommend using condoms to avoid contracting the virus through sexual contact. Classes teach both children and adults the basic facts about AIDS prevention, and counseling is available for HIV-positive patients and their families. In general, the campaign's messages are designed to foster an understanding of the disease and an acceptance of AIDS victims in Iranian society.

time when state support of public health is inadequate. Others consider Islamic clinics to be a sign of the rise of political Islam and a way for Muslim groups to gain legitimacy.

The practice of modern medicine in the Islamic world continues to grow and progress. In 2000 the World Health Organization (WHO) assessed the health systems in its 191 member states based on a variety of factors, including the general health of the population. Many countries in the Middle East and North Africa ranked high, with Oman, Saudi Arabia, United Arab Emirates, and Morocco scoring in the top 20 percent. WHO officials pointed to Oman, which had a poorly performing health care system in the early 1970s, as an example of a country that has benefited from government investment in medical services.

Despite such progress, many parts of the Islamic world still face serious health issues. Malnutrition plagues the countries of Afghanistan, Yemen, Nigeria, and Bangladesh. Following the Persian Gulf War in 1991, the health care system of Iraq suffered a major setback. Most hospitals still lack the water and electricity necessary to treat patients properly. Unsafe drinking water and poor sanitation threaten the health of many Iraqis. (*See also* **Dietary Rules; Medicine; Science.**)

Hijab

* **Qur'an** book of the holy scriptures of Islam

See color plate 13, vol. 1.

The Arabic word *hijab*, which literally means "a screen or curtain," can refer both to the traditional head, face, or body covering worn by Muslim women and to the practice of keeping women separate from men. Although the Qur'an* stresses modesty for women, it does not specifically require them to keep their heads or faces covered. Nonetheless, many Muslims believe the practice of veiling is supported by statements such as, "Say to the believing women that they should . . . draw their shawls over their bosoms and not display their beauty."

Veiling—the practice of covering a woman's head, face, or body—did not originate with Muslims. The tradition existed in the Middle East for centuries before Islam began in the early 600s. In ancient Mesopotamia and Persia, veiling was a sign of status. The veil distinguished respectable women from slaves and prostitutes. The practice of veiling gradually spread to upper-class Arab women, and eventually it became widespread among Muslim women in cities throughout the Middle East. In rural areas, women were much slower to adopt veiling because the garments interfered with their work in the fields.

In some parts of the Muslim world, both women and men have adopted Western-style dress. However, beginning in the 1970s, many Muslim women returned to veiling as part of an overall return to traditional Islamic values. Veiling became a symbol of Islamic identity. In the 1980s, the Islamic movement began to focus more on nationalism* and on resisting Western control. Veiling came to represent Muslim resistance to foreign domination.

Outsiders often regard veiling as a symbol of the inferior status of women in Islamic countries. Opponents of veiling, both Muslim and non-Muslim, link the practice with the oppression of women, claiming that it denies women the right to dress as they choose. Supporters of veiling, by contrast, argue that the practice enables women to emphasize their intellectual and personal qualities rather than their physical appearance. They argue that Western dress is far more oppressive to women because it turns them into sex objects. (*See also* **Clothing; Women; Women and Reform; Women in the Qur'an.**)

Hijrah

The term *hijrah* means "emigration," the process of moving from one place to another. In Islamic history, the original Hijrah occurred in 622 when Muhammad and his community of followers moved from Mecca to Medina to avoid the growing hostility to their preachings. Muhammad's arrival in Medina marks the formal beginning of the Islamic community (*ummah*), and 622 denotes the first year of the Muslim calendar.

Hijrah is an important Islamic concept, symbolizing a journey made for religious reasons, often to escape persecution. Muslims may undertake a hijrah individually or as part of a group. The journey symbolizes hope in the face of opposition, and Muslims display their devotion to Islam through their willingness to endure the hardships of moving. Hijrah can also mean abandoning sinful behavior to pursue righteousness. In Sufism*, hijrah represents a spiritual journey of returning to Allah.

Throughout history, Muslims have applied *hijrah* to a variety of situations, validating the historical experiences of Islam. Political groups invoked the concept when they opposed colonial rule. Muslims leaving Russia and the Balkan states in the 1800s called their migrations hijrah. In the 1920s, Indian Muslims moving from British-controlled India to Afghanistan also used the term. Saudi Arabian officials claimed hijrah when resettling Bedouin* tribes to expand their state's territory. Muslims who move to America also view themselves as following hijrah.

More recently, hijrah has assumed a broader meaning. Various groups have invoked the term when calling for a withdrawal from perceived un-Islamic influences, such as secularism*, socialism*, capitalism*, and the modernization and westernization of Muslim states. Hijrah has also come to describe the search for a better way of life through education or a new job. (*See also* **Mecca; Medina; Muhammad.**)

* **Sufism** Islamic mysticism, which seeks to develop spirituality through discipline of the mind and body

* **Bedouin** nomad of the desert, especially in North Africa, Syria, and Arabia

* **secularism** belief that religion should be separate from other aspects of human life and society, especially politics

* **socialism** economic system in which the government owns and operates the means of production and the distribution of goods

* **capitalism** economic system in which businesses are privately owned and operated and where competition exists in a free market environment

Historians

The Islamic tradition of writing history dates back to the 700s. Muslim historians have produced compilations of hadith*, biographies, digests, epic poems, collections of anecdotes, and descriptive chronicles. In the twenty-first century, the study of history continues as a major scholarly pursuit throughout the Islamic world.

* **hadith** reports of the words and deeds of Muhammad (not in the Qur'an but accepted as guides for Muslim behavior)

* **Qur'an** book of the holy scriptures of Islam

* **caliph** religious and political leader of an Islamic state

* **Shi'i** refers to Muslims who believe that Muhammad chose Ali ibn Abi Talib and his descendants as the spiritual-political leaders of the Muslim community

* **imam** spiritual-political leader in Shi'i Islam, one who is regarded as directly descended from Muhammad; also, one who leads prayers

* **dynasty** succession of rulers from the same family or group

Early Historians. The first Muslim historians depicted the rise of Islam and gave an overview of its principles. They used the Qur'an* and hadith to write biographies about the Prophet, creating *sirah* (historical accounts of Muhammad's life) and *akhbar* (stories or narratives about Muslim conquest and other heroic events). Biographers worked to determine the accuracy of their sources, rejecting hadith that seemed of dubious origin. They often incorporated aspects of Christian and Jewish history into their work, including the lives of the prophets, of whom they considered Muhammad to be the last. The Qur'an itself contains much Jewish and Christian lore, which Muslim historians used in their writing.

Other historians focused on certain regions or on various caliphs*. Some created works based on the teachings of certain Islamic sects. In the 800s, the Ismailis (a Shi'i* group) developed a cyclic view of history. They claimed that seven prophets would appear on earth, each followed by seven imams*. Muhammad served as the sixth prophet, and Ismail was the last imam. Ismail's son would return at the end of the world to serve as the seventh and final prophet.

Pioneering Persian historian Ibn Jarir al-Tabari (839–923) produced a 30-volume history that provides a wealth of information on the early Islamic world, beginning with the Creation and ending with the early years of the Abbasid caliphate. Al-Tabari reportedly planned to write a 300-volume work, but modified his plan to spare his students. The Persian poet Firdawsi produced another history, the *Book of Kings*, in 1010. This epic poem includes an account of Persian kings dating back to mythical times and a biography of the great hero Rustam, who fought many mythical monsters and married a princess. It is said that the sultan Mahmud of Ghazni (Afghanistan) bought the epic, paying Firdawsi only enough for a bath and a drink. This prompted the author to write a satire about Mahmud's stinginess, which he sold for five times the amount he had received for the epic. Just as Mahmud was about to make amends by sending him a large gift, Firdawsi died.

Possibly the best known Muslim historian is Abd al-Rahman Ibn Khaldun (1332–1406), who served as an official in various North African states. Ibn Khaldun developed many theories of history and society, concentrating especially on nomadic populations and the qualities that enabled them to survive. He presented highly influential ideas on the nature of rulers and the laws that govern communities in the introduction, or *Muqaddimah*, to his multivolume universal history.

Other historians concentrated on particular dynasties* or eras. Mughal kings hired historians to write about their conquests. Ottoman rulers similarly used historians to link their rule with a glorious past, as well as to record everyday court and military events. Mustafa Ali (1541–1599) is among the most prominent Ottoman historians. His most famous work, *Kunh al-Akhbar*, covers ancient world history, early Islamic society, a history of Turkish peoples, and the rise of the Ottoman Empire. In the 1500s and 1600s, several Egyptian writers also produced local histories, while other Islamic authors described such subjects as the conquests of Alexander the Great and the voyages of Sinbad. Many wrote in verse, using such forms as the rhyming couplet.

Introduction of New Research Methods. In the modern era, increased intellectual interaction between Europeans and Muslims influenced

Islamic historical writing. Europeans had developed new research methods and writing techniques and had brought them to the Muslim world during colonial expansion. The first influential European text came from a team of scholars sent to Egypt with Napoleon's army in 1798. They produced the massive *Descriptions de l'Egypte*, which influenced the study of ancient history in both Egypt and the West.

Reforms in education also led to changes in historical writing. In the early 1800s, the Egyptian ruler Muhammad Ali worked to modernize education. He encouraged scholars to translate European works, including histories by Montesquieu and Voltaire, into Arabic and Turkish. Cairo became the center for the development of a new historical style. Scholars combined old and new methodologies, as illustrated in Ali Mubarak's 20-volume encyclopedia of Egypt.

In the years following World War I (1914–1919), a growing number of Muslim historians traveled to Europe to study in Western universities. They began to produce works in multiple languages, writing in French or English for European readers, and in Arabic, Persian, or Turkish for a Muslim audience. Their work often raised significant questions about interpretation. For example, Taha Husayn's analysis of the authenticity of pre-Islamic poetry generated fierce controversy over a culturally revered body of literature. Some new works, however, became enormously successful. Muhammad Husayn Haykal combined modern historical methods and traditional sources to create a biography of the Prophet that continues to be read around the world.

Modern historical writing reflects issues affecting the authors' homelands. Many writers voiced their concerns about the threat that Western influence posed to the Islamic identity. Egyptian historians described the political struggles in their country following the arrival of the Europeans in the 1800s. Other Muslim historians produced landmark works, such as Kemal Inal's biography of the last 37 grand viziers* of the Ottoman Empire and Kurd Ali's history of Syria.

Contemporary Historical Writing. Historical writing continued to evolve in the late 1990s. Muslim historians moved beyond the framework of foreign domination. Influenced by Marxism*, they began to include the concepts of class and class struggle into their works.

The use of professional standards also increased among Muslim historians. Many institutions of higher learning grew after World War II (1939–1945). Universities needed professors to teach the flood of students, and professors needed advanced research degrees. Muslim historians flocked to Europe and the United States to earn their doctorates. These scholars produced dissertations* on a wide range of Islamic topics.

The academic study of history continues to expand. Several Muslim countries developed or improved their research archives, and Muslim historians secured teaching positions at American and European universities. Beginning in the 1970s, some Muslim historians began to criticize elements of early Islamic society as well as the accuracy of early historical writings. In many countries, rulers suppressed these writings and discouraged Muslim historians from publishing controversial material. (*See also* **Arabic Language and Literature; Ibn Khaldun; Muhammad; Universities.**)

A Dangerous Profession

Historians in Islamic societies have sometimes encountered fatal opposition. One of Iran's most noted historians, Ahmad Kasravi (1890–1946), taught history at the University of Tehran. Kasravi produced several important works on pre-Seljuk dynasties and modern Iran. He also criticized many aspects of Iranian culture, calling for reforms and inspiring the formation of a new political party. Kasravi drew bitter opposition from religious leaders for his sharp criticisms of Shi'i Islamic practices. Some clerics, such as Ayatollah Ruhollah Khomeini, criticized Kasravi in their own writings. Others sought to permanently silence the historian. In 1946 the Fidaiyani Islam, an extremist organization, murdered Ahmad Kasravi.

* **vizier** Muslim minister of state

* **Marxism** political philosophy that rejects capitalism and advocates a classless society

* **dissertation** extended written treatment of a particular subject

Glossary

ablution ritual washing that Muslims must perform before prayer

adhan Muslim call to prayer that occurs five times daily

Allah God

Allahu akbar "God is most great," beginning of Muslim call to prayer

amir military commander, governor, or prince; **amirate** office or realm of authority of an amir

aqidah Islamic creed, which consists of the five articles of faith: belief in God, angels, prophets, scriptures, and the Last Day (or Day of Judgment)

arabesque artistic style that uses foliage, fruit, or figural outlines to produce an intricate pattern of interlaced lines

ayatollah highest-ranking legal scholar among some Shi'i Muslims

burqa traditional garment worn by some Muslim women that covers the whole body, leaving only the eyes visible

caliph religious and political leader of an Islamic state; **caliphate** office and government of the caliph

chador veil worn by Muslim women in public that covers the whole body except the face, hands, and feet

Crusades during the Middle Ages, the holy wars declared by the pope against non-Christians, mostly Muslims

dar al-harb "Land of War;" place where inhabitants do not practice Islam

dar al-Islam "Land of Islam;" place where Islamic law is observed

da'wah call to Islam; refers to efforts to convert people to Islam or to draw Muslim individuals and communities back to God

dawlah Arabic for "state"

dhikr Sufi chant for the remembrance of God

dhimmi non-Muslims under the protection of Muslim law; typically applied to People of the Book, particularly Christians and Jews

Dhu al-Hijjah last month of the Islamic calendar and month of pilgrimage to Mecca

Eid al-Adha Feast of the Sacrifice, celebration commemorating Abraham's willingness to sacrifice his son to God; comes at the end of the pilgrimage to Mecca

Eid al-Fitr Feast of the Breaking of the Fast of Ramadan; celebration that ends the holy month of Ramadan

fatwa opinion issued by an Islamic legal scholar in response to a question posed by an individual or a court of law

fiqh human efforts to understand and codify divine law

Five Pillars of Islam five acts required of all Muslims: pledging one's faith, praying five times daily, putting aside a portion of one's wealth for the poor, fasting during the month of Ramadan, and making a pilgrimage to the holy city of Mecca

hadith reports of the words and deeds of Muhammad (not in the Qur'an, but accepted as guides for Muslim behavior)

hajj pilgrimage to Mecca that Muslims who are physically and financially able are required to make once in their lifetime

halal permissible; acceptable under Islamic law

haram illegal; prohibited by Islamic law

harem room in a Muslim household where the women live; also, female members of a Muslim household

heresy belief that is contrary to established religious doctrine or practice

hijab refers to the traditional head, face, or body covering worn by Muslim women

Hijrah celebrated emigration of Muhammad from Mecca in 622, which marks the first year of the Islamic calendar

hudud punishments prescribed by the Qur'an for specific crimes

ijma consensus of scholars on issues of law

ijtihad use of independent reasoning, rather than precedent, to interpret Islamic law

imam spiritual-political leader in Shi'i Islam, one who is regarded as directly descended from Muhammad; also, one who leads prayers

iman in Arabic, "faith"

Glossary

insha'a Allah Arabic phrase meaning "if God wills"

intifadah Arabic word for "uprising"

jami congregational mosque used specifically for Friday prayers

jihad literally "striving"; war in defense of Islam

jinn spirit beings

jizyah tax imposed by Muslims on non-Muslims

kaffiyah head cloth worn by some Muslim men

kalam in Arabic, "speech"; refers to the field of theology

kalam Allah in Arabic, "God's speech"; refers to the Qur'an

khan honorific title used for leaders in certain Islamic societies

khutbah sermon delivered at Friday prayers

kohl black powder applied to the edge of the eyelids

Kufic angular style of Arabic calligraphy

kuttab Islamic elementary school

loya jirga tribal council in Afghanistan

madhhab school of legal thought

madrasah religious college or university; also religious school for young students

Mahdi "divinely guided" imam who Muslims believe will return to earth to restore the faith and establish a just government

marabout African term for Sufi leader

mashhad gravesite of a martyr

masjid mosque; place for Muslim communal affairs

Mawlid an-Nabi Muhammad's birthday

mihrab niche, or recess, in a mosque indicating the direction of Mecca

minaret tall, slender tower of a Muslim mosque from which the faithful are called to prayer

minbar mosque platform used for the Friday sermon

monotheism belief that there is only one God

mosque Muslim place of worship

muezzin person who calls the faithful to prayer

mufti scholar who interprets Islamic law and issues fatwas

Muharram first month of the Islamic calendar

mujahidin literally "warriors of God"; refers to Muslim fighters in proclaimed jihads, such as the war against the Soviet invasion of Afghanistan

mujtahid legal scholar who interprets law according to independent reasoning (ijtihad)

mullah Muslim cleric or learned man

musalla informal areas and open air spaces for prayer

mutah a type of marriage contract allowing temporary marriage; prohibited in Sunni Islam.

mystic one who seeks to experience spiritual enlightenment and truth through various physical and spiritual disciplines

nabi "one who announces"; Arabic term for prophet

Pan-Islamic refers to the movement to unify all Islamic peoples

People of the Book for Muslims, religious group with written scriptures, mainly Christians and Jews

polygyny practice of having more than one wife at the same time

polytheism belief in more than one god

pre-Islamic refers to the Arabian peninsula or to the Arabic language before the founding of Islam in the early 600s

prophet one who announces divinely inspired revelations

qadi judge who administers Islamic law

qibla direction of prayer indicated by the mihrab (niche) in the wall of a mosque

qiyas type of reasoning that involves the use of analogy, or comparison based on resemblance

Qur'an book of the holy scriptures of Islam

Ramadan ninth month of the Islamic calendar and holy month during which Muslim adults fast and abstain from sex from sunrise to sunset

revelation message from God to humans transmitted through a prophet

sadaqah voluntary charitable offering of an amount beyond what is required; may enable a Muslim to atone for sins or other offenses

salat prayer; one of the five Pillars of Islam

sawm fasting; one of the five Pillars of Islam

sayyid honorific title equivalent to lord or sir; descendant of Muhammad

scripture sacred writings believed to contain revelations from God

shah king (Persian); ruler of Iran

shahadah profession of faith: "There is no God but God (Allah), and Muhammad is the messenger of God"

shahid martyr, or one who dies for his or her religious beliefs

shari'ah Islamic law as established in the Qur'an and sunnah, the exemplary behavior of the Prophet Muhammad

sharif nobleman; descendant of Muhammad

shaykh tribal elder; also, title of honor given to those who are considered especially learned and pious

Shi'ism branch of Islam that believes that Muhammad chose Ali ibn Abi Talib and his descendants as the spiritual-political leaders of the Muslim community

shura consultation; advisory council to the head of state

Sufism Islamic mysticism, which seeks to develop spirituality through discipline of the mind and body

sultan political and military ruler of a Muslim dynasty or state

sunnah literally "the trodden path"; Islamic customs based on the exemplary behavior of Muhammad

Sunni refers to the largest branch of the Muslim community; the name derives from sunnah, the exemplary behavior of the Prophet Muhammad

surah chapter of the Qur'an

talaq type of divorce in which a husband repeats the words "I divorce you" three times

taqiyah act of concealing one's true religious beliefs in order to prevent death or injury to oneself or other Muslims

taqwa piety, virtue, and awareness or reverence of God

tariqah path followed by Sufis to attain oneness with God; Sufi brotherhood

tawhid refers to the oneness or unity of God; monotheism

tazir punishments not required in the Qur'an but administered by an Islamic judge

ta'ziyah Shi'i religious drama about the martyrdom of Husayn ibn Ali, Muhammad's grandson

ulama religious scholars

ummah Muslim community

vizier Muslim minister of state

waqf donation of property for charitable causes

zakat charity; one of the five Pillars of Islam

zawiyah Sufi center that serves as a place of worship and a welfare institution

ziyadah in a mosque, the wall that holds the facilities for ablution, or ritual cleansing

People and Places

Abbas I (ruled 1588–1629) Shah of Safavid empire of Iran

Abbasids (750–1258) Dynasty that controlled the caliphate after the Umayyads; established capital in Baghdad in 762

Abd al-Qadir (1808–1883) Sufi poet; led uprising in Algeria against French 1832–1847

Abduh, Muhammad (1849–1905) Egyptian scholar and architect of Islamic modernism

Abraham Patriarch of Judaism, Christianity, and Islam; father of Ismail

Abu Bakr (ca. 573–634) Companion and follower of Muhammad; served as the first caliph from 632 to 634

Abu Hanifah (699–767) Legal scholar who founded the Hanafi, one of the four Sunni schools of law

Afghani, Jamal al-Din al- (1838–1897) Political activist and writer, best known for his role in the Pan-Islamic movement

Ahmad Khan, Sayyid (1817–1898) Islamic writer and reformer in British India who sought to modernize the interpretation of Islam

A'ishah (614–678) Muhammad's third and youngest wife; daughter of Abu Bakr, one of the Prophet's most important supporters

Akbar, Jalaludin Muhammad (1542–1605) Mughal emperor who expanded the realm and improved the efficiency of government

Alawi Minority Shi'i sect in Syria and Turkey

Ali ibn Abi Talib (ca. 597–661) Cousin and son-in-law of Muhammad who became the fourth caliph; conflicts over succession and Ali's assassination ultimately led to the division of Muslims into Shi'is and Sunnis

Andalusia Southernmost region of Spain controlled by Muslims from 711 to 1492

Arafat, Yasir (1929–) Founder and leader of Palestinian Liberation Organization

Ash'ari, Abu al-Hasan al- (ca. 873–935) Theologian who founded the Ash'ari school of Islamic thought

Assad, Hafiz al- (1928–2000) President of Syria from 1971 to 2000

Atatürk, Mustafa Kemal (1881–1938) Revolutionary leader and founder of modern Turkish state

Banna, Hasan al- (1906–1949) Founder of Muslim Brotherhood and Egyptian reformer

Bedouins Desert nomads, especially in North Africa, Syria, and Arabia

Beg, Toghril (died 1063) Early Seljuk leader who conquered Iran and Iraq

Berbers North-African ethnic group, primarily Muslim

Bin Laden, Osama (1957–) Islamic militant from Saudi Arabia; head of the al-Qaeda network

Byzantine Empire (330–1453) Eastern Christian Empire based in Constantinople

Caucacus Region of southern Europe between Black and Caspian Seas

Córdoba Caliphate in Muslim Spain from 756 to 1016; also important city and cultural center

Dan Fodio, Usuman (ca. 1754–1817) Founder and ruler of Sokoto caliphate in Nigeria

Druze Offshoot of Shi'i Islam, found mainly in Lebanon and Syria

Elijah Muhammad (1897–1975) Longtime leader of the Nation of Islam, militant religious group promoting the development of African American society

Farabi, Abu Nasr al- (870–950) Arab scholar, regarded as father of Islamic political science

Farrakhan, Louis (1933–) Leader of Nation of Islam, militant religious group promoting the development of African American society

Fatimah (ca. 605–633) Daughter of Muhammad and wife of Ali ibn Abi Talib

Fatimid Dynasty (909–1171) Family claiming descent from Fatimah that established caliphate that controlled North Africa; extended rule as far as Syria

Gasprinskii, Ismail Bey (1851–1914) Reformer who worked to help Turkish Muslims living under Russian rule in Crimea

Ghazali, Abu Hamid al- (1058–1111) Influential Muslim thinker who studied many areas of religion and science

Ghazali, Zaynab al- (1917–) Founder of Muslim Women's Association

Gulf States Refers to four nations on the Persian Gulf—Bahrain, Kuwait, Qatar, and the United Arab Emirates

Hagar In Bible, wife of Abraham and mother of Ismail; revered by Muslims

Harun al-Rashid (764–809) Fifth and most famous Abbasid caliph; ruled from 786 to 809

Holy Land Refers to ancient Palestine, land containing sacred sites of Muslims, Jews, and Christians

Husayn ibn Ali (626–680) Grandson of Muhammad and third Shi'i imam; led unsuccessful revolt against caliphs and died in battle; revered as a martyr by Shi'is

Hussein, Saddam (1937–) President of Iraq from 1979 to 2003

Ibn Abd al-Wahhab, Muhammad (1703–1791) Saudi Arabian reformer who founded Wahhabi movement

Ibn al-Arabi (1165–1240) Sufi mystic and poet in Muslim Spain

Ibn Battutah (died ca. 1368) Arab who traveled widely throughout the Muslim world, including West Africa and Southeast Asia

Ibn Hanbal (died 855) Muslim jurist and theologian; founded the Hanbali school, one of the major Sunni schools of law

Ibn Khaldun (1332–1406) Scholar who wrote on society and politics in the Arab world; regarded by some as the founder of sociology

Ibn Rushd (1126–1198) Philosopher and physician in Muslim Spain, known as Averroës in West; gained recognition for his writings on Aristotle

Ibn Sina (980–1037) Philosopher and physician, known as Avicenna in West; wrote the influential *Canon of Medicine*

Ibn Taymiyah (1263–1328) Hanbali jurist and reformer who advocated *ijtihad*; still influential among Islamic reformers

Iqbal, Muhammad (1876–1938) Poet and philosopher from India who advocated the creation of a separate state for Muslims

Ismail Son of Abraham and Hagar, called Ishmael in the Bible; considered the father of the Arab nation

Jafar al-Sadiq (died ca. 756) Shi'i imam who founded the Jafari school of Islamic law

Jinnah, Mohammad Ali (1876–1948) Indian who led Muslim League at time of partition; revered as a founder of Pakistan

Kaaba Shrine in Mecca considered the most sacred place in the Muslim world

Karbala Iraqi city containing the tomb of Husayn ibn Ali; important shrine and pilgrimage site for Shi'i Muslims

Kashmir Contested territory between India and Pakistan

Khadija (565–ca. 623) Muhammad's first wife and supporter

Khayyam, Umar (1038–1131) Persian mathematician and poet

Khomeini, Ruhollah al-Musavi (1902–1989) Leader of Iran's Islamic Revolution in 1979 and the country's political and religious leader during the 1980s

Maghrib, al- coastal region of North African countries of Tunisia, Algeria, Morocco, and Libya

Malcolm X (1925–1965) Controversial African American leader, assassinated by opponents in the Nation of Islam

Malik ibn Anas (ca. 713–795) Scholar who founded the Maliki school, one of the main Sunni schools of Islamic law

Mamluk State (1250–1517) Islamic state based in Egypt, ruled by slave soldiers; controlled Syria and parts of Asia Minor and Arabia

Maryam Jameelah (1934–) American convert to Islam who became a prominent critic of Western society

Mawdudi, Sayyid Abu al-Ala (1903–1979) Founder of Jamaat-i Islami revivalist movement calling for return to traditional Islamic values

Mecca Birthplace of Muhammad and site of Kaaba; most important pilgrimage destination for Muslims

Mehmed II (1432–1461) Ottoman sultan who conquered Byzantine Constantinople in 1453

Mongols Nomadic people from Central Asia who established an empire in the early 1200s that lasted about 200 years; at its peak the empire included much of Asia, Russia, eastern Europe and Middle East

Mughal Empire (1520s–1857) Muslim empire on subcontinent of India founded by Babur; British deposed the last emperor

Moors North African Muslims who conquered Spain

Muhammad (ca. 570–632) The Prophet of Islam, viewed by Muslims as God's messenger

Mulla Sadra (1571–ca. 1640) Influential Persian philosopher

Nasser, Gamal Abdel (1918–1970) Nationalist leader who seized control of Egypt in 1952 and became its president in 1956

Ottoman Empire Large Turkish empire established in the early 1300s that eventually controlled much of the Balkans and the Middle East; disintegrated after World War I (1914–1918)

Pahlavi, Muhammad Reza Shah (1919–1980) Last monarch of Iran, overthrown by Islamic Revolution in 1979

Palestine Historic region on the eastern Mediterranean that includes modern Israel and western Jordan, as well as the city of Jerusalem

Persia name foreigners used for Iran until 1935

Qaddafi, Mu'ammar al- (1942–) Ruler of Libya since 1969

Qom Site of the tomb of Fatimah and major Shi'i pilgrimage site in Iran

Qutb, Sayyid (1906–1966) Influential thinker associated with Muslim Brotherhood; regarded by many as founder of militant Islamic politics

Rashid Rida, Muhammad (1865–1935) Syrian reformer who advocated the establishment of a modern Islamic state based on a reinterpretation of Islamic law

Rumi (died 1273) Persian religious poet; his followers founded the Sufi order known as Mawlawiyah (also known as Mevlevis and Whirling Dervishes) that incorporates dance in its rituals

Rushdie, Salman (1947–) British-Indian author who wrote The Satanic Verses (1988), considered by many Muslims to be blasphemous

Sadat, Anwar el- (1918–1981) President of Egypt 1970–1981; assassinated by Islamic extremists

Sadr, Musa al- (1928–ca. 1978) Iranian cleric who led Shi'i movement in Lebanon; disappeared in 1978

Safavid Dynasty (1501–1722) Ruled Iran and parts of present-day Iraq; converted country to Shi'ism and founded the city of Isfahan

Saladin (1137–1193) Muslim leader who defeated the Fatimids in Egypt in 1171 and founded the Ayyubid dynasty; defeated the Crusaders, ending Christian occupation of Jerusalem

Seljuks (1038–1193) Turkic dynasty that ruled Iran and Iraq and parts of Central Asia; established a sultanate in Turkey that lasted until the Mongols invaded in 1243

Shafi'i, Muhammad (767–820) Jurist who founded the Shafi'i school, one of the major Sunni schools of Islamic law

Sokoto Caliphate Islamic state in Nigeria, founded in the 1800s by Usuman Dan Fodio

Suleyman (1520–1566) Sultan during the peak of the Ottoman Empire; called the Lawgiver in the East and the Magnificent in the West

Tamerlane (Timur Lang) (1336–1405) Mongol chieftain who came to power in Iran and conquered large areas of the Islamic world, including Anatolia and parts of Syria and India

Turabi, Hasan al- (1932–) Sudanese political leader who led efforts to form an Islamic state in Sudan

Umar ibn al-Khattab (ruled 634–644) Close friend of Muhammad and the second caliph; began expansion of Islamic empire

Umayyad Dynasty (661–750) Ruled Islamic caliphate; expanded the empire westward through North Africa and into Spain

Warith Deen Muhammad (1933–) Son of Nation of Islam leader Elijah Muhammad; assumed leadership of the organization in 1975

Zaynab (627–684) Granddaughter of Muhammad and daughter of Ali and Fatimah